Collins
Spanish
Grammar

HarperCollins Publishers
Westerhill Road
Bishopbriggs
Glasgow
G64 2QT
Great Britain

First Edition 2004

Reprint 10 9 8 7 6 5

© HarperCollins Publishers 2004

ISBN-13 978-0-00-719645-6
ISBN-10 0-00-719645-8

www.collins.co.uk

A catalogue record for this book is available
from the British Library

Typeset by Davidson's Prepress, Glasgow

Printed in Italy by Rotolito Lombarda SpA

Acknowledgements
We would like to thank those authors and
publishers who kindly gave permission for
copyright material to be used in the Collins
Word Web. We would also like to thank
Times Newspapers Ltd for providing
valuable data.

PUBLISHING DIRECTOR
Lorna Knight

EDITORIAL DIRECTOR
Michela Clari

MANAGING EDITOR
Maree Airlie

CONTRIBUTORS
Cordelia Lilly
José María Ruiz Vaca
Fernando León Solís
Wendy Lee
Di Larkin
Jeremy Butterfield

We would like to give special thanks to Di
Larkin, Foreign Languages Consultant, and
Irene Muir, Faculty Head, Belmont House
School, for all their advice on teaching
practice in today's classroom. Their
contributions have been invaluable in the
writing of this book.

CONTENTS

Note on trademarks
Entered words which we have reason to believe constitute trademarks have been
designated as such. However, neither the presence nor the absence of such designation
should be regarded as affecting the legal status of any trademark.

FOREWORD FOR LANGUAGE TEACHERS

The *Easy Learning Spanish Grammar* is designed to be used with both young and adult learners, as a group reference book to complement your course book during classes, or as a recommended text for self-study and homework/coursework.

The text specifically targets learners from *ab initio* to intermediate or GCSE level, and therefore its structural content and vocabulary have been matched to the relevant specifications up to and including Higher GCSE.

The approach aims to develop knowledge and understanding of grammar and your learners' ability to apply it by:

- defining parts of speech at the start of each major section with examples in English to clarify concepts
- minimizing the use of grammar terminology and providing clear explanations of terms both within the text and in the **Glossary**
- illustrating points with examples (and their translations) based on topics and contexts which are relevant to beginner and intermediate course content

The text helps you develop positive attitudes to grammar learning in your classes by:

- giving clear, easy-to-follow explanations
- prioritizing content according to relevant specifications for the levels
- sequencing points to reflect course content, e.g. verb tenses
- highlighting useful **Tips** to deal with common difficulties
- summarizing **Key points** at the end of sections to consolidate learning

In addition to fostering success and building a thorough foundation in Spanish grammar, the optional **Grammar Extra** sections will encourage and challenge your learners to further their studies to higher and advanced levels.

INTRODUCTION FOR STUDENTS

Whether you are starting to learn Spanish for the very first time, brushing up on topics you have studied in class, or revising for your GCSE exams, the *Easy Learning Spanish Grammar* is here to help. This easy-to-use guide takes you through all the basics you will need to speak and understand modern, everyday Spanish.

Newcomers can sometimes struggle with the technical terms they come across when they start to explore the grammar of a new language. The *Easy Learning Spanish Grammar* explains how to get to grips with all the parts of speech you will need to know, using simple language and cutting out jargon.

The text is divided into sections, each dealing with a particular area of grammar. Each section can be studied individually, as numerous cross-references in the text guide you to relevant points in other sections of the book for further information.

Every major section begins with an explanation of the area of grammar covered on the following pages. For quick reference, these definitions are also collected together on pages viii–xii in a glossary of essential grammar terms.

What is a verb?
A **verb** is a 'doing' word which describes what someone or something does, what someone or something is, or what happens to them, for example, *be*, *sing*, *live*.

Each grammar point in the text is followed by simple examples of real Spanish, complete with English translations, helping you understand the rules. Underlining has been used in examples throughout the text to highlight the grammatical point being explained.

➤ In orders and instructions telling someone <u>TO DO</u> something, the pronoun joins onto the end of the verb to form one word.

| **Ayúda<u>me</u>.** | Help me. |
| **Acompáña<u>nos</u>.** | Come with us. |

In Spanish, as with any foreign language, there are certain pitfalls which have to be avoided. **Tips** and **Information** notes throughout the text are useful reminders of the things that often trip learners up.

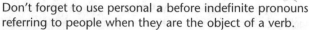

Tip

Don't forget to use personal **a** before indefinite pronouns referring to people when they are the object of a verb.

¿Viste <u>a</u> alguien?	Did you see anybody?
No vi <u>a</u> nadie.	I didn't see anybody.

Key points sum up all the important facts about a particular area of grammar, to save you time when you are revising and help you focus on the main grammatical points.

> ### Key points
> ✔ Like other adjectives, Spanish indefinite adjectives (such as **otro** and **todo**), must agree with what they describe.
> ✔ They go before the noun to which they relate.

If you think you would like to continue with your Spanish studies to a higher level, check out the **Grammar Extra** sections. These are intended for advanced students who are interested in knowing a little more about the structures they will come across beyond GCSE.

Grammar Extra!

por is often combined with other Spanish prepositions and words, usually to show movement.

Saltó <u>por encima</u> de la mesa.	She jumped over the table.
Nadamos <u>por debajo del</u> puente.	We swam under the bridge.
Pasaron <u>por delante de</u> Correos.	They went past the post office.

Finally, the supplement at the end of the book contains **Verb Tables**, where 83 important Spanish verbs (both regular and irregular) are conjugated in full. Examples show you how to use these verbs in your own work. If you are unsure how a verb is conjugated in Spanish, you can look up the **Verb Index** on pages 85–91 to find a cross-reference to a model verb.

We hope that you will enjoy using the *Easy Learning Spanish Grammar* and find it useful in the course of your studies.

GLOSSARY OF GRAMMAR TERMS

ABSTRACT NOUN a word used to refer to a quality, idea, feeling or experience, rather than a physical object, for example, *size, reason, happiness*. Compare with **concrete noun**.

ACTIVE a form of the verb that is used when the subject of the verb is the person or thing doing the action, for example, *I wrote a letter*. Compare with **passive**.

ADJECTIVE a 'describing' word that tells you more about a person or thing, such as their appearance, colour, size or other qualities, for example, *pretty, blue, big*.

ADVERB a word usually used with verbs, adjectives or other adverbs that gives more information about when, where, how or in what circumstances something happens or to what degree something is true, for example, *quickly, happily, now, extremely, very*.

AGREE (to) in the case of adjectives and pronouns, to have the correct word ending or form according to whether what is referred to is masculine, feminine, singular or plural; in the case of verbs, to have the form which goes with the person or thing carrying out the action.

APOSTROPHE s an ending ('s) added to a noun to show who or what someone or something belongs to, for example, *Danielle's dog, the doctor's wife, the book's cover*.

ARTICLE a word like *the, a* and *an*, which is used in front of a noun. See also **definite article, indefinite article**.

AUXILIARY VERB a verb such as *be, have* or *do* used with a main verb to form tenses, negatives and questions.

BASE FORM the form of the verb without any endings added to it, for example, *walk, have, be, go*.

CARDINAL NUMBER a number used in counting, for example, *one, seven, ninety*. Compare with **ordinal number**.

CLAUSE a group of words containing a verb.

COMPARATIVE an adjective or adverb with *-er* on the end of it or *more* or *less* in front of it that is used to compare people, things or actions, for example, *slower, less important, more carefully*.

COMPOUND NOUN a word for a living being, thing or idea, which is made up of two or more words, for example, *tin-opener, railway station*.

CONCRETE NOUN a word that refers to an object you can touch with your hand, rather than to a quality or idea, for example, *ball, map, apples*. Compare with **abstract noun**.

CONDITIONAL a verb form used to talk about things that would happen or would be true under certain conditions, for example, *I would help you if I could*. It is also used to say what you would like or need, for example, *Could you give me the bill?*

CONJUGATE (to) to give a verb different endings according to whether you are referring to *I, you, they* and so on, and according to whether you are referring to the present, past or future, for example, *I have, she had, they will have*.

CONJUGATION a group of verbs which have the same endings as each other or change according to the same pattern.

CONJUNCTION a word such as *and*, *because* or *but* that links two words or phrases of a similar type or two parts of a sentence, for example, *Diane and I have been friends for years; I left because I was bored.*

CONSONANT a letter that isn't a vowel, for example, *b, f, m, s, v* and so on. Compare with **vowel.**

CONTINUOUS TENSE a verb tense formed using *to be* and the *-ing* form of the main verb, for example, *They're swimming* (present continuous); *He was eating* (past continuous).

DEFINITE ARTICLE the word *the.* Compare with **indefinite article.**

DEMONSTRATIVE ADJECTIVE one of the words *this, that, these* and *those* used with a noun to refer to particular peope or things, for example, *this woman, that dog.*

DEMONSTRATIVE PRONOUN one of the words *this, that, these* and *those* used instead of a noun to point out people or things, for example, *That looks fun.*

DIRECT OBJECT a noun or pronoun used with verbs to show who or what is acted on by the verb. For example, in *He wrote a letter* and *He wrote me a letter, letter* is the direct object. Compare **indirect object.**

DIRECT OBJECT PRONOUN a word such as *me, him, us* and *them* which is used instead of a noun to stand in for the person or thing most directly affected by the action expressed by the verb. Compare with **indirect object pronoun.**

ENDING a form added to a verb, for example, *go —> goes,* and to adjectives and nouns depending on whether they refer to masculine, feminine, singular or plural things.

EXCLAMATION a word, phrase or sentence that you use to show you are surprised, shocked, angry and so on,

for example, *Wow!; How dare you!; What a surprise!*

FEMININE a form of noun, pronoun or adjective that is used to refer to a living being, thing or idea that is not classed as masculine.

FUTURE a verb tense used to talk about something that will happen or will be true.

GENDER whether a noun, pronoun or adjective is feminine or masculine.

GERUND a verb form in English ending in *-ing,* for example, *eating, sleeping.*

IMPERATIVE the form of a verb used when giving orders and instructions, for example, *Shut the door!; Sit down!; Don't go!; Let's eat.*

IMPERFECT one of the verb tenses used to talk about the past, especially in descriptions, and to say what was happening or used to happen, for example, *It was sunny at the weekend; We were living in Spain at the time; I used to walk to school.* Compare to **preterite.**

IMPERSONAL VERB a verb whose subject is *it,* but where the *it* does not refer to any specific thing, for example, *It's raining; It's 10 o'clock.*

INDEFINITE ADJECTIVE one of a small group of adjectives used to talk about people or things in a general way, without saying who or what they are, for example, *several, all, every.*

INDEFINITE ARTICLE the words *a* and *an.* Compare with **definite article.**

INDICATIVE ordinary verb forms that aren't subjunctive, such as the present, preterite or future. Compare with **subjunctive.**

INDEFINITE PRONOUN a small group of pronouns such as *everything, nobody* and *something,* which are used to refer to people or things in a general way, without saying exactly who or what they are.

INDIRECT OBJECT a noun or pronoun used with verbs to show who benefits or is harmed by an action. For example, in *I gave the carrot to the rabbit,* the rabbit is the indirect object and *the carrot* is the direct object. Compare with **direct object.**

INDIRECT OBJECT PRONOUN a pronoun used with verbs to show who benefits or is harmed by an action. For example, in *I gave him the carrot* and *I gave it to him, him* is the indirect object and the *carrot* and *it* are the direct objects. Compare with **direct object pronoun.**

INDIRECT QUESTION a question that is embedded in another question or instruction such as *Can you tell me what time it is?; Tell me why you did it.* Also used for reported speech such as *He asked me why I did it.*

INDIRECT SPEECH the words you use to report what someone has said when you aren't using their actual words, for example, *He said that he was going out.* Also called **reported speech.**

INFINITIVE a form of the verb that hasn't any endings added to it and doesn't relate to any particular tense. In English the infinitive is usually shown with *to,* as in *to speak, to eat.*

INTERROGATIVE ADJECTIVE a question word used with a noun, for example, *What instruments do you play?; Which shoes do you like?*

INTERROGATIVE PRONOUN one of the words *who, whose, whom, what* and *which* when they are used instead of a noun to ask questions, for example, *What's that?; Who's coming?*

INTRANSITIVE VERB a type of verb that does not take a direct object, for example, *to sleep, to rise, to swim.* Compare with **transitive verb.**

INVARIABLE used to describe a form which does not change.

IRREGULAR VERB a verb whose forms do not follow a general pattern. Compare with **regular verb.**

MASCULINE a form of noun, pronoun or adjective that is used to refer to a living being, thing or idea that is not classed as feminine.

NEGATIVE a question or statement which contains a word such as *not, never* or *nothing,* and is used to say that something is not happening, is not true or is absent, for example, *I never eat meat; Don't you love me?* Compare with **positive.**

NOUN a 'naming' word for a living being, thing or idea, for example, *woman, desk, happiness, Andrew.*

NOUN GROUP, NOUN PHRASE a word or group of words that acts as the subject or object of a verb, or as the object of a preposition, for example, *my older sister; the man next door; that big house on the corner.*

NUMBER used to say how many things you are referring to or where something comes in a sequence. See also **ordinal number** and **cardinal number.** Also the condition of being singular or plural.

OBJECT a noun or pronoun which refers to a person or thing that is affected by the action described by the verb. Compare with **direct object, indirect object** and **subject.**

OBJECT PRONOUN one of the set of pronouns including *me, him* and *them,* which are used instead of the noun as the object of a verb or preposition. Compare with **subject pronoun.**

ORDINAL NUMBER a number used to indicate where something comes in an order or sequence, for example, *first, fifth, sixteenth*. Compare with **cardinal number**.

PART OF SPEECH a word class, for example, *noun, verb, adjective, preposition, pronoun*.

PASSIVE a form of the verb that is used when the subject of the verb is the person or thing that is affected by the action, for example, *we were told*.

PAST PARTICIPLE a verb form which is used to form perfect and pluperfect tenses and passives, for example, *watched, swum*. Some past participles are also used as adjectives, for example, *a broken watch*.

PAST PERFECT see **pluperfect**.

PERFECT a verb form used to talk about what has or hasn't happened, for example, *I've broken my glasses; We haven't spoken about it*.

PERSON one of the three classes: the first person (*I, we*), the second person (*you* singular and *you* plural), and the third person (*he, she, it* and *they*).

PERSONAL PRONOUN one of the group of words including *I, you* and *they* which are used to refer to you, the people you are talking to, or the people or things you are talking about.

PLUPERFECT one of the verb tenses used to describe something that had happened or had been true at a point in the past, for example, *I'd forgotten to finish my homework*. Also called **past perfect**.

PLURAL the form of a word which is used to refer to more than one person or thing. Compare with **singular**.

POSITIVE a positive sentence or instruction is one that does not contain a negative word such as *not*. Compare with **negative**.

POSSESSIVE ADJECTIVE one of the words *my, your, his, her, its, our* or *their*, used with a noun to show who it belongs to.

POSSESSIVE PRONOUN one of the words *mine, yours, hers, his, ours* or *theirs*, used instead of a noun to show who something belongs to.

PREPOSITION is a word such as *at, for, with, into* or *from*, which is usually followed by a noun, pronoun or, in English, a word ending in *-ing*. Prepositions show how people and things relate to the rest of the sentence, for example, *She's at home; a tool for cutting grass; It's from David*.

PRESENT a verb form used to talk about what is true at the moment, what happens regularly, and what is happening now, for example, *I'm a student; I travel to college by train; I'm studying languages*.

PRESENT PARTICIPLE a verb form in English ending in *-ing*, for example, *eating, sleeping*.

PRETERITE a verb form used to talk about actions that were completed in the past in Spanish. It often corresponds to the ordinary past tense in English, for example, *I bought a new bike; Mary went to the shops on Friday; I typed two reports yesterday*.

PRONOUN a word which you use instead of a noun, when you do not need or want to name someone or something directly, for example, *it, you, none*.

PROPER NOUN the name of a person, place, organization or thing. Proper nouns are always written with a capital letter, for example, *Kevin, Glasgow, Europe, London Eye*.

QUESTION WORD a word such as *why, where, who, which* or *how* which is used to ask a question.

RADICAL-CHANGING VERBS in Spanish, verbs which change their stem or root in certain tenses and in certain persons.

REFLEXIVE PRONOUN a word ending in -self or -selves, such as myself or themselves, which refers back to the subject, for example, He hurt himself; Take care of yourself.

REFLEXIVE VERB a verb where the subject and object are the same, and where the action 'reflects back' on the subject. A reflexive verb is used with a reflexive pronoun such as myself, yourself, herself, for example, I washed myself; He shaved himself.

REGULAR VERB a verb whose forms follow a general pattern or the normal rules. Compare with **irregular verb**.

RELATIVE PRONOUN a word such as that, who or which, when it is used to link two parts of a sentence together.

REPORTED SPEECH see **indirect speech**.

SENTENCE a group of words which usually has a verb and a subject. In writing, a sentence begins with a capital and ends with a full stop, question mark or exclamation mark.

SIMPLE TENSE a verb tense in which the verb form is made up of one word, rather than being formed from to have and a past participle or to be and an -ing form; for example, She plays tennis; He wrote a book.

SINGULAR the form of a word which is used to refer to one person or thing. Compare with **plural**.

STEM the main part of a verb to which endings are added.

SUBJECT a noun or pronoun that refers to the person or thing doing the action or being in the state described by the verb, for example, My cat doesn't drink milk. Compare with **object**.

SUBJECT PRONOUN a word such as I, he, she and they which carries out the action described by the verb. Pronouns stand in for nouns when it is clear who is being talked about, for example, My brother isn't here at the moment. He'll be back in an hour. Compare with **object pronoun**.

SUBJUNCTIVE a verb form used in certain circumstances to indicate some sort of feeling, or to show doubt about whether something will happen or whether something is true. It is only used occasionally in modern English, for example, If I were you, I wouldn't bother; So be it.

SUPERLATIVE an adjective or adverb with -est on the end of it or most or least in front of it that is used to compare people, things or actions, for example, thinnest, most quickly, least interesting.

SYLLABLE consonant+vowel units that make up the sounds of a word, for example, ca-the-dral (3 syllables), im-po-ssi-ble (4 syllables).

TENSE the form of a verb which shows whether you are referring to the past, present or future.

TRANSITIVE VERB a type of verb that takes a direct object, for example, to spend, to raise, to waste. Compare with **intransitive verb**.

VERB a 'doing' word which describes what someone or something does, is, or what happens to them, for example, be, sing, live.

VOWEL one of the letters a, e, i, o or u. Compare with **consonant**.

NOUNS

What is a noun?
A **noun** is a 'naming' word for a living being, thing or idea, for example, *woman, desk, happiness, Andrew.*

Using nouns

➤ In Spanish, all nouns are either <u>masculine</u> or <u>feminine</u>. This is called their <u>gender</u>. Even words for things have a gender.

➤ Whenever you are using a noun, you need to know whether it is masculine or feminine as this affects the form of other words used with it, such as:

- adjectives that describe it
- articles (such as **el** or **una**) that go before it

⇨ *For more information on **Articles** and **Adjectives**, see pages 10 and 19.*

➤ You can find information about gender by looking the word up in a dictionary. When you come across a new noun, always learn the word for *the* or *a* that goes with it to help you remember its gender.

- **el** or **un** before a noun tells you it is masculine
- **la** or **una** before a noun tells you it is feminine

➤ We refer to something as <u>singular</u> when we are talking about just one of them, and as <u>plural</u> when we are talking about more than one. The singular is the form of the noun you will usually find when you look a noun up in the dictionary. As in English, nouns in Spanish change their form in the plural.

➤ Adjectives, articles and pronouns are also affected by whether a noun is singular or plural.

Tip
Remember that you have to use the right word for *the*, *a* and so on according to the gender of the Spanish noun.

Gender

1 Nouns referring to people

➤ Most nouns referring to men and boys are <u>masculine</u>.

el hombre	the man
el rey	the king

➤ Most nouns referring to women and girls are <u>feminine</u>.

la mujer	the woman
la reina	the queen

➤ When the same word is used to refer to either men/boys or women/girls, its gender usually changes depending on the sex of the person it refers to.

el estudiante	the (male) student
la estudiante	the (female) student
el belga	the Belgian (man)
la belga	the Belgian (woman)

Grammar Extra!

Some words for people have only <u>one</u> possible gender, whether they refer to a male or a female.

la persona	the (male or female) person
la víctima	the (male or female) victim

➤ In English, we can sometimes make a word masculine or feminine by changing the ending, for example, English<u>man</u> and English<u>woman</u> or prince and prin<u>cess</u>. In Spanish, very often the ending of a noun changes depending on whether it refers to a man or a woman.

el camarero	the waiter
la camarera	the waitress
el empleado	the employee (*male*)
la empleada	the employee (*female*)
el inglés	the Englishman
la inglesa	the Englishwoman

Tip

Note that a noun ending in -o is usually <u>masculine</u>, and a noun ending in -a is usually <u>feminine</u>.

➪ *For more information on **Masculine and feminine forms of words**, see page 5.*

2 Nouns referring to animals

➤ In English we can choose between words like *bull* or *cow*, depending on the sex of the animal. In Spanish too there are sometimes separate words for male and female animals.

<u>el</u> toro	the bull
<u>la</u> vaca	the cow

➤ Sometimes, the same word with different endings is used for male and female animals.

<u>el</u> perr<u>o</u>	the (male) dog
<u>la</u> perr<u>a</u>	the (female) dog, bitch
<u>el</u> gat<u>o</u>	the (male) cat
<u>la</u> gat<u>a</u>	the (female) cat

Tip

When you do not know or care what sex the animal is, you can usually use the <u>masculine form</u> as a general word.

➤ Words for other animals don't change according to the sex of the animal. Just learn the Spanish word with its gender, which is always the same.

<u>el</u> sapo	the toad
<u>el</u> hámster	the hamster
<u>la</u> cobaya	the guinea pig
<u>la</u> tortuga	the tortoise

3 Nouns referring to things

➤ In English, we call all things – for example, *table, car, book, apple* – 'it'. In Spanish, however, things are either <u>masculine</u> or <u>feminine</u>. As things don't divide into sexes the way humans and animals do, there are no physical clues to help you with their gender in Spanish. Try to learn the gender as you learn the word.

➤ There are lots of rules to help you. Certain endings are usually found on masculine nouns, while other endings are usually found on feminine nouns.

4 NOUNS

➤ The following ending is usually found on <u>masculine nouns</u>.

Masculine ending	Examples
-o	**el** libr**o** the book **el** periódic**o** the newspaper BUT: **la** mano the hand **la** foto the photo **la** moto the motorbike **la** radio the radio (*although in parts of Latin America, it is* **el** *radio*)

➤ The following types of word are also masculine.

- names of the days of the week and the months of the year
  Te veré el lunes.   I'll see you on Monday.
- the names of languages
  el inglés   English
  el español   Spanish
  Estudio el español.   I'm studying Spanish.
- the names of rivers, mountains amd seas
  el Ebro   the Ebro
  el Everest   Everest
  el Atlántico   the Atlantic

➤ The following endings are usually found on <u>feminine nouns</u>.

Feminine ending	Examples
-a	**la** cas**a** the house **la** car**a** the face BUT: **el** día the day **el** mapa the map **el** planeta the planet **el** tranvía the tram and many words ending in -ma (**el** problema the problem, **el** programa the programme, **el** sistema the system, **el** clima the climate)
-ción -sión	**la** lec**ción** the lesson **la** esta**ción** the station **la** expre**sión** the expression
-dad -tad -tud	**la** ciu**dad** the city **la** liber**tad** freedom **la** multi**tud** the crowd

For further explanation of grammatical terms, please see pages viii-xii.

Grammar Extra!

Some words have different meanings depending on whether they are masculine or feminine.

Masculine	Meaning	Feminine	Meaning
el capital	the capital (meaning *money*)	la capital	the capital (meaning *city*)
el cometa	the comet	la cometa	the kite
el cura	the priest	la cura	the cure
el guía	the guide (*man*)	la guía	the guidebook; the guide (*woman*)

Invirtieron mucho capital.   They invested a lot of capital.
Viven en la capital.   They live in the capital.

4   Masculine and feminine forms of words

➤ Like English, Spanish sometimes has very different words for males and females.

el hombre	the man
la mujer	the woman
el rey	the king
la reina	the queen

➤ Many Spanish words can be used to talk about men or women simply by changing the ending. For example, if the word for the male ends in -o, you can almost always make it feminine by changing the -o to -a.

el amigo	the (male) friend
la amiga	the (female) friend
el hermano	the brother
la hermana	the sister
el empleado	the (male) employee
la empleada	the (female) employee
el viudo	the widower
la viuda	the widow

[i] Note that some words referring to people end in -a in the masculine as well as in the feminine. Only the article (el or la, un or una) can tell you what gender the noun is.

el dentista	the (male) dentist
la dentista	the (female) dentist
el deportista	the sportsman
la deportista	the sportswoman

➤ Many masculine nouns ending in a consonant (any letter other than a vowel) become feminine by adding an -**a**.

<u>el</u> **español**	the Spanish man
<u>la</u> **español<u>a</u>**	the Spanish woman
<u>el</u> **profesor**	the (male) teacher
<u>la</u> **profesor<u>a</u>**	the (female) teacher

Típ

If the last vowel of the masculine word has an accent, this is dropped in the feminine form.

<u>un</u> **ingl<u>és</u>**	an Englishman
<u>una</u> **ingl<u>esa</u>**	an Englishwoman
<u>un</u> **franc<u>és</u>**	a Frenchman
<u>una</u> **franc<u>esa</u>**	a Frenchwoman

⇨ *For more information about **Spelling** and **Stress**, see pages 196 and 200.*

Key points

✔ The ending of a Spanish word often helps you work out its gender: for instance, if a word ends in -**o**, it is probably masculine; if it ends in -**a**, it is probably feminine.

✔ These endings generally mean that the noun is feminine: -**ción**, -**sión**, -**dad**, -**tad**, -**tud**

✔ Days of the week and months of the year are masculine. So are languages, mountains and seas.

✔ You can change the ending of some nouns from -**o** to -**a** to make a masculine noun feminine.

Forming plurals

1 Plurals ending in -s and -es

➤ In English we usually make nouns plural by adding an -s to the end (*garden* → *gardens*; *house* → *houses*), although we do have some nouns which are <u>irregular</u> and do not follow this pattern (*mouse* → *mice*; *child* → *children*).

Tip

Remember that you have to use **los** (for <u>masculine nouns</u>) or **las** (for <u>feminine nouns</u>) with plural nouns in Spanish. Any adjective that goes with the noun also has to agree with it, as does any pronoun that replaces it.

⇨ *For more information on **Articles**, **Adjectives** and **Pronouns**, see pages 10, 19 and 41.*

➤ To form the plural in Spanish, add -s to most nouns ending in a vowel (*a*, *e*, *i*, *o* or *u*) which doesn't have an accent.

el libro	the book
los libros	the books
el hombre	the man
los hombres	the men
la profesora	the (female) teacher
las profesoras	the (female) teachers

➤ Add -es to singular nouns ending in a consonant (any letter other than a vowel).

el profesor	the (male) teacher
los profesores	the (male/male and female) teachers
la ciudad	the town/city
las ciudades	the towns/cities

i Note that some foreign words (that is, words which have come from another language, such as English) ending in a consonant just add -s.

el jersey	the jersey
los jerseys	the jerseys

➤ Words ending in -s which have an unstressed final vowel do not change in the plural.

el paraguas	the umbrella
los paraguas	the umbrellas
el lunes	(on) Monday
los lunes	(on) Mondays

⇨ *For more information on* **Stress**, *see page 200.*

➤ Some singular nouns ending in an accented vowel add -es in the plural while other very common ones add -s.

el jabalí	the boar
<u>los</u> **jabalíes**	the boars
el café	the café
<u>los</u> **cafés**	the cafés
el sofá	the sofa
<u>los</u> **sofás**	the sofas

Grammar Extra!

When nouns are made up of two separate words, they are called <u>compound nouns</u>, for example, **el abrelatas** (meaning *the tin-opener*) and **el hombre rana** (meaning *the frogman*). Some of these nouns don't change in the plural, for example, **los abrelatas**, while others do, for example, **los hombres rana**. It is always best to check in a dictionary to see what the plural is.

2	**Spelling changes with plurals ending in -es**

➤ Singular nouns which end in an accented vowel and either -n or -s drop the accent in the plural.

la canción	the song
las canciones	the songs
el autobús	the bus
los autobuses	the buses

➤ Singular nouns of more than one syllable which end in -en and don't already have an accent, add one in the plural.

el examen	the exam
los exámenes	the exams

el joven	the youth
los jóvenes	young people

➤ Singular nouns ending in -z change to -c in the plural.

la luz	the light
las luces	the lights
la vez	the times
las veces	the times

⇨ *For further information on **Spelling** and **Stress**, see pages 196 and 200.*

3 **Plural versus singular**

➤ A few words relating to clothing that are plural in English can be singular in Spanish.

una braga	(a pair of) knickers
un slip	(a pair of) underpants
un pantalón	(a pair of) trousers

➤ A few common words behave differently in Spanish from the way they behave in English.

un mueble	a piece of furniture
unos muebles	some furniture
una noticia	a piece of news
unas noticias	some news
un consejo	a piece of advice
unos consejos	some advice

Key points

✔ Add -s to form the plural of a noun ending in an unaccented vowel.

✔ Add -es to form the plural of most nouns ending in a consonant.

✔ Drop the accent when adding plural -es to nouns ending in an accented vowel + -n or -s.

✔ Add an accent when adding plural -es to words of more than one syllable ending in -en.

✔ Change -z to -c when forming the plural of words like luz.

✔ A few common words are plural in English but not in Spanish.

ARTICLES

What is an article?
In English, an **article** is one of the words *the, a,* and *an* which is given in front of a noun.

Different types of article

➤ There are two types of article:

- the <u>definite</u> article: *the* in English. This is used to identify a particular thing or person.

  I'm going to <u>the</u> supermarket.
  That's <u>the</u> woman I was talking to.

- the <u>indefinite</u> article: *a* or *an* in English, whose plural is *some* or *any* (or no word at all). This is used to refer to something unspecific, or that you do not really know about.

  Is there <u>a</u> supermarket near here?
  I need <u>a</u> day off.

The definite article: el, la, los and las

1 **The basic rules**

➤ In English, there is only <u>one</u> definite article: *the*. In Spanish, you have to choose between <u>four</u> definite articles: **el, la, los** and **las**. Which one you choose depends on the noun which follows.

➤ In Spanish, all nouns (including words for things) are either masculine or feminine – this is called their <u>gender</u>. And just as in English they can also be either singular or plural. You must bear this in mind when deciding which Spanish word to use for *the*.

⇨ *For more information on* **Nouns**, *see page 1.*

➤ **el** is used before <u>masculine singular nouns</u>.

el niño	the boy
el periódico	the newspaper

➤ **la** is used before <u>feminine singular nouns</u>.

la niña	the girl
la revista	the magazine

> *Tip*
>
> To help you speak and write correct Spanish, always learn the <u>article</u> or the <u>gender</u> together with the noun when learning vocabulary. A good dictionary will also give you this information.

➤ **los** and **las** are used before <u>plural nouns</u>. **los** is used with masculine plural words, and **las** is used with feminine plural words.

los niños	the boys
las niñas	the girls
los periódicos	the newspapers
las revistas	the magazines

ℹ Note that you use **el** instead of **la** immediately before a feminine singular word beginning with **a** or **ha** when the stress falls on the beginning of the word. This is because **la** sounds wrong before the '*a*' sound. <u>BUT</u> if you add an adjective in front of the noun, you use **la** instead, since the two '*a*' sounds do not come next to each other.

el agua	the water
el hacha	the axe
la misma agua	the same water
la mejor hacha	the best axe

To the → al

2   a and de with the definite article

➤ If a is followed by el, the two words become al.

al cine	to the cinema	*a + el → al*
al empleado	to the employee *(to)*	
al hospital	to the hospital	
Vio **al** camarero.	He saw the waiter.	

➤ If de is followed by el, the two words become del.

del departamento	of/from the department	*de + el → del*
del autor	of/from the author	
del presidente	of/from the president	*of / from the → del*

3   Using the definite article

➤ el, la, los and las are often used in Spanish in the same way as *the* is used in English. However, there are some cases where the article is used in Spanish but not in English.

➤ The definite article <u>IS</u> used in Spanish:

- when talking about people, animals and things in a general way

Me gustan <u>los</u> animales.	I like animals.
Están subiendo <u>los</u> precios.	Prices are going up.
Me gusta <u>el</u> chocolate.	I like chocolate.
No me gusta <u>el</u> café.	I don't like coffee.
<u>El</u> azúcar es dulce.	Sugar is sweet.

- when talking about abstract qualities, for example, *time, hope, darkness, violence*

<u>El</u> tiempo es oro.	Time is money.
Admiro <u>la</u> sinceridad en la gente.	I admire honesty in people.

[i] Note that the definite article is <u>NOT</u> used in certain set phrases consisting of **tener** and a noun or after certain prepositions.

tener hambre	to be hungry	*(literally: to have hunger)*
sin duda	no doubt	*(literally: without doubt)*
con cuidado	carefully	*(literally: with care)*

⇨ *For more information on **Prepositions**, see page 178.*

- when talking about colours

  El azul es mi color favorito.   Blue is my favourite colour.

- when talking about parts of the body – you do not use *my, your, his* and so on as you would in English

  Tiene los ojos verdes.   He's got green eyes.
  No puedo mover las piernas.   I can't move my legs.

i Note that possession is often shown by a personal pronoun in Spanish.

  La cabeza me da vueltas.   My head is spinning.
  Lávate las manos.   Wash your hands.

⇨ *For more information on **Personal pronouns**, see page 42.*

- when using someone's title – for example, *Doctor, Mr* – but talking ABOUT someone rather than to them.

  El doctor Vidal no está.   Dr Vidal isn't here.
  El señor Pelayo vive aquí.   Mr Pelayo lives here.

- when talking about institutions, such as school or church

en el colegio	at school
en la universidad	at university
en la iglesia	at church
en el hospital	in hospital
en la cárcel	in prison

- when talking about meals, games or sports

  La cena es a las nueve.   Dinner is at nine o'clock.
  Me gusta el tenis.   I like tennis.
  No me gusta el ajedrez.   I don't like chess.

- when talking about days of the week and dates, where we use the preposition *on* in English

  Te veo el lunes.   I'll see you on Monday.
  Los lunes tenemos muchos   We have a lot of homework on
  deberes.   Mondays.
  Nací el 17 de marzo.   I was born on 17 March.

- when talking about the time

  Es la una.   It's one o'clock.
  Son las tres.   It's three o'clock.
  Son las cuatro y media.   It's half past four.

- when talking about prices and rates

  Cuesta dos euros el kilo.   It costs two euros a kilo.
  20 euros la hora   20 euros an hour

Key points

✔ Before masculine singular nouns → use **el**.

✔ Before feminine singular nouns → use **la**.

✔ Before feminine singular nouns starting with stressed **a** or **ha** → use **el**.

✔ Before masculine plural nouns → use **los**.

✔ Before feminine plural nouns → use **las**.

✔ **a + el → al**

✔ **de + el → del**

✔ There are some important cases when you would use a definite article in Spanish when you wouldn't in English; for example, when talking about:
  - things in a general way
  - abstract qualities
  - colours
  - parts of the body
  - someone with a title in front of their name
  - institutions
  - meals, games or sports
  - the time, days of the week and dates (*using the preposition <u>on</u> in English*)
  - prices and rates

The indefinite article: un, una, unos and unas

1   The basic rules

➤ In English, the indefinite article is *a*, which changes to *an* when it comes before a vowel or a vowel sound, for example, *an apple*. In the plural, we use *some* or *any*.

➤ In Spanish, you have to choose between <u>four</u> indefinite articles: **un**, **una**, **unos** and **unas**. Which one you choose depends on the noun that follows.

➤ In Spanish, all nouns (including words for things) are either masculine or feminine – this is called their <u>gender</u>. And, just as in English, they can also be either singular or plural. You must bear this in mind when deciding which Spanish word to use for *a*.

⇨   *For more information on* **Nouns**, *see page 1.*

➤ **un** is used before <u>masculine singular nouns</u>.

<u>un</u> **niño**	a boy
<u>un</u> **periódico**	a newspaper

➤ **una** is used before <u>feminine singular nouns</u>.

<u>una</u> **niña**	a girl
<u>una</u> **revista**	a magazine

➤ **unos** is used before <u>masculine plural nouns</u>.

<u>unos</u> **niños**	some boys
<u>unos</u> **periódicos**	some newspapers

➤ **unas** is used before <u>feminine plural nouns</u>.

unas niñas	some girls
unas revistas	some magazines

i   Note that you use **un** instead of **una** immediately before a feminine singular word beginning with **a** or **ha** when the stress falls on the beginning of the word. This is because **una** sounds wrong before the '*a*' sound.

un ave	a bird

2   Using the indefinite article

➤ The indefinite article is often used in Spanish in the same way as it is in English. However, there are some cases where the article is not used in Spanish but is in English, and vice versa.

➤ The indefinite article is <u>NOT</u> used in Spanish:
- when you say what someone's job is

Es profesor.	He's <u>a</u> teacher.
Mi madre es enfermera.	My mother is <u>a</u> nurse.

- after **tener**, **buscar**, or **llevar (puesto)** when you are only likely *to have*, *be looking for* or *be wearing* one of the items in question

No tengo coche.	I haven't got <u>a</u> car.
¿Llevaba sombrero?	Was he wearing <u>a</u> hat?

[*i*] Note that when you use an adjective to describe the noun, you <u>DO</u> use an article in Spanish too.

Es <u>un</u> buen médico.	He's <u>a</u> good doctor.
Tiene <u>una</u> novia española.	He has a Spanish girlfriend.
Busca <u>un</u> piso pequeño.	He's looking for a little flat.

➤ The indefinite article is <u>NOT</u> used in Spanish with the words **otro**, **cierto**, **cien**, **mil**, **sin**, and **qué**.

otro libro	another book
cierta calle	<u>a</u> certain street
cien soldados	<u>a</u> hundred soldiers
mil años	<u>a</u> thousand years
sin casa	without <u>a</u> house
¡Qué sorpresa!	What <u>a</u> surprise!

➤ The indefinite article <u>IS</u> used in Spanish but <u>NOT</u> in English when an abstract noun, such as **inteligencia** (meaning *intelligence*) or **tiempo** (meaning *time*) has an adjective with it.

Posee <u>una</u> gran inteligencia.	He possesses great intelligence.

Key points

✔ Before masculine singular nouns → use **un**.

✔ Before feminine singular nouns → use **una**.

✔ Before feminine singular nouns starting with stressed **a** or **ha** → use **un**.

✔ Before masculine plural nouns → use **unos**.

✔ Before feminine plural nouns → use **unas**

✔ You do not use an indefinite article in Spanish for saying what someone's job is.

✔ You do not use an indefinite article in Spanish with the words **otro**, **cierto**, **cien**, **mil**, **sin**, and **qué**.

The article lo

➤ Unlike the other Spanish articles, and articles in English, **lo** is <u>NOT</u> used with a noun.

➤ **lo** can be used with a masculine singular adjective or past participle (the **-ado** and **-ido** forms of regular verbs) to form a noun.

<u>Lo único</u> que no me gusta ...	The only thing I don't like ...
Esto es <u>lo importante</u>.	That's the important thing.
<u>Lo bueno</u> de eso es que ...	The good thing about it is that ...
Sentimos mucho <u>lo ocurrido.</u>	We are very sorry about what happened.

⇨ *For more information on the **Past participle**, see page 115.*

➤ **lo** is also used in a number of very common phrases:

- **a lo mejor** maybe, perhaps

  <u>A lo mejor</u> ha salido. Perhaps he's gone out.

- **por lo menos** at least

  Hubo <u>por lo menos</u> cincuenta heridos. At least fifty people were injured.

- **por lo general** generally

  <u>Por lo general</u> me acuesto temprano. I generally go to bed early.

➤ **lo** can also be used with **que** to make **lo que** (meaning *what*).

Vi <u>lo que</u> pasó.	I saw what happened.
<u>Lo que</u> más me gusta es nadar.	What I like best is swimming.

Grammar Extra!

lo can be used with de followed by a noun phrase to refer back to something the speaker and listener both know about.

Lo de tu hermano me preocupa mucho.	<u>That business with your brother</u> worries me a lot.
Lo de ayer es mejor que lo olvides.	It would be best to forget <u>what happened yesterday.</u>

lo can be used with an adjective followed by **que** to emphasize how big/small/beautiful and so on something is or was. The adjective must agree with the noun it describes.

No sabíamos <u>lo pequeña que</u> era la casa.	We didn't know <u>how small</u> the house was.
No te imaginas <u>lo simpáticos que</u> son.	You can't imagine <u>how nice</u> they are.

lo can also be used in a similar way with an adverb followed by **que**.

Sé <u>lo mucho que</u> te gusta la música.	I know <u>how much</u> you like music.

Key points

✔ **lo** is classed as an article in Spanish, but is not used with nouns.

✔ You can use **lo** with a masculine adjective or past participle to form a noun.

✔ You also use **lo** in a number of common phrases.

✔ **lo que** can be used to mean *what* in English.

(ADJECTIVES)

> **What is an adjective?**
> An **adjective** is a 'describing' word that tells you more about a person or thing, such as their appearance, colour, size or other qualities, for example, *pretty*, *blue*, *big*.

Using adjectives

➤ Adjectives are words like *clever*, *expensive* and *silly* that tell you more about a noun (a living being, thing or idea). They can also tell you more about a pronoun, such as *he* or *they*. Adjectives are sometimes called 'describing words'. They can be used right next to a noun they are describing, or can be separated from the noun by a verb like *be*, *look*, *feel* and so on.

    a <u>clever</u> girl
    an <u>expensive</u> coat
    a <u>silly</u> idea
    He's just being <u>silly</u>.

⇨ *For more information on **Nouns** and **Pronouns**, see pages 1 and 41.*

➤ In English, the only time an adjective changes its form is when you are making a comparison.

    She's <u>cleverer</u> than her brother.
    That's the <u>silliest</u> idea I've ever heard!

➤ In Spanish, however, most adjectives <u>agree</u> with what they are describing. This means that their endings change depending on whether the person or thing you are referring to is masculine or feminine, singular or plural.

un chico <u>rubio</u>	a fair boy
una chica <u>rubia</u>	a fair girl
unos chicos <u>rubios</u>	some fair boys
unas chicas <u>rubias</u>	some fair girls

➤ In English adjectives come <u>BEFORE</u> the noun they describe, but in Spanish you usually put them <u>AFTER</u> it.

    una casa <u>blanca</u>   a <u>white</u> house

⇨ *For more information on **Word order with adjectives**, see page 24.*

Making adjectives agree

1 Forming feminine adjectives

➤ The form of the adjective shown in dictionaries is generally the masculine singular form. This means that you need to know how to change its form to make it agree with the person or thing it is describing.

➤ Adjectives ending in -o in the masculine change to -a for the feminine.

mi hermano <u>pequeño</u>	my little brother
mi hermana <u>pequeña</u>	my little sister

➤ Adjectives ending in any vowel other than -o (that is: *a, e, i* or *u*) or ending in a vowel with an accent on it do <u>NOT</u> change for the feminine.

el vestido <u>verde</u>	the green dress
la blusa <u>verde</u>	the green blouse
un pantalón <u>caqui</u>	some khaki trousers
una camisa <u>caqui</u>	a khaki shirt
un médico <u>iraquí</u>	an Iraqi doctor
una familia <u>iraquí</u>	an Iraqi family

➤ Adjectives ending in a consonant (any letter other than a vowel) do <u>NOT</u> change for the feminine except in the following cases:

- Adjectives of nationality or place ending in a consonant add -a for the feminine. If there is an accent on the final vowel in the masculine, they lose this in the feminine.

un periódico <u>inglés</u>	an English newspaper
una revista <u>inglesa</u>	an English magazine
el equipo <u>francés</u>	the French team
la cocina <u>francesa</u>	French cooking
el vino <u>español</u>	Spanish wine
la lengua <u>española</u>	the Spanish language

i Note that these adjectives do not start with a capital letter in Spanish.

- Adjectives ending in -or in the masculine usually change to -ora for the feminine.

un niño <u>encantador</u>	a charming little boy
una niña <u>encantadora</u>	a charming little girl

i Note that a few adjectives ending in -or used in comparisons – such as **mejor** (meaning *better, best*), **peor** (meaning *worse, worst*), **mayor** (meaning *older, bigger*), **superior** (meaning *upper, top*), **inferior** (meaning *lower, inferior*) as well as **exterior** (meaning *outside, foreign*) and **posterior** (meaning *rear*) do not change in the feminine.

- Adjectives ending in -án, -ón and -ín in the masculine change to -ana, -ona and -ina (without an accent) in the feminine.

un gesto <u>burlón</u>	a mocking gesture
una sonrisa <u>burlona</u>	a mocking smile
un hombre <u>parlanchín</u>	a chatty man
una mujer <u>parlanchina</u>	a chatty woman

➤ Adjectives ending in a consonant but which do not fall into the above categories do <u>NOT</u> change in the feminine.

un chico <u>joven</u>	a young boy
una chica <u>joven</u>	a young girl
un final <u>feliz</u>	a happy ending
una infancia <u>feliz</u>	a happy childhood

2 Forming plural adjectives

➤ Adjectives ending in an unaccented vowel (*a, e, i, o* or *u*) in the singular add -s in the plural.

el <u>último</u> tren	the last train
los <u>últimos</u> trenes	the last trains
una casa <u>vieja</u>	an old house
unas casas <u>viejas</u>	some old houses
una chica muy <u>habladora</u>	a very chatty girl
unas chicas muy <u>habladoras</u>	some very chatty girls
una pintora <u>francesa</u>	a French (woman) painter
unas pintoras <u>francesas</u>	some French (women) painters
una mesa <u>verde</u>	a green table
unas mesas <u>verdes</u>	some green tables

➤ Adjectives ending in a consonant in the masculine or feminine singular add -es in the plural. If there is an accent on the <u>FINAL</u> syllable in the singular, they lose it in the plural.

un chico muy <u>hablador</u>	a very chatty boy
unos chicos muy <u>habladores</u>	some very chatty boys
un pintor <u>francés</u>	a French painter
unos pintores <u>franceses</u>	some French painters

un examen <u>fácil</u>	an easy exam
unos exámenes <u>fáciles</u>	some easy exams
la tendencia <u>actual</u>	the current trend
las tendencias <u>actuales</u>	the current trends

➤ -z at the end of a singular adjective changes to -ces in the plural.

un día <u>feliz</u>	a happy day
unos días <u>felices</u>	happy days

Típ

When an adjective describes a mixture of both masculine and feminine nouns, use the <u>masculine plural</u> form of the adjective.

El pan y la fruta son <u>baratos.</u>   Bread and fruit are cheap.

Grammar Extra!

Adjectives ending in an accented vowel in the singular add -es in the plural.

un médico <u>iraní</u>	an Iranian doctor
unos médicos <u>iraníes</u>	some Iranian doctors

---

3 Invariable adjectives

➤ A small number of adjectives do not change in the feminine or plural. They are called <u>invariable</u> because their form <u>NEVER</u> changes, no matter what they are describing. These adjectives are often made up of more than one word – for example **azul marino** (meaning *navy blue*) – or come from the names of things – for example **naranja** (meaning *orange*).

las chaquetas <u>azul marino</u>	navy-blue jackets
los vestidos <u>naranja</u>	orange dresses

4 Short forms for adjectives

➤ The following adjectives drop the final -o before a <u>masculine singular noun</u>.

bueno	→	buen	→	un <u>buen</u> libro	a good book
malo	→	mal	→	<u>mal</u> tiempo	bad weather
alguno	→	algún	→	<u>algún</u> libro	some book
ninguno	→	ningún	→	<u>ningún</u> hombre	no man
uno	→	un	→	<u>un</u> día	one day
primero	→	primer	→	el <u>primer</u> hijo	the first child
tercero	→	tercer	→	el <u>tercer</u> hijo	the third child

For further explanation of grammatical terms, please see pages viii-xii.

[*i*] Note that the adjectives **alguno** and **ninguno** add accents when they are shortened to become **algún** and **ningún**.

➤ **grande** (meaning *big, great*) is shortened to **gran** before a <u>singular noun</u>.

un gran actor	a great actor
una gran sorpresa	a big surprise

➤ **ciento** (meaning *a hundred*) changes to **cien** before all <u>plural nouns</u> as well as before **mil** (meaning *thousand*) and **millones** (meaning *millions*).

cien años	a hundred years
cien millones	a hundred million

[*i*] Note that you use the form **ciento** before other numbers.

ciento tres	one hundred and three

⇨ *For more information on **Numbers**, see page 206.*

Grammar Extra!

➤ **cualquiera** drops the final **a** before any noun.

<u>**cualquier**</u> **día**	any day
a <u>**cualquier**</u> **hora**	any time

Key points

✔ Most Spanish adjectives change their form according to whether the person or thing they are describing is masculine or feminine, singular or plural.

✔ In Spanish, adjectives usually go after the noun they describe.

✔ Don't forget to make adjectives agree with the person or thing they describe – they change for the feminine and plural forms:
un chico español
una chica española
unos chicos españoles
unas chicas españolas

✔ Some adjectives never change their form.

✔ Some adjectives drop the final -o before a masculine singular noun.

✔ **grande** and **ciento** also change before certain nouns.

Word order with adjectives

➤ When adjectives are used right beside the noun they are describing, they go <u>BEFORE</u> it in English. Spanish adjectives usually go <u>AFTER</u> the noun.

una corbata <u>azul</u>	a <u>blue</u> tie
una palabra <u>española</u>	a <u>Spanish</u> word
la página <u>siguiente</u>	the <u>following</u> page
la hora <u>exacta</u>	the <u>precise</u> time

➤ When you have two or more adjectives after the noun, you use y (meaning *and*) between the last two.

un hombre alto <u>y</u> delgado   a tall, slim man

➤ A number of types of Spanish adjectives go <u>BEFORE</u> the noun:

- demonstrative adjectives
  <u>este</u> sombrero   this hat

- possessive adjectives (mi, tu, su and so on)
  <u>mi</u> padre   my father

- numbers
  <u>tres</u> días   three days

- interrogative adjectives
  ¿<u>qué</u> hombré?   which man?

- adjectives used in exclamations
  ¡<u>Qué</u> lástima!   What a pity!

- indefinite adjectives
  <u>cada</u> día   every day

- shortened adjectives
  <u>mal</u> tiempo   bad weather

➤ Some adjectives can go both <u>BEFORE</u> and <u>AFTER</u> the noun, but their meaning changes depending on where they go.

Adjective	Before Noun	Examples	After Noun	Examples
antiguo	former	**un antiguo colega** a former colleague	old, ancient	**la historia antigua** ancient history
diferente	various	**diferentes idiomas** various languages	different	**personas diferentes** different people
grande	great	**un gran pintor** a great painter	big	**una casa grande** a big house
medio	half	**medio melón** half a melon	average	**la nota media** the average mark
mismo	same	**la misma respuesta** the same answer	self, very, precisely	**yo mismo** myself **eso mismo** precisely that
nuevo	new	**mi nuevo coche** my new car (= *new to me*)	brand new	**unos zapatos nuevos** some (brand) new shoes
pobre	poor (= *wretched*)	**esa pobre mujer** that poor woman	poor (= *not rich*)	**un país pobre** a poor country
viejo	old (= *long-standing*)	**un viejo amigo** an old friend	old (= *aged*)	**esas toallas viejas** those old towels

---

Key points

✔ Most Spanish adjectives go after the noun.

✔ Certain types of adjectives in Spanish go before the noun.

✔ Some adjectives can go before or after the noun – the meaning changes according to the position in the sentence.

Comparatives and superlatives of adjectives

1 Making comparisons using comparative adjectives

> **What is a comparative adjective?**
> A **comparative adjective** in English is one with *-er* on the end of it or
> *more* or *less* in front of it, that is used to compare people or things, for
> example, *cleverer, less important, more beautiful.*

➤ In Spanish, to say something is *cheaper, more expensive* and so on, you use
más (meaning *more*) before the adjective.

Esta bicicleta es <u>más barata</u>.	This bicycle is cheaper.
La verde es <u>más cara</u>.	The green one is more expensive.

➤ To say something is *less expensive, less beautiful* and so on, you use **menos**
(meaning *less*) before the adjective.

La verde es <u>menos cara</u>.	The green one is less expensive.

➤ To introduce the person or thing you are making the comparison with,
use **que** (meaning *than*).

Es <u>más</u> alto <u>que</u> mi hermano.	He's taller than my brother.
La otra bicicleta es <u>más</u> cara <u>que</u> ésta.	The other bicycle is more expensive than this one.
Esta bicicleta es <u>menos</u> cara <u>que</u> la otra.	This bicycle is less expensive than the other one.

Grammar Extra!

When *than* in English is followed by a verbal construction, use <u>de lo que</u> rather than
que alone.

      Está <u>más</u> cansada <u>de lo que</u> parece.   She is more tired than she seems.

---

2 Making comparisons using superlative adjectives

> **What is a superlative adjective?**
> A **superlative adjective** in English is one with *-est* on the end of it or
> *most* or *least* in front of it, that is used to compare people or things, for
> example, *thinnest, most beautiful, least interesting.*

➤ In Spanish, to say something is *the cheapest, the most expensive* and so on, you use **el/la/los/las** (+ noun) + **más** + adjective.

el caballo más viejo	the oldest horse
la casa más pequeña	the smallest house
los hoteles más baratos	the cheapest hotels
las manzanas más caras	the most expensive apples
¿Quién es el más alto?	Who's the tallest?

➤ To say something is *the least expensive, the least intelligent* and so on, you use **el/la/los/las** (+ noun) + **menos** + adjective.

el hombre menos simpático	the least likeable man
la niña menos habladora	the least talkative girl
los cuadros menos bonitos	the least attractive paintings
las empleadas menos trabajadoras	the least hardworking (female) employees
¿Quién es el menos trabajador?	Who's the least hardworking?

Tip

In phrases like *the cleverest girl in the school* and *the tallest man in the world*, you use **de** to translate *in*.

el hombre más alto del mundo the tallest man in the world

3 | **Irregular comparatives and superlatives**

➤ Just as English has some irregular comparative and superlative forms – *better* instead of '*more good*', and *worst* instead of '*most bad*' – Spanish also has a few irregular forms.

Adjective	Meaning	Comparative	Meaning	Superlative	Meaning
bueno	good	**mejor**	better	**el mejor**	the best
malo	bad	**peor**	worse	**el peor**	the worst
grande	big	**mayor**	older	**el mayor**	the oldest
pequeño	small	**menor**	younger	**el menor**	the youngest

Éste es mejor que el otro.	This one is better than the other one.
Es el mejor de todos.	It's the best of the lot.
Hoy me siento peor.	I feel worse today.
la peor alumna de la clase	the worst student in the class

[i] Note that mejor, peor, mayor and menor don't change their endings in the feminine. In the plural, they become mejores, peores, mayores and menores. Don't forget to use el, la, los or las as appropriate, depending on whether the person or thing described is masculine or feminine, singular or plural.

Tip

más grande and más pequeño are used mainly to talk about the actual size of something.

Este plato es <u>más grande</u> que aquél.	This plate is bigger than that one.
Mi casa es <u>más pequeña</u> que la tuya.	My house is smaller than yours.

mayor and menor are used mainly to talk about age.

mis hermanos <u>mayores</u>	my older brothers
la hija <u>menor</u>	the youngest daughter

---

[4] **Other ways of making comparisons**

➤ To say *as … as* (for example, *as pretty as, not as pretty as*) you use tan … como in Spanish.

Pedro es <u>tan</u> alto <u>como</u> Miguel.	Pedro is as tall as Miguel.
No es <u>tan</u> guapa <u>como</u> su madre.	She isn't as pretty as her mother.
No es <u>tan</u> grande <u>como</u> yo creía.	It isn't as big as I thought.

Grammar Extra!

You use tanto with a noun rather than tan with an adjective in some expressions. This is because in Spanish you would use a noun where in English we would use an adjective.

Pablo tiene <u>tanto</u> miedo <u>como</u> yo.	Pablo is as frightened as I am.
Yo no tengo <u>tanta</u> hambre <u>como</u> tú.	I'm not as hungry as you are.

➤ To make an adjective stronger, you can use muy (meaning *very*).

Este libro es <u>muy</u> interesante.	This book is very interesting.

For further explanation of grammatical terms, please see pages viii-xii.

Grammar Extra!

For even more emphasis, you can add -ísimo (meaning *really, extremely*) to the end of an adjective. Take off the final vowel if the adjective already ends in one. For example, delgado (meaning *thin*) becomes delgadísimo (meaning *really thin*).

Se ha comprado un coche <u>carísimo</u>.	He's bought himself a really expensive car.
Está <u>delgadísima</u>.	She's looking really thin.

If you add -ísimo, you need to take off any other accent. For example, fácil (meaning *easy*) becomes facilísimo (meaning *extremely easy*) and rápido (meaning *fast*) becomes rapidísimo (meaning *extremely fast*).

Es <u>facilísimo</u> de hacer.	It's really easy to make.
un coche <u>rapidísimo</u>	an extremely fast car

When the adjective ends in -co, -go or -z, spelling changes are required to keep the same sound. For example, rico (meaning *rich*) becomes riquísimo (meaning *extremely rich*) and feroz (meaning *fierce*) becomes ferocísimo (meaning *extremely fierce*).

Se hizo <u>riquísimo</u>.	He became extremely rich.
un tigre <u>ferocísimo</u>	an extremely fierce tiger

⇨ *For more information on **Spelling** and **Stress**, see pages 196 and 200.*

Key points

✔ Comparative adjectives in Spanish are formed by:
 • más + adjective + que
 • menos + adjective + que

✔ Superlative adjectives in Spanish are formed by:
 • el/la/los/las + más + adjective
 • el/la/los/las + menos + adjective

✔ There are a few irregular comparative and superlative forms in Spanish.

✔ You can use tan ... como to say *as ... as*.

✔ To make an adjective stronger, use muy.

Demonstrative adjectives

> **What is a demonstrative adjective?**
> A **demonstrative adjective** is one of the words *this, that, these* and *those*
> used with a noun in English to point out a particular thing or person, for
> example, *this* woman, *that* dog.

1 Using demonstrative adjectives

➤ Just as in English, Spanish demonstrative adjectives go <u>BEFORE</u> the noun.
Like other adjectives in Spanish, they have to change for the feminine and
plural forms.

	Masculine	Feminine	Meaning
Singular	este	esta	this
	ese	esa	that (*close by*)
	aquel	aquella	that (*further away*)
Plural	estos	estas	these
	esos	esas	those (*close by*)
	aquellos	aquellas	those (*further away*)

➤ Use **este/esta/estos/estas** (meaning *this/these*) to talk about things and
people that are near <u>you</u>.

> **Este** bolígrafo no escribe.   This pen isn't working.
> **Me he comprado estos libros.**   I've bought these books.

➤ Use **ese/esa/esos/esas** and **aquel/aquella/aquellos/aquellas** (meaning
that/those) to talk about things that are further away.

> **Esa** revista es muy mala.   That magazine is very bad.
> **¿Conoces a esos señores?**   Do you know those gentlemen?
> **No le gusta aquella muñeca.**   She doesn't like that doll.
> **Siga usted hasta aquellos**   Carry on until you reach those
> **árboles.**   trees (over there).

2 ese or aquel?

➤ In English we use *that* and *those* to talk about anything that is not close by,
but in Spanish you need to be a bit more precise.

➤ Use **ese/esa/esos/esas**:

- to talk about things and people that are nearer to the person you are talking to than to you

<u>ese</u> papel en el que escribes	that paper you're writing on
¿Por qué te has puesto <u>esas</u> medias?	Why are you wearing those tights?

- to talk about things and people that aren't very far away

No me gustan <u>esos</u> cuadros.	I don't like those pictures.

➤ Use **aquel/aquella/aquellos/aquellas** to talk about things that are further away.

Me gusta más <u>aquella</u> mesa.	I prefer that table (over there).

Grammar Extra!

You should use **ese/esa/esos/esas** when you are talking about a definite date, month or year.

¿1999? No me acuerdo de dónde pasamos las vacaciones <u>ese</u> año.	1999? I can't remember where we went on holiday that year.

You should use **aquel/aquella/aquellos/aquellas** when you are talking about something in the past and not mentioning a definite date.

<u>aquellas</u> vacaciones que pasamos en Francia	those holidays we had in France

---

Key points

- ✔ <u>this</u> + noun = **este/esta** + noun
- ✔ <u>these</u> + noun = **estos/estas** + noun
- ✔ <u>that</u> + noun = **ese/esa** + noun (*when the object is not far away from you or the person you're talking to*)
- ✔ <u>that</u> + noun = **aquel/aquella** + noun (*when the object is more distant*)
- ✔ <u>those</u> + noun = **esos/esas** + noun (*when the objects are not far away from you or the person you're talking to*)
- ✔ <u>those</u> + noun = **aquellos/aquellas** + noun (*when the objects are more distant*)

Interrogative adjectives

> **What is an interrogative adjective?**
> An **interrogative adjective** is one of the question words and expressions used with a noun such as *which, what, how much* and *how many;* for example, *Which shirt are you going to wear?; How much time have we got?*

➤ In Spanish the interrogative adjectives are **qué** (meaning *which* or *what*) and **cuánto/cuánta/cuántos/cuántas** (meaning *how much/how many*). Note that like all other Spanish question words, **qué** and **cuánto** have accents on them.

➤ **¿qué?** (meaning *which?* or *what?*) doesn't change for the feminine and plural forms.

¿Qué libro te gusta más?	Which book do you like best?
¿Qué clase de diccionario necesitas?	What kind of dictionary do you need?
¿Qué instrumentos tocas?	What instruments do you play?
¿Qué ofertas has recibido?	What offers have you received?

➤ **¿cuánto?** means the same as *how much?* in English. It changes to **¿cuánta?** in the feminine form.

¿Cuánto dinero te queda?	How much money have you got left?
¿Cuánta lluvia ha caído?	How much rain have we had?

i Note that with **gente** (meaning *people*), which is a feminine singular noun, **cuánta** must be used.

¿Cuánta gente ha venido?	How many people came?

➤ **¿cuántos?** means the same as *how many?* in English. It changes to **¿cuántas?** in the feminine plural.

¿Cuántos bolígrafos quieres?	How many pens would you like?
¿Cuántas personas van a venir?	How many people are coming?

> *Tip*
> Don't forget to add the opening upside-down question mark in Spanish questions.

Grammar Extra!

In English we can say, *Tell me what time it is, He asked me how much sugar there was* and *I don't know which dress to choose* to express doubt, report a question, or ask a question in a roundabout or indirect way. In Spanish you can use qué and cuánto/cuánta/cuántos/ cuántas in the same way.

Dime <u>qué</u> hora es.	Tell me what time it is.
Me preguntó <u>cuánto</u> azúcar había.	He asked me how much sugar there was.
No sé <u>qué</u> vestido escoger.	I don't know which dress to choose.
No sé a <u>qué</u> hora llegó.	I don't know what time she arrived.
Dime <u>cuántas</u> postales quieres.	Tell me how many postcards you'd like.

Adjectives used in exclamations

➤ In Spanish ¡qué...! is often used where we might say *What a ...!* in English.

¡Qué lástima!	What a pity!
¡Qué sorpresa!	What a surprise!

Tip

Don't forget to add the opening upside-down exclamation mark in Spanish exclamations.

Grammar Extra!

¡qué...! combines with tan or más and an adjective in Spanish to mean *What (a)...!* in English.

¡Qué día tan *or* **más bonito!**	What a lovely day!
¡Qué tiempo tan *or* **más malo!**	What awful weather!
¡Qué pasteles tan *or* **más ricos!**	What delicious cakes!

In Spanish cuánto/cuánta/cuántos/cuántas can be used to mean *What a lot of ...!* in English.

¡Cuánto dinero!	What a lot of money!
¡Cuánta gente!	What a lot of people!
¡Cuántos autobuses!	What a lot of buses!
¡Cuánto tiempo!	What a long time!

For further explanation of grammatical terms, please see pages viii-xii.

Possessive adjectives (1)

What is a possessive adjective?
In English a **possessive adjective** is one of the words *my, your, his, her, its, our* or *their* used with a noun to show that one person or thing belongs to another.

➤ Like other adjectives in Spanish, possessive adjectives have to change for the feminine and plural forms.

Singular		Plural		Meaning
masculine	feminine	masculine	feminine	
mi	mi	mis	mis	my
tu	tu	tus	tus	your (*belonging to someone you address as tú*)
su	su	sus	sus	his; her; its; your (*belonging to someone you address as usted*)
nuestro	nuestra	nuestros	nuestras	our
vuestro	vuestra	vuestros	vuestras	your (*belonging to people you address as vosotros/vosotras*)
su	su	sus	sus	their; your (*belonging to people you address as ustedes*)

⇨ *For more information on **Ways of saying 'you' in Spanish**, see page 44.*

¿Dónde está <u>tu</u> hermana?	Where's your sister?
José ha perdido <u>su</u> cartera.	José has lost his wallet.
¿Dónde están **nuestros** pasaportes?	Where are our passports?
¿Por qué no traéis a **vuestros** hijos?	Why don't you bring your children?
Mis tíos están vendiendo <u>su</u> casa.	My uncle and aunt are selling their house.

Tip

Possessive adjectives agree with what they describe NOT with the person who owns that thing.

Pablo ha perdido <u>su</u> bolígrafo.	Pablo has lost his pen.
Pablo ha perdido <u>sus</u> bolígrafos.	Pablo has lost his pens.

[i] Note that possessive adjectives aren't normally used with parts of the body. You usually use the <u>definite article</u> instead.

Tiene <u>los</u> ojos verdes.	He's got green eyes.
No puedo mover <u>las</u> piernas.	I can't move my legs.

⇨ *For more information on **Articles**, see page 10.*

Típ

As **su** and **sus** can mean *his*, *her*, *its*, *your* or *their*, it can sometimes be a bit confusing. When you need to avoid confusion, you can say the Spanish equivalent of *of him* and so on.

<u>su</u> casa	→	**la casa <u>de él</u>**	his house *(literally: the house of him)*
<u>sus</u> amigos	→	**los amigos <u>de usted</u>**	your friends *(literally: the friends of you)*
<u>sus</u> coches	→	**los coches <u>de ellos</u>**	their cars *(literally: the cars of them)*
<u>su</u> abrigo	→	**el abrigo <u>de ella</u>**	her coat *(literally: the coat of her)*

⇨ *For more information on **Personal pronouns**, see page 42.*

Key points

✔ The Spanish possessive adjectives are:
  • mi/tu/su/nuestro/vuestro/su with a masculine singular noun
  • mi/tu/su/nuestra/vuestra/su with a feminine singular noun
  • mis/tus/sus/nuestros/vuestros/sus with a masculine plural noun
  • mis/tus/sus/nuestras/vuestras/sus with a feminine plural noun

✔ Possessive adjectives come before the noun they refer to. They agree with what they describe, rather than with the person who owns that thing.

✔ Possessive adjectives are not usually used with parts of the body. Use el/la/los or las as appropriate instead.

✔ To avoid confusion, it is sometimes clearer to use el coche de él/ella/ellas/ellos/usted and so on rather than su coche.

Possessive adjectives (2)

➤ In Spanish, there is a second set of possessive adjectives, which mean (of) mine, (of) yours and so on. Like other adjectives in Spanish, they change in the feminine and plural forms.

Singular		Plural		Meaning
masculine	feminine	masculine	feminine	
mío	mía	míos	mías	mine/of mine
tuyo	tuya	tuyos	tuyas	yours/of yours (*belonging to* tú)
suyo	suya	suyos	suyas	his/of his; hers/of hers; of its; yours/of yours (*belonging to* usted)
nuestro	nuestra	nuestros	nuestras	ours/of ours
vuestro	vuestra	vuestros	vuestras	yours/of yours (*belonging to* vosotros/as)
suyo	suya	suyos	suyas	theirs/of theirs; yours/of yours (*belonging to* ustedes)

⇨ *For more information on **Ways of saying 'you' in Spanish**, see page 44.*

un amigo <u>mío</u>	a (male) friend of mine, one of my (male) friends
una revista <u>tuya</u>	a magazine of yours, one of your magazines
una tía <u>suya</u>	an aunt of his/hers/theirs/yours, one of his/her/their/your aunts
una amiga <u>nuestra</u>	a (female) friend of ours, one of our friends
¿De quién es esta bufanda? – Es <u>mía</u>.	Whose scarf is this? – It's mine.

ℹ️ Note that unlike the other possessive adjectives, these adjectives go <u>AFTER</u> the noun they describe.

un amigo <u>vuestro</u>	a (male) friend of yours, one of your friends

Tip

Possessive adjectives agree with what they describe <u>NOT</u> with the person who owns that thing.

Estos apuntes son <u>míos</u>.   These notes are mine.

Grammar Extra!

mío/mía and so on are also used in exclamations and when addressing someone. In this case they mean the same as *my* in English.

¡Dios <u>mío</u>!	My God!
amor <u>mío</u>	my love
Muy señor <u>mío</u>	Dear Sir
hija <u>mía</u>	my dear daughter

Indefinite adjectives

> **What is an indefinite adjective?**
> An **indefinite adjective** is one of a small group of adjectives used to talk about people or things in a general way without saying exactly who or what they are, for example, *several, all, every*.

➤ In English indefinite adjectives do not change, but in Spanish most indefinite adjectives change for the feminine and plural forms.

Singular		Plural		Meaning
masculine	feminine	masculine	feminine	
algún	alguna	algunos	algunas	some; any
cada	cada			each; every
mismo	misma	mismos	mismas	same
mucho	mucha	muchos	muchas	a lot of
otro	otra	otros	otras	another; other
poco	poca	pocos	pocas	little; few
tanto	tanta	tantos	tantas	so much; so many
todo	toda	todos	todas	all; every
		varios	varias	several

algún día	some day
el **mismo** día	the same day
las **mismas** películas	the same films
otro coche	another car
mucha gente	a lot of people
otra manzana	another apple
pocos amigos	few friends

i Note that you can never use **otro** (meaning *other* or *another*) with **un** or **una**.

¿Me das **otra** manzana?	Will you give me another apple?
¿Tienes **otro** jersey?	Have you got another jumper?

Tip

Some and *any* are usually not translated before nouns that you can't count like bread, butter, water.

Hay pan en la mesa.	There's some bread on the table.
¿Quieres café?	Would you like some coffee?
¿Hay leche?	Is there any milk?
No hay mantequilla.	There isn't any butter.

➤ todo/toda/todos/todas (meaning *all* or *every*) can be followed by:

- a definite article (el, la, los, las)

  Han estudiado durante <u>toda la noche</u>.   They've been studying all night.

  Vienen <u>todos los</u> días.   They come every day.

- a demonstrative adjective (este, ese, aquel and so on)

  Ha llovido <u>toda esta</u> semana.   It has rained all this week.

- a possessive adjective (mi, tu, su and so on)

  Pondré en orden <u>todos mis</u> libros.   I'll sort out all my books.

- a place name.

  Lo sabe <u>todo Madrid</u>.   The whole of Madrid knows it.

➪ *For more information on **Articles**, **Demonstrative adjectives** and **Possessive adjectives**, see pages 10, 30 and 35.*

➤ As in English, Spanish indefinite adjectives come <u>BEFORE</u> the noun they describe.

  las <u>mismas</u> películas   the same films

Key points

✔ Like other adjectives, Spanish indefinite adjectives (such as otro and todo) must agree with what they describe.

✔ They go before the noun to which they relate.

PRONOUNS

What is a pronoun?
A **pronoun** is a word you use instead of a noun, when you do not need or want to name someone or something directly, for example, *it, you, none.*

➤ There are several different types of pronoun:
- <u>Personal pronouns</u> such as *I, you, he, her* and *they,* which are used to refer to you, the person you are talking to, or other people and things. They can be either <u>subject pronouns</u> (*I, you, he* and so on) or <u>object pronouns</u> (*him, her, them,* and so on).
- <u>Possessive pronouns</u> like *mine* and *yours,* which show who someone or something belongs to.
- <u>Indefinite pronouns</u> like *someone* or *nothing,* which refer to people or things in a general way without saying exactly who or what they are.
- <u>Relative pronouns</u> like *who, which* or *that,* which link two parts of a sentence together.
- <u>Interrogative pronouns</u> like *who, what* or *which,* which are used in questions.
- <u>Demonstrative pronouns</u> like *this* or *those,* which point things or people out.
- <u>Reflexive pronouns</u>, a type of object pronoun that forms part of Spanish reflexive verbs like **lavarse** (meaning *to wash*) or **llamarse** (meaning *to be called*).

➩ *For more information on **Reflexive verbs**, see page 91.*

➤ Pronouns often stand in for a noun to save repeating it.
> I finished my homework and gave <u>it</u> to my teacher.
> Do you remember Jack? I saw <u>him</u> at the weekend.

➤ Word order with personal pronouns is usually different in Spanish and English.

Personal pronouns: subject

> **What is a subject pronoun?**
> A **subject pronoun** is a word such as *I, he, she* and *they*, that carries out
> the action expressed by the verb. Pronouns stand in for nouns when it is
> clear who or what is being talked about, for example, *My brother isn't here
> at the moment. He'll be back in an hour.*

1 Using subject pronouns

➤ Here are the Spanish subject pronouns:

Singular	Meaning	Plural	Meaning
yo	I	**nosotros** (*masculine*)	we
tú	you	**nosotras** (*feminine*)	we
él	he	**vosotros** (*masculine*)	you
ella	she	**vosotras** (*feminine*)	you
usted (Vd.)	you	**ellos** (*masculine*)	they
		ellas (*feminine*)	they
		ustedes (Vds.)	you

i Note that there is an accent on **tú** (*you*) and **él** (*he*) so that they are
not confused with **tu** (*your*) and **el** (*the*).

> *Tip*
> The abbreviations **Vd.** and **Vds.** are often used instead of **usted**
> and **ustedes**.

➤ In English we use subject pronouns all the time – *I walk, you eat, they are
going.* In Spanish you don't need them if the verb endings and context
make it clear who the subject is. For example **hablo español** can only
mean *I speak Spanish* since the -**o** ending on the verb is only used with *I*.
Similarly, **hablamos francés** can only mean *we speak French* since the -**amos**
ending is only used with *we*. So the subject pronouns are not needed in
these examples.

Tengo un hermano.	I've got a brother.
Tenemos dos coches.	We've got two cars.

i Note that **usted/Vd.** and **ustedes/Vds.** are often used for politeness, even if they are not really needed.

> **¿Conoce <u>usted</u> al señor Martín?** Do you know Mr Martín?
> **Pasen <u>ustedes</u> por aquí.** Please come this way.

⟹ *For more information on **Ways of saying 'you' in Spanish**, see page 44.*

➤ Spanish subject pronouns are normally only used:
  - for emphasis

    > **¿Y <u>tú</u> qué piensas?** What do <u>you</u> think about it?
    > **<u>Ellos</u> sí que llegaron tarde.** <u>They</u> really did arrive late.

  - for contrast or clarity

    > **<u>Yo</u> estudio español pero <u>él</u> estudia francés.** I study Spanish but <u>he</u> studies French.
    > **<u>Él</u> lo hizo pero <u>ella</u> no.** <u>He</u> did it but <u>she</u> didn't.

  - after **ser** (meaning *to be*)

    > **Soy <u>yo</u>.** It's <u>me</u>.
    > **¿Eres <u>tú</u>?** Is that <u>you</u>?

  - in comparisons after **que** and **como**

    > **Enrique es más alto que <u>yo</u>.** Enrique is taller than <u>I</u> am *or* than me.
    > **Antonio no es tan alto como <u>tú</u>.** Antonio isn't as tall as <u>you</u> (are).

⟹ *For more information on **Making comparisons**, see page 26.*

  - on their own without a verb

    > **¿Quién dijo eso? – <u>Él</u>.** Who said that? – <u>He</u> did.
    > **¿Quién quiere venir? – <u>Yo</u>.** Who wants to come? – <u>I</u> do.

  - after certain prepositions

    > **Es para <u>ella</u>.** It's for <u>her</u>.

⟹ *For more information on **Pronouns after prepositions**, see page 54.*

i Note that *it* used as the subject, and *they* referring to things, are <u>NEVER</u> translated into Spanish.

> **¿Qué es? – Es una sorpresa.** What is it? – <u>It</u>'s a surprise.
> **¿Qué son? – Son abrelatas.** What are they? – <u>They</u> are tin openers.

2 Ways of saying *'you'* in Spanish

➤ In English we have only <u>one</u> way of saying *you*. In Spanish, there are <u>several</u> words to choose from. The word you use depends on:
  - whether you are talking to one person or more than one person
  - whether you are talking to a friend or family member, or someone else.

➤ If you are talking to one person <u>you know well</u>, such as a friend, a young person or a relative, use **tú**.

➤ If you are talking to one person <u>you do not know so well</u>, such as your teacher, your boss or a stranger, use the polite form, **usted**.

➤ If you are talking to <u>more than one person</u> you know well, use **vosotros** (or **vosotras**, if you are talking to women only) in Spain. Use **ustedes** instead in Latin America.

➤ Use **ustedes** if you are talking to more than one person <u>you do not know so well</u>.

> *Tip*
>
> Remember that adjectives describing **tú** and **usted** should be feminine if you're talking to a woman or girl, while adjectives describing **ustedes** should be feminine plural if you're talking to women or girls only.

3 Using the plural subject pronouns

➤ When you are talking about males only, use **nosotros**, **vosotros** or **ellos**.

<u>**Nosotros**</u> **no somos italianos.**	<u>We</u> are not Italian.

➤ When you are talking about females only, use **nosotras**, **vosotras** or **ellas**.

Hablé con mis hermanas.	I spoke to my sisters.
<u>**Ellas**</u> **estaban de acuerdo conmigo.**	<u>They</u> agreed with me.

➤ When you are talking about both males and females, use **nosotros**, **vosotros** or **ellos**.

<u>**Ellos**</u> **sí que llegaron tarde.**	<u>They</u> really did arrive late.

Key points

✔ The Spanish subject pronouns are: yo, tú, él, ella, usted in the singular, and nosotros/nosotras, vosotros/vosotras, ellos/ellas, ustedes in the plural.

✔ Don't use the subject pronouns (other than usted and ustedes) with verbs except for emphasis or clarity.

✔ Make sure you choose the correct form of the verb.

✔ Do use the subject pronouns:
  • after ser (meaning to be)
  • in comparisons after que and como
  • in one-word answers to questions.

✔ Choose the word for you carefully. Remember to think about how many people you are talking to and your relationship with them when deciding between tú, vosotros, vosotras, usted and ustedes.

✔ It as the subject of the verb, and they when it refers to things are NOT translated in Spanish.

✔ Use masculine plural forms (nosotros, vosotros, ellos) for groups made up of men and women.

✔ Remember to make any adjectives describing the subject agree.

Personal pronouns: direct object

> **What is a direct object pronoun?**
> A **direct object pronoun** is a word such as *me, him, us* and *them,* which is used instead of the noun to stand in for the person or thing most directly affected by the action expressed by the verb.

1 Using direct object pronouns

➤ Direct object pronouns stand in for nouns when it is clear who or what is being talked about, and save having to repeat the noun.

>   I've lost my glasses. Have you seen <u>them</u>?
>   'Have you met Jo?' – 'Yes, I really like <u>her</u>!'

➤ Here are the Spanish direct object pronouns:

Singular	Meaning	Plural	Meaning
me	me	nos	us
te	you (*relating to* **tú**)	os	you (*relating to* **vosotros/vosotras**)
lo	him it (*masculine*) you (*relating to* **usted** *– masculine*)	los	them (*masculine*) you (*relating to* **ustedes** *– masculine*)
la	her it (*feminine*) you (*relating to* **usted** *– feminine*)	las	them (*feminine*) you (*relating to* **ustedes** *– feminine*)

>   **Te** quiero.   I love you.
>   **No los toques.**   Don't touch them.

[*i*] Note that you cannot use the Spanish direct object pronouns on their own without a verb or after a preposition such as **a** or **de**.

⇨ *For more information on **Pronouns after prepositions**, see page 54.*

2 **Word order with direct object pronouns**

➤ The direct object pronoun usually comes <u>BEFORE</u> the verb.

¿Las ve usted?	Can you see them?
¿No me oís?	Can't you hear me?
Tu hija no nos conoce.	Your daughter doesn't know us.
¿Lo has visto?	Have you seen it?

➤ In orders and instructions telling someone <u>TO DO</u> something, the pronoun joins onto the end of the verb to form one word.

Ayúdame.	Help me.
Acompáñanos.	Come with us.

[*i*] Note that you will often need to add a written accent to preserve the spoken stress when adding pronouns to the end of verbs.

⇨ *For more information on **Stress**, see page 200.*

➤ In orders and instructions telling someone <u>NOT TO DO</u> something, the pronoun does <u>NOT</u> join onto the end of the verb.

No los toques.	Don't touch them.

➤ If the pronoun is the object of an infinitive (the *to* form of the verb) or a gerund (the *-ing* form of the verb), you always add the pronoun to the end of the verb to form one word, unless the infinitive or gerund follows another verb. Again, you may have to add a written accent to preserve the stress.

Se fue después de arreglarlo.	He left after fixing it.
Practicándolo, aprenderás.	You'll learn by practising it.

⇨ *For more information on **Verbs** and **Gerunds**, see pages 69 and 125.*

➤ Where an infinitive or gerund follows another verb, you can put the pronoun either at the end of the infinitive or gerund, or before the other verb.

Vienen a vernos *or* **Nos vienen a ver.**	They are coming to see us.
Está comiéndolo *or* **Lo está comiendo.**	He's eating it.

⇨ *For further information on the **Order of object pronouns**, see page 52.*

3 **Special use of lo**

➤ lo is sometimes used to refer back to an idea or information that has already been given. The word *it* is often missed out in English.

¿Va a venir María? – No lo sé.	Is María coming? – I don't know.
Habían comido ya pero no nos lo dijeron.	They had already eaten, but they didn't tell us.
Yo conduzco de prisa pero él lo hace despacio.	I drive fast but he drives slowly.

Key points

✔ The Spanish direct object pronouns are: me, te, lo, la in the singular, and nos, os, los, las in the plural.

✔ The object pronoun usually comes before the verb.

✔ Object pronouns are joined to the end of infinitives, gerunds or verbs instructing someone to do something.

✔ If an infinitive or gerund follows another verb, you can choose whether to add the object pronoun to the end of the infinitive or gerund or to put it before the first verb.

✔ lo is sometimes used to refer back to an idea or information that has already been given.

Personal pronouns: indirect object

> **What is an indirect object pronoun?**
> An **indirect object pronoun** is used instead of a noun to show the person
> or thing an action is intended to benefit or harm, for example, *me* in
> *He gave me a book.; Can you get me a towel?; He wrote to me.*

1   **Using indirect object pronouns**

➤ It is important to understand the difference between direct and indirect
  object pronouns in English, as they can have different forms in Spanish.

➤ You can usually test whether an object is a direct object or an indirect one
  by asking questions about the action using *what* and *who*:

  ● an indirect object answers the question *who ... to?* or *who ... for?*, equally
    what ... to? or *what ... for?*

    He gave me a book. → *Who did he give the book to?* → me
    (=*indirect object pronoun*)

    Can you get me a towel? → *Who can you get a towel for?* → me
    (=*indirect object pronoun*)

    We got some varnish for it. → *What did you get the varnish for?* → it
    (=*indirect object pronoun*)

  ● if something answers the question *what* or *who*, then it is the direct
    object and <u>NOT</u> the indirect object.

    He gave me a book. → *What did he give me?* → a book
    (=*direct object*)

    I saw Mandy. → *Who did you see?* → Mandy
    (=*direct object*)

    We got some varnish for it. → *What did you get?* → some varnish
    (=*direct object*)

i Note that a verb won't necessarily have both a direct and an indirect object.

➤   Here are the Spanish indirect object pronouns:

Singular	Meaning	Plural	Meaning
me	me, to me, for me	nos	us, to us, for us
te	you, to you, for you (*relating to tú*)	os	you, to you, for you (*relating to vosotros/vosotras*)
le	him, to him, for him her, to her, for her it, to it, for it you, to you, for you (*relating to usted*)	les	them, to them, for them you, to you, for you (*relating to ustedes*)

➤ The pronouns shown in the table are used instead of using the preposition **a** with a noun.

>**Estoy escribiendo <u>a Teresa</u>**. I am writing to Teresa. →
>**<u>Le</u> estoy escribiendo**. I am writing to her.
>**Compra un regalo <u>a los niños</u>**. Buy the children a present. →
>**Cómpra<u>les</u> un regalo**. Buy them a present.

➤ Some Spanish verbs like **mirar** (meaning *to look at*), **esperar** (meaning *to wait for*) and **buscar** (meaning *to look for*) take a direct object, because the Spanish construction is different from the English.

Grammar Extra!

You should usually use direct object pronouns rather than indirect object pronouns when replacing personal **a** + <u>noun</u>.

>**Vi <u>a Teresa</u>. → <u>La</u> vi.**   I saw Teresa. → I saw her.

➡ *For more information on **Personal** a, see page 182.*

---

2 | **Word order with indirect object pronouns**

➤ The indirect object pronoun usually comes <u>BEFORE</u> the verb.

Sofía <u>os</u> ha escrito.	Sophie has written to you.
¿<u>Os</u> ha escrito Sofía?	Has Sofía written to you?
Carlos no <u>nos</u> habla.	Carlos doesn't speak to us.
¿Qué <u>te</u> pedían?	What were they asking you for?

➤ In orders and instructions telling someone <u>TO DO</u> something, the pronoun goes on the end of the verb to form one word.

Respónde<u>me</u>.	Answer me.
Di<u>me</u> la respuesta.	Tell me the answer.

[ℹ] Note that you will often need to add a written accent to preserve the spoken stress.

➡ *For more information on **Stress**, see page 200.*

➤ In orders and instructions telling someone <u>NOT TO DO</u> something, the pronoun does not join onto the end of the verb.

>**No <u>me</u> digas la respuesta.**   Don't tell me the answer.

➤ If the pronoun is the object of an infinitive (the *to* form of the verb) or a gerund (the *-ing* form of the verb), you always add the pronoun to the end of the verb to form one word, unless the infinitive or gerund follows another verb. Again, you may have to add a written accent to preserve the stress.

Eso de dar<u>le</u> tu dirección no fue muy prudente.	It wasn't very wise to give him your address.
Gritándo<u>le</u> tanto lo vas a asustar.	You'll frighten him by shouting at him like that.

➤ Where an infinitive or gerund follows another verb, you can put the pronoun either at the end of the infinitive or gerund, or before the other verb.

Quiero decir<u>te</u> algo. *or* **<u>Te</u> quiero decir algo.**	I want to tell you something.
Estoy escribiéndo<u>le</u>. *or* **<u>Le</u> estoy escribiendo.**	I am writing to him/her.

⇨ *For further information on the **Order of object pronouns**, see page 52.*

*For further information on the **Order of object pronouns**, see page 52.*

Key points

✔ The Spanish indirect object pronouns are: **me, te, le** in the singular, and **nos, os, les** in the plural.

✔ They can replace the preposition **a** (meaning *to*) + noun.

✔ Like the direct object pronoun, the indirect object pronoun usually comes before the verb.

✔ Object pronouns are joined to the end of infinitives, gerunds or verbs instructing someone to do something.

✔ If an infinitive or gerund follows another verb, you can choose whether to add the object pronoun to the end of the infinitive or gerund or to put it before the first verb.

Order of object pronouns

➤ Two object pronouns are often used together in the same sentence; for example: *he gave me them* or *he gave them to me*. In Spanish, you should always put the indirect object pronoun BEFORE the direct object pronoun.

Indirect		Direct
me	BEFORE	lo
te		la
nos		los
os		las

Ana <u>os lo</u> mandará mañana.	Ana will send it to you tomorrow.
¿<u>Te los</u> ha enseñado mi hermana?	Has my sister shown them to you?
No <u>me lo</u> digas.	Don't tell me (that).
Todos estaban pidiéndo<u>telo</u>.	They were all asking you for it.
No quiere prestár<u>nosla</u>.	He won't lend it to us.

➤ You have to use **se** instead of **le** (*to him, to her, to you*) and **les** (*to them, to you*), when you are using the object pronouns **lo, la, los,** or **las**.

<u>Se</u> lo di ayer.	I gave it to him/her/you/them yesterday.
<u>Se</u> las enviaré.	I'll send them to him/her/you/them.

Key points

✔ When combining two object pronouns, put the indirect object pronoun before the direct object pronoun.

✔ Use **se** as the indirect object pronoun rather than **le** or **les** when there is more than one object pronoun.

For further explanation of grammatical terms, please see pages viii-xii.

Further information on object pronouns

➤ The object pronoun le can mean *(to) him, (to) her* and *(to) you;* les can mean *(to) them* and *(to) you,* and se can mean all of these things, which could lead to some confusion.

➤ To make it clear which one is meant, a él (meaning *to him*), a ella (meaning *to her*), a usted (meaning *to you*) and so on can be added to the phrase.

A ella le escriben mucho.	They write to her often.
A ellos se lo van a mandar pronto.	They will be sending it to them soon.

➤ When a noun object comes before the verb, the corresponding object pronoun must be used too.

A tu hermano lo conozco bien. I know your brother well.
(*literally: Your brother I know him well.*)

A María la vemos algunas veces. We sometimes see María.
(*literally: María we see her sometimes.*)

➤ Indirect object pronouns are often used in constructions with the definite article with parts of the body or items of clothing to show who they belong to. In English, we'd use a possessive adjective.

La chaqueta le estaba ancha.	His jacket was too loose.
Me duele el tobillo.	My ankle's sore.

⇨ *For more information on **The definite article** and **Possessive adjectives**, see pages 11, 35 and 37.*

➤ Indirect object pronouns can also be used in certain common phrases which use reflexive verbs.

Se me ha perdido el bolígrafo. I have lost my pen.

⇨ *For more information on **Reflexive verbs**, see page 91.*

[*i*] Note that in Spain, you will often hear le and les used instead of lo and los as direct object pronouns when referring to men and boys. It is probably better not to copy this practice since it is considered incorrect in some varieties of Spanish, particularly Latin American ones.

Pronouns after prepositions

➤ In English, we use *me, you, him* and so on after a preposition, for example, *he came <u>towards me</u>; it's <u>for you</u>; books <u>by him</u>*. In Spanish, there is a special set of pronouns which are used after prepositions.

➤ The pronouns used after a preposition in Spanish are the same as the subject pronouns, except for the forms **mí** (meaning *me*) **ti** (meaning *you*), and **sí** (meaning *himself, herself, yourself, themselves, yourselves*).

Singular	Meaning	Plural	Meaning
mí	me	**nosotros**	us (*masculine*)
ti	you	**nosotras**	us (*feminine*)
él	him	**vosotros**	you (*masculine*)
ella	her	**vosotras**	you (*feminine*)
usted (Vd.)	you	**ellos**	them (*masculine*)
sí	himself	**ellas**	them (*feminine*)
	herself	**ustedes (Vds.)**	you
	yourself	**sí**	themselves
			yourselves

Pienso <u>en ti</u>.	I think about you.
¿Son <u>para mí</u>?	Are they for me?
No he sabido nada <u>de él</u>.	I haven't heard from him.
Es <u>para ella</u>.	It's for her.
Iban <u>hacia ellos</u>.	They were going towards them.
Volveréis <u>sin nosotros</u>.	You'll come back without us.
Volaban <u>sobre vosotros</u>.	They were flying above you.

[*i*] Note that **mí**, **sí** and **él** each have an accent, to distinguish them from **mi** (meaning *my*) , **si** (meaning *if*), and **el** (meaning *the*), but **ti** does not have an accent.

➤ These pronouns are often used for emphasis.

¿A <u>ti</u> no te escriben?	Don't they write to <u>you</u>?
Me lo manda a <u>mí</u>, no a <u>ti</u>.	She's sending it to <u>me</u>, not to you.

➤ **con** (meaning *with*) combines with **mí**, **ti** and **sí** to form:

- **conmigo** with me

  Ven <u>conmigo</u>. Come with me.

- **contigo** with you

  Me gusta estar <u>contigo</u>. I like being with you.

- **consigo**   with himself/herself/yourself/themselves/yourselves
  Lo trajeron <u>consigo</u>.   They brought it with them.

➤ entre, hasta, salvo, menos and según are always used with the <u>subject pronouns</u> (yo and tú), rather than with the object pronouns (mí and ti).

- **entre**   between, among
  <u>entre</u> tú y yo   between you and me
- **hasta**   even, including
  <u>Hasta</u> yo puedo hacerlo.   Even I can do it.
- **menos**   except
  todos <u>menos</u> yo   everybody except me
- **salvo**   except
  todos <u>salvo</u> yo   everyone except me
- **según**   according to
  <u>según</u> tú   according to you

⇨ *For more information on **Subject pronouns**, see page 42.*

For more information on **Subject pronouns**, see page 42.

Key points

✔ Most prepositions are followed by the forms: mí, ti, sí and so on.

✔ con combines with mí, ti and sí to form conmigo, contigo and consigo.

✔ entre, hasta, menos, salvo and según are followed by the subject pronouns yo and tú.

Possessive pronouns

> **What is a possessive pronoun?**
> A **possessive pronoun** is one of the words *mine, yours, hers, his, ours* or *theirs,* which are used instead of a noun to show that one person or thing belongs to another, for example, *Ask Carole if this pen is hers.; Mine's the blue one.*

➤ Here are the Spanish possessive pronouns:

Masculine singular	Feminine singular	Masculine plural	Feminine plural	Meaning
el mío	la mía	los míos	las mías	mine
el tuyo	la tuya	los tuyos	las tuyas	yours (*belonging to* tú)
el suyo	la suya	los suyos	las suyas	his; hers; its; yours (*belonging to* usted)
el nuestro	la nuestra	los nuestros	las nuestras	ours
el vuestro	la vuestra	los vuestros	las vuestras	yours (*belonging to* vosotros/vosotras)
el suyo	la suya	los suyos	las suyas	theirs; yours (*belonging to* ustedes)

⇨ *For more information on **Ways of saying 'you' in Spanish**, see page 44.*

Pregunta a Cristina si este bolígrafo es el suyo.
Ask Cristina if this pen is hers.

¿Qué equipo ha ganado, el suyo o el nuestro?
Which team won – theirs or ours?

Mi perro es más joven que el tuyo.
My dog is younger than yours.

Daniel pensó que esos libros eran los suyos.
Daniel thought those books were his.

Si no tienes lápices, te prestaré los míos.
If you haven't got any pencils, I'll lend you mine.

Las habitaciones son más pequeñas que las vuestras.
The rooms are smaller than yours.

Típ

In Spanish, possessive pronouns agree with what they describe, <u>NOT</u> with the person who owns that thing. For example, el suyo can mean *his*, *hers*, *yours* or *theirs*, but can only be used to replace a masculine singular noun.

i Note that the prepositions a and de combine with the article el to form al and del, for example, a + el mío becomes al mío, and de + el mío becomes del mío.

Prefiero tu coche <u>al mío</u>.	I prefer your car to mine.
Su coche se parece <u>al vuestro</u>.	His/Her/Their car looks like yours.
Mi piso está encima <u>del tuyo</u>.	My flat is above yours.
Su colegio está cerca <u>del nuestro</u>.	His/Her/Your/Their school is near ours.

➤ Instead of el suyo/la suya/los suyos/las suyas, it is sometimes clearer to say el/la/los/las de usted, el/la/los/las de ustedes, el/la/los/las de ellos and so on. You choose between el/la/los/las to agree with the noun referred to.

mi libro y <u>el de</u> usted	my book and yours

➤ el/la/los/las de can also be used with a name or other noun referring to somebody.

Juan tiene un coche bonito pero yo prefiero <u>el de</u> Ana.	Juan's got a nice car, but I prefer Ana's.
Ellos tienen una casa bonita pero yo prefiero <u>la del</u> médico.	They've got a nice house but I prefer the doctor's.

Key points

✔ The Spanish possessive pronouns are el mío, el tuyo, el suyo, el nuestro, el vuestro and el suyo when they stand in for a masculine noun. If they stand in for a feminine or a plural noun, their forms change accordingly.

✔ In Spanish, the pronoun you choose has to agree with the noun it replaces, and <u>not</u> with the person who owns that thing.

✔ el/la/los/las de are used with a noun or pronoun to mean the *one(s) belonging to ...*

Indefinite pronouns

> **What is an indefinite pronoun?**
> An **indefinite pronoun** is one of a small group of pronouns such as *everything, nobody* and *something* which are used to refer to people or things in a general way without saying exactly who or what they are.

➤ Here are the most common Spanish indefinite pronouns:
- algo   something, anything

Tengo <u>algo</u> para ti.	I have something for you.
¿Viste <u>algo</u>?	Did you see anything?

- alguien   somebody, anybody

<u>Alguien</u> me lo ha dicho.	Somebody told me.
¿Has visto a <u>alguien</u>?	Have you seen anybody?

> *Tip*
>
> Don't forget to use personal a before indefinite pronouns referring to people when they are the object of a verb.
>
> | | |
> |---|---|
> | ¿Viste <u>a</u> alguien? | Did you see anybody? |
> | No vi <u>a</u> nadie. | I didn't see anybody. |
>
> ⇨ *For more information on **Personal** a, see page 182.*

- alguno/alguna/algunos/algunas   some, a few

<u>Algunos</u> de los niños ya saben leer.	Some of the children can already read.

- cada uno/una   each (one), everybody

Le dio una manzana a <u>cada uno</u>.	She gave each one an apple.
¡<u>Cada uno</u> a su casa!	Everybody home!

- cualquiera   anybody; any

<u>Cualquiera</u> puede hacerlo.	Anybody can do it.
<u>Cualquiera</u> de las explicaciones vale.	Any of the explanations is valid.

  - mucho/mucha/muchos/muchas   much; many

<u>Muchas</u> de las casas no tenían jardín.	Many of the houses didn't have a garden.

- **nada** nothing, anything

¿Qué tienes en la mano?	What have you got in your hand?
– <u>Nada</u>.	– Nothing.
No dijo <u>nada</u>.	He didn't say anything.

- **nadie** nobody, anybody

¿A quién ves? – A <u>nadie</u>.	Who can you see? – Nobody.
No quiere ver a <u>nadie</u>.	He doesn't want to see anybody.

Tip

Don't forget to use personal **a** before indefinite pronouns referring to people when they are the object of a verb.

¿Viste <u>a</u> alguien?	Did you see anybody?
No vi <u>a</u> nadie.	I didn't see anybody.

⇨ *For more information on **Personal a**, see page 182.*

- **ninguno/ninguna** none, any

¿Cuántas tienes? – <u>Ninguna</u>.	How many have you got? – None.
No me queda <u>ninguno</u>.	I haven't any left *or* I have none left.

- **otro/otra/otros/otras** another one; others

No me gusta este modelo.	I don't like this model. Have you got another?
¿Tienes <u>otro</u>?	

☐ Note that you can never put **un** or **una** before **otro** or **otra**.

- **poco/poca/pocos/pocas** little; few

sólo unos <u>pocos</u>	only a few

- **tanto/tanta/tantos/tantas** so much; so many

¿Se oía mucho ruido?	Was there a lot of noise? – Not so much.
– No <u>tanto</u>.	

- **todo/toda/todos/todas** all; everything

Lo ha estropeado <u>todo</u>.	He has spoiled everything.
<u>Todo</u> va bien.	It's all going well.

- **uno ... el otro/una ... la otra** (the) one ... the other

<u>Uno</u> dijo que sí y <u>el otro</u> que no.	One said yes while the other said no.

- unos ... los otros/unas ... las otras   some ... the others

<u>Unos</u> cuestan 30 euros, <u>los otros</u> 40 euros.	Some cost 30 euros, the others 40 euros.

- varios/varias several

<u>Varios</u> de ellos me gustan mucho.	I like several of them very much.

Tip

Don't forget to make those pronouns that have feminine and plural forms agree with the noun they refer to.

He perdido mi goma pero tengo <u>otra</u>.	I've lost my rubber but I've got another one.

---

[i] Note that algo, alguien and alguno can <u>NEVER</u> be used after a negative such as no. Instead you must use the appropriate negative pronouns, nada, nadie, ninguno.

<u>No</u> veo a <u>nadie</u>.	I can't see anybody.
<u>No</u> tengo <u>nada</u> que hacer.	I haven't got anything to do.

➤ You use nada, nadie and ninguno on their own without no to answer questions.

¿Qué pasa? – <u>Nada</u>.	What's happening? – Nothing.
¿Quién habló? – <u>Nadie</u>.	Who spoke? – Nobody.
¿Cuántos quedan? – <u>Ninguno</u>.	How many are there left? – None.

➤ You also use nada, nadie and ninguno on their own without no when they come before a verb.

<u>Nada</u> lo asusta.	Nothing frightens him.
<u>Nadie</u> habló.	Nobody spoke.
<u>Ninguno</u> de mis amigos quiso venir.	None of my friends wanted to come.

⇨ *For more information on **Negatives**, see page 157.*

Key points

✔ Where indefinite pronouns have alternative endings, they must agree with the noun they refer to.

✔ *Anything* is usually translated by algo in questions and by nada in sentences containing no.

✔ *Anybody* is usually translated by alguien in questions and by nadie in sentences containing no.

✔ When nada, nadie or ninguno come <u>after</u> the verb, remember to put no before it. When they come <u>before</u> the verb, don't use no.

For further explanation of grammatical terms, please see pages viii-xii.

Relative pronouns

> **What is a relative pronoun?**
> In English, a **relative pronoun** is one of the words *who, which* and *that* (and the more formal *whom*) which can be used to introduce information that makes it clear which person or thing is being talked about, for example, *The man who has just come in is Ann's boyfriend.; The vase that you broke was quite valuable.*
> Relative pronouns can also introduce further information about someone or something, for example, *Peter, who is a brilliant painter, wants to study art.; Jane's house, which was built in 1890, needs a lot of repairs.*

1 Relative pronouns referring to people

➤ In English, we use the relative pronouns *who, whom* and *that* to talk about people. In Spanish, **que** is used.

el hombre que vino ayer	the man who came yesterday
Mi hermano, que tiene veinte años, es mecánico.	My brother, who is twenty, is a mechanic.
el hombre que vi en la calle	the man (that) I saw in the street

> *Tip*
>
> In English we often miss out the relative pronouns *who, whom* and *that*. For example, we can say both *the friends that I see most*, or *the friends I see most*.
>
> In Spanish, you can **NEVER** miss out **que** in this way.

➤ When the relative pronoun is used with a preposition, use **el/la/los/las que** or **quien/quienes** which must agree with the noun it replaces; **el que** changes for the feminine and plural forms, **quien** changes only in the plural.

➤ Here are the Spanish relative pronouns referring to people that are used after a preposition:

	Masculine	Feminine	Meaning
Singular	el que quien	la que quien	who, that, whom
Plural	los que quienes	las que quienes	who, that, whom

las mujeres con <u>las que</u> or **con <u>quienes</u> estaba hablando**	the women (that) she was talking to
La chica de <u>la que</u> or de **<u>quien</u> te hablé llega mañana.**	The girl (that) I told you about is coming tomorrow.
los niños de <u>los que</u> or **de <u>quienes</u> se ocupa usted**	the children (that) you look after

[*i*] Note that when **de** is used with **el que**, they combine to become **del que**. When **a** is used with **el que**, they combine to become **al que**.

el chico <u>del que</u> te hablé	the boy I told you about
Vive con un hombre <u>al que</u> adora.	She lives with a man she adores.

Tip

In English, we often put prepositions at the end of the sentence, for example, *the man she was talking to*. In Spanish, you can <u>never</u> put a preposition at the end of a sentence.

el hombre <u>con el que</u> or **<u>con quien</u> estaba hablando**	the man she was talking to

⇨ *For more information on **Prepositions**, see page 178.*

---

2 <u>Relative pronouns referring to things</u>

➤ In English, we use the relative pronouns *which* and *that* to talk about things. In Spanish, **que** is used.

la novela <u>que</u> ganó el premio	the novel <u>that</u> or <u>which</u> won the prize
el coche <u>que</u> compré	the car (<u>that</u> or <u>which</u>) I bought

---

Tip

In English, we often miss out the relative pronouns *which* and *that*. For example, we can say both *the house <u>which</u> we want to buy*, or *the house we want to buy*.

In Spanish, you can <u>NEVER</u> miss out **que** in this way.

➤ When the relative pronoun is used with a preposition, use el/la/los/las que, which must agree with the noun it replaces. Here are the Spanish relative pronouns referring to things that are used after a preposition:

	Masculine	Feminine	Meaning
Singular	el que	la que	which, that
Plural	los que	las que	which, that

<blockquote>

la tienda a <u>la que</u> siempre va   the shop (that or which) she always goes to

los temas de <u>los que</u> habla   the subjects he talks about

</blockquote>

[i] Note that when de is used with el que, they combine to become del que. When a is used with el que, they combine to become al que.

<blockquote>

el programa <u>del que</u> te hablé   the programme I told you about

el banco <u>al que</u> fuiste   the bank you went to

</blockquote>

➤ The neuter form lo que is used when referring to the whole of the previous part of the sentence.

<blockquote>

Todo estaba en silencio, <u>lo que</u> me pareció raro.   All was silent, which I thought was odd.

</blockquote>

⇨ *For more information on lo que, see page 17.*

Tip

In English, we often put prepositions at the end of the sentence, for example, *the shop she always goes to*. In Spanish, you can <u>never</u> put a preposition at the end of a sentence.

la tienda <u>a la que</u> siempre va   the shop she always goes <u>to</u>

la película <u>de la que</u> te hablaba   the film I was telling you <u>about</u>

Grammar Extra!

In English we can use *whose* to show possession, for example, *the woman whose son is ill*. In Spanish you use cuyo/cuya/cuyos/cuyas; cuyo is actually an adjective and must agree with the noun it describes <u>NOT</u> with the person who owns that thing.

La mujer, <u>cuyo</u> nombre era Antonia, estaba jubilada.	The woman, whose name was Antonia, was retired.
el señor en <u>cuya</u> casa me alojé	the gentleman whose house I stayed in

In your reading, you may come across the forms el cual/la cual/los cuales/las cuales which are a more formal alternative to el que/la que/los que/las que after a preposition.

las mujeres con <u>las cuales</u> estaba hablando	the women (that or who) she was talking to
la ventana desde <u>la cual</u> nos observaban	the window from which they were watching us

el cual/la cual/los cuales/las cuales are also useful to make it clear who you are talking about in other cases where the pronoun does not immediately follow the person or thing it refers to.

El padre de Elena, <u>el cual</u> tiene mucho dinero, es ...	Elena's father, who has a lot of money, is ...

---

3 | **Other uses of el que, la que, los que, las que**

➤ You can use el que, la que, los que, las que to mean *the one(s) (who/which)* or *those who*.

Esa película es <u>la que</u> quiero ver.	That film is the one I want to see.
<u>los que</u> quieren irse	those who want to leave

> **Key points**
> ✔ que can refer to both people and things in Spanish.
> ✔ In English we often miss out the relative pronouns *who*, *which* and *that*, but in Spanish you can never miss out que.
> ✔ After a preposition you use el que/la que/los que/las que or quien/quienes if you are referring to people; you use el que/la que/los que/las que if you are referring to things. el que and quien agree with the nouns they replace.
> ✔ a + el que → al que
> de + el que → del que
> ✔ <u>Never</u> put the preposition at the end of the sentence in Spanish.
> ✔ el que/la que/los que and las que are also used to mean *the one(s) who/which* or *those who*.

For further explanation of grammatical terms, please see pages viii-xii.

Interrogative pronouns

> **What is an interrogative pronoun?**
> In English, an **interrogative pronoun** is one of the words *who, which, whose, whom,* and *what* when they are used without a noun to ask questions.

➤ These are the interrogative pronouns in Spanish:

Singular	Plural	Meaning
¿qué?	¿qué?	what?
¿cuál?	¿cuáles?	which? which one(s)?; what?
¿quién?	¿quiénes?	who? (*as subject or after a preposition*)
¿cuánto?/¿cuánta?	¿cuántos?/¿cuántas?	how much? how many?

[*i*] Note that question words have an accent on them in Spanish.

1 ¿qué?

➤ ¿qué? is the equivalent of *what?* in English.

¿**Qué** están haciendo?	What are they doing?
¿**Qué** dices?	What are you saying?
¿Para <u>qué</u> lo quieres?	What do you want it for?

➤ You can use ¿por qué? in the same way as *why?* in English.

¿<u>Por qué</u> no vienes?	Why don't you come?

2 ¿cuál?, ¿cuáles?

➤ ¿cuál? and ¿cuáles? are usually the equivalent of *which?* in English and are used when there is a choice between two or more things.

¿<u>Cuál</u> de estos vestidos te gusta más?	Which of these dresses do you like best?
¿<u>Cuáles</u> quieres?	Which (ones) do you want?

[*i*] Note that you don't use cuál before a noun; use qué instead.

¿<u>Qué</u> libro es más interesante?	Which book is more interesting?

➪ *For more information on **Interrogative adjectives**, see page 32.*

3 | qué es or cuál es?

➤ You should only use ¿qué es ...? (meaning *what is...?*) and ¿qué son ...? (meaning *what are...?*) when you are asking someone to define, explain or classify something.

¿Qué es esto?	What is this?
¿Qué son los genes?	What are genes?

➤ Use ¿cuál es ...? and ¿cuáles son...? (also meaning *what is ...?* and *what are ...?*) when you want someone to specify a particular detail, number, name and so on.

¿Cuál es la capital de España?	What is the capital of Spain?
¿Cuál es tu consejo?	What's your advice?

4 | ¿quién?

➤ ¿quién? and ¿quiénes? are the equivalent of *who?* in English when it is the subject of the verb or when used with a preposition.

¿Quién ganó la carrera?	Who won the race?
¿Con quiénes los viste?	Who did you see them with?
¿A quién se lo diste?	Who did you give it to?

➤ ¿a quién? and ¿a quiénes? are the equivalent of *who(m)?* when it is the object of the verb.

¿A quién viste?	Who did you see? *or* Whom did you see?
¿A quiénes ayudaste?	Who did you help? *or* Whom did you help?

➤ ¿de quién? and ¿de quiénes? are the equivalent of *whose?* in English.

¿De quién es este libro?	Whose is this book? *or* Whose books are these?
¿De quiénes son estos coches?	Whose are these cars? *or* Whose cars are these?

5 | ¿cuánto?, ¿cuántos?

➤ ¿cuánto? (*masculine*) and ¿cuánta? (*feminine*) are the equivalent of *how much* in English. ¿cuántos? (*masculine plural*) and ¿cuántas? (*feminine plural*) are the equivalent of *how many?*

¿Cuánto es?	How much is it?
¿Cuántos tienes?	How many have you got?

Demonstrative pronouns

> **What is a demonstrative pronoun?**
> In English a **demonstrative pronoun** is one of the words *this, that, these,* and *those* used instead of a noun to point people or things out, for example, *That* looks fun.

1 Using demonstrative pronouns

➤ These are the demonstrative pronouns in Spanish:

	Masculine	Feminine	Neuter	Meaning
Singular	éste	ésta	esto	this, this one
	ése	ésa	eso	that, that one (*close by*)
	aquél	aquélla	aquello	that, that one (*further away*)
Plural	éstos	éstas		these, these ones
	ésos	ésas		those, those ones (*close by*)
	aquéllos	aquéllas		those, those ones (*further away*)

➤ The demonstrative pronouns in Spanish have to agree with the noun that they are replacing.

¿Qué abrigo te gusta más? – **Éste** de aquí.	Which coat do you like best? – This one here.
Aquella casa era más grande que **ésta**.	That house was bigger than this one.
estos libros y **aquéllos**	these books and those (over there)
Quiero estas sandalias y **ésas**.	I'd like these sandals and those ones.

2 ¿ése or aquél?

➤ In English we use *that* and *those* to talk about anything that is not close by. In Spanish, you need to be a bit more precise.

➤ Use ése/ésa and so on to indicate things and people that are nearer to the person you're talking to than to you.

Me gusta más **ése** que tienes en la mano.	I prefer the one you've got in your hand.

➤ Use ése/ésa and so on to indicate things and people that aren't very far away.

Si quieres ver una película, podemos ir a **ésa** que dijiste.	If you want to see a film, we can go and see that one you mentioned.

➤ Use **aquél/aquélla** and so on to talk about things that are further away.

Aquélla al fondo de la calle es mi casa.	My house is that one at the end of the street.

ⓘ Note that the masculine and feminine forms of demonstrative <u>pronouns</u> usually have an accent, to distinguish them from demonstrative <u>adjectives</u>. Compare:

este bolígrafo	this pen	**éste**	this one
esa mesa	that table	**ésa**	that one

⇨ *For more information on **Demonstrative adjectives**, see page 30.*

➤ The neuter forms (**esto, eso, aquello**) are used to talk about an object you don't recognize or about an idea or statement.

¿Qué es <u>eso</u> que llevas en la mano?	What's that you've got in your hand?
No puedo creer que <u>esto</u> me esté pasando a mí.	I can't believe this is really happening to me.
<u>Aquello</u> sí que me gustó.	I really did like that.

ⓘ Note that the neuter forms of demonstrative pronouns do <u>NOT</u> have an accent.

Key points

✔ Spanish demonstrative pronouns agree with the noun they are replacing.

✔ Masculine and feminine demonstrative pronouns usually have an accent on them in both the singular and the plural.

✔ In Spanish you have to choose the correct pronoun to emphasize the difference between something that is close to you and something that is further away:
  • **éste/ésta/éstos** and **éstas** (meaning *this/these*) are used to indicate things and people that are very close.
  • **ése/ésa/ésos** and **ésas** (meaning *that/those*) are used to indicate things and people that are near the person you are talking to or that aren't too far away.
  • **aquél/aquélla/aquéllos/aquéllas** (meaning *that/those*) are used to indicate things and people that are further away.

✔ The neuter pronouns (**esto, eso** and **aquello**) are used to talk about things you don't recognize or to refer to statements or ideas. They don't have an accent.

VERBS

What is a verb?
A **verb** is a 'doing' word which describes what someone or something does, what someone or something is, or what happens to them, for example, *be, sing, live*.

Overview of verbs

➤ Verbs are frequently used with a noun, with somebody's name or, particularly in English, with a pronoun such as *I, you* or *she*. They can relate to the present, the past and the future; this is called their <u>tense</u>.

⇨ *For more information on **Nouns** and **Pronouns**, see pages 1 and 41.*

➤ Verbs are either:
  • **regular**; their forms follow the normal rules
  • **irregular**; their forms do not follow normal rules

➤ Almost all verbs have a form called the <u>infinitive</u>. This is a base form of the verb (for example, *walk, see, hear*) that hasn't had any endings added to it and doesn't relate to any particular tense. In English, the infinitive is usually shown with *to*, as in *to speak, to eat, to live*.

➤ In Spanish, the infinitive is always made up of just one word (never two as in *to speak* in English) and ends in **-ar**, **-er** or **-ir**: for example, **hablar** (meaning *to speak*), **comer** (meaning *to eat*) and **vivir** (meaning *to live*). All Spanish verbs belong to one of these three types, which are called <u>conjugations</u>. We will look at each of these three conjugations in turn on the next few pages.

➤ Regular English verbs have other forms apart from the infinitive: a form ending in *-s* (*walks*), a form ending in *-ing* (*walking*), and a form ending in -ed (*walked*).

➤ Spanish verbs have many more forms than this, which are made up of endings added to a <u>stem</u>. The stem of a verb can usually be worked out from the infinitive.

➤ Spanish verb endings change depending on who or what is doing the action and on when the action takes place. In fact, the ending is very often the only thing that shows you <u>who</u> is doing the action, as the Spanish equivalents of *I, you, he* and so on (**yo, tú, él** and so on) are not used very much. So, both **hablo** on its own and **yo hablo** mean *I speak*. Sometimes there is a name or a noun in the sentence to make it clear who is doing the action.

<u>**José**</u> **habla español.**	<u>José</u> speaks Spanish.
<u>**El profesor**</u> **habla español.**	<u>The teacher</u> speaks Spanish.

⇨ *For more information on **Subject pronouns**, see page 42.*

➤ Spanish verb forms also change depending on whether you are talking about the present, past or future, so (**yo**) **hablaré** means *I will speak* while (**yo**) **hablé** means *I spoke*.

➤ Some verbs in Spanish do not follow the usual patterns. These <u>irregular verbs</u> include some very common and important verbs like **ir** (meaning *to go*), **ser** and **estar** (meaning *to be*) and **hacer** (meaning *to do* or *to make*). Other verbs are only slightly irregular, changing their stems in certain tenses.

⇨ *For **Verb Tables**, see supplement.*

> **Key points**
> ✔ Spanish verbs have different forms depending on who or what is doing the action and on the tense.
> ✔ Spanish verb forms are made up of a stem and an ending. The stem is usually based on the infinitive of the verb. The ending depends on who or what is doing the action and on when the action takes place.
> ✔ Regular verbs follow the standard patterns for **-ar**, **-er** and **-ir** verbs. Irregular verbs do not.

The present tenses

> **What are the present tenses?**
> The **present tenses** are the verb forms that are used to talk about what is true at the moment, what happens regularly and what is happening now; for example, *I'm a student*; *I travel to college by train*; *I'm studying languages*.

➤ In English, there are two tenses you can use to talk about the present:

- the present simple tense
  I live here.
  They get up early.

- the present continuous tense
  He is eating an apple.
  You aren't working very hard.

➤ In Spanish, there is also a present simple and a present continuous tense. As in English, the present simple in Spanish is used to talk about:

- things that are generally true
  En invierno hace frío.   It's cold in winter.

- things that are true at the moment
  Carlos no come carne.   Carlos doesn't eat meat.

- things that happen at intervals
  A menudo vamos al cine.   We often go to the cinema.

➤ The present continuous tense in Spanish is used to talk about things that are happening right now or at the time of writing:

  Marta está viendo la televisión.   Marta is watching television.

➤ However, there are times where the use of the present tenses in the two languages is not exactly the same.

⇨ *For more information on the use of the **Present tenses**, see pages 79 and 84.*

The present simple tense

1 | Forming the present simple tense of regular -ar verbs

➤ If the infinitive of the Spanish verb ends in **-ar**, it means that the verb belongs to the <u>first conjugation</u>, for example, **hablar**, **lavar**, **llamar**.

➤ To know which form of the verb to use in Spanish, you need to work out what the stem of the verb is and then add the correct ending. The stem of regular **-ar** verbs in the present simple tense is formed by taking the <u>infinitive</u> and chopping off **-ar**.

Infinitive	Stem (without -ar)
hablar (*to speak*)	habl-
lavar (*to wash*)	lav-

➤ Now you know how to find the stem of a verb you can add the correct ending. The one you choose will depend on who or what is doing the action.

i Note that as the ending generally makes it clear who is doing the action, you usually don't need to add a subject pronoun such as **yo** (meaning *I*), **tú** (meaning *you*) as well.

⤷ *For more information on **Subject pronouns**, see page 42.*

➤ Here are the present simple endings for regular **-ar** verbs:

Present simple endings	Present simple of hablar	Meaning: *to speak*
-o	(yo) habl<u>o</u>	I speak
-as	(tú) habl<u>as</u>	you speak
-a	(él/ella) habl<u>a</u>	he/she/it speaks
	(usted) habl<u>a</u>	you speak
-amos	(nosotros/nosotras) habl<u>amos</u>	we speak
-áis	(vosotros/vosotras) habl<u>áis</u>	you speak
-an	(ellos/ellas) habl<u>an</u> (ustedes) habl<u>an</u>	they speak you speak

➤ You use the **él/ella** (*third person singular*) form of the verb with nouns and with people's names, when you are just talking about one person, animal or thing.

Lydia estudi<u>a</u> medicina.	Lydia studies *or* is studying medicine.
Mi profesor me ayud<u>a</u> mucho.	My teacher helps me a lot.

➤ You use the **ellos/ellas** (*third person plural*) form of the verb with nouns and with people's names, when you are talking about more than one person, animal or thing.

Lydia y Carlos estudian medicina.	Lydia and Carlos study *or* are studying medicine.
Mis profesores me ayudan mucho.	My teachers help me a lot.

[i] Note that even though you use the **él/ella** and **ellos/ellas** forms of the verb to talk about things in Spanish, you should never include the pronouns **él, ella, ellos** or **ellas** themselves in the sentence when referring to things.

Funciona bien.	It works well.
Funcionan bien.	They work well.

➪ *For more information on **Ways of saying 'you' in Spanish**, see page 44.*

Key points

✔ Verbs ending in -ar belong to the first conjugation. Regular -ar verbs form their present tense stem by losing the -ar.

✔ The present tense endings for regular -ar verbs are: -o, -as, -a, -amos, -áis, -an.

✔ You usually don't need to give a pronoun in Spanish as the ending of the verb makes it clear who or what is doing the action.

---

2 **Forming the present simple tense of regular -er verbs**

➤ If the infinitive of the Spanish verb ends in -**er**, it means that the verb belongs to the second conjugation, for example, **comer, depender**.

➤ The stem of regular -**er** verbs in the present simple tense is formed by taking the infinitive and chopping off -**er**.

Infinitive	Stem (without -er)
comer (*to eat*)	com-
depender (*to depend*)	depend-

➤ Now add the correct ending, depending on who or what is doing the action.

[i] Note that as the ending generally makes it clear who is doing the action, you usually don't need to add a subject pronoun such as **yo** (meaning *I*) or **tú** (meaning *you*) as well.

➪ *For more information on **Subject pronouns**, see page 42.*

➤ Here are the present simple endings for regular -er verbs:

Present simple endings	Present simple of comer	Meaning: *to eat*
-o	(yo) com<u>o</u>	I eat
-es	(tú) com<u>es</u>	you eat
-e	(él/ella) com<u>e</u>	he/she/it eats
	(usted) com<u>e</u>	you eat
-emos	(nosotros/nosotras) com<u>emos</u>	we eat
-éis	(vosotros/vosotras) com<u>éis</u>	you eat
-en	(ellos/ellas) com<u>en</u>	they eat
	(ustedes) com<u>en</u>	you eat

➤ You use the él/ella (*third person singular*) form of the verb with nouns and with people's names, when you are just talking about one person, animal or thing.

> **Juan com<u>e</u> demasiado.**   Juan eats too much.
>
> **Mi padre me deb<u>e</u> 15 euros.**   My father owes me 15 euros.

➤ You use the ellos/ellas (*third person plural*) form of the verb with nouns and with people's names, when you talking about more than one person, animal or thing.

> **Juan y Pedro com<u>en</u> demasiado.**   Juan and Pedro eat too much.
>
> **Mis padres me deb<u>en</u> 15 euros.**   My parents owe me 15 euros.

[*i*] Note that even though you use the él/ella and ellos/ellas forms of the verb to talk about things in Spanish, you should <u>never</u> include the pronouns él, ella, ellos or ellas themselves in the sentence when referring to things.

> **Depende.**   It depends.

⇨ *For more information on **Ways of saying 'you' in Spanish**, see page 44.*

Key points

✔ Verbs ending in -er belong to the second conjugation. Regular -er verbs form their present tense stem by losing the -er.

✔ The present tense endings for regular -er verbs are: -o, -es, -e, -emos, -éis, -en.

✔ You usually don't need to give a pronoun in Spanish as the ending of the verb makes it clear who or what is doing the action.

---

3 | Forming the present simple tense of regular -ir verbs

➤ If the infinitive of the Spanish verb ends in -ir, it means that the verb belongs to the <u>third conjugation</u>, for example, **vivir**, **recibir**.

➤ The stem of regular -ir verbs in the present simple tense is formed by taking the <u>infinitive</u> and chopping off -ir.

Infinitive	Stem (without -ir)
vivir (*to live*)	viv-
recibir (*to receive*)	recib-

➤ Now add the correct ending depending on who or what is doing the action.

[*i*] Note that as the ending generally makes it clear who is doing the action, you usually don't need to add a subject pronoun such as **yo** (meaning *I*) or **tú** (meaning *you*) as well.

⇨ *For more information on **Subject pronouns**, see page 42.*

➤ Here are the present simple endings for regular -ir verbs:

Present simple endings	Present simple of vivir	Meaning: *to live*
-o	(yo) viv<u>o</u>	I live
-es	(tú) viv<u>es</u>	you live
-e	(él/ella) viv<u>e</u>	he/she/it lives
	(usted) viv<u>e</u>	you live
-imos	(nosotros/nosotras) viv<u>imos</u>	we live
-ís	(vosotros/vosotras) viv<u>ís</u>	you live
-en	(ellos/ellas) viv<u>en</u>	they live
	(ustedes) viv<u>en</u>	you live

➤ You use the **él/ella** (*third person singular*) form of the verb with nouns and with people's names, when you are just talking about one person, animal or thing.

> **Javier viv<u>e</u> aquí.**　　　　Javier lives here.
> **Mi padre recib<u>e</u> muchas cartas.**　My father gets a lot of letters.

➤ You use the **ellos/ellas** (*third person plural*) form of the verb with nouns and with people's names, when you talking about more than one person, animal or thing.

> **Javier y Antonia viv<u>en</u> aquí.**　　Javier and Antonia live here.
> **Mis padres recib<u>en</u> muchas cartas.**　My parents get a lot of letters.

i Note that even though you use the él/ella and ellos/ellas forms of the
verb to talk about things in Spanish, you should <u>never</u> include the
pronouns él, ella, ellos or ellas themselves in the sentence when
referring to things.

| **Ocurrió ayer.** | It happened yesterday. |

⇨ *For more information on* ***Ways of saying 'you' in Spanish****, see page 44.*

Key points

✔ Verbs ending in -ir belong to the third conjugation. Regular -ir
verbs form their present tense stem by losing the -ir.

✔ The present tense endings for regular -ir verbs are: - o, -es, -e,
-imos, -ís, -en.

✔ You usually don't need to give a pronoun in Spanish as the
ending of the verb makes it clear who or what is doing the action.

---

4 **Forming the present simple tense of less regular verbs**

➤ Many Spanish verbs do not follow the regular patterns shown previously.
There are lots of verbs that change their <u>stem</u> in the present tense when the
stress is on the stem. This means that all forms are affected in the present
simple <u>APART FROM</u> the nosotros and vosotros forms. Such verbs are often
called <u>radical-changing verbs</u>, meaning root-changing verbs.

➤ For example, some verbs containing an -o in the stem change it to -ue in
the present simple for all forms <u>APART FROM</u> the nosotros/nosotras and
vosotros/vosotras forms.

	encontrar *to find*	recordar *to remember*	poder *to be able*	dormir *to sleep*
(yo)	enc**ue**ntro	rec**ue**rdo	p**ue**do	d**ue**rmo
(tú)	enc**ue**ntras	rec**ue**rdas	p**ue**des	d**ue**rmes
(él/ella/usted)	enc**ue**ntra	rec**ue**rda	p**ue**de	d**ue**rme
(nosotros/as)	enc**o**ntramos	rec**o**rdamos	p**o**demos	d**o**rmimos
(vosotros/as)	enc**o**ntráis	rec**o**rdáis	p**o**déis	d**o**rmís
(ellos/ellas/ustedes)	enc**ue**ntran	rec**ue**rdan	p**ue**den	d**ue**rmen

➤ Other verbs containing an -e in the stem change it to -ie for all forms
<u>APART FROM</u> the **nosotros/nosotras** and **vosotros/vosotras** forms.

	cerrar to close	pensar to think	entender to understand	perder to lose	preferir to prefer
(yo)	cierro	pienso	entiendo	pierdo	prefiero
(tú)	cierras	piensas	entiendes	pierdes	prefieres
(él/ella/usted)	cierra	piensa	entiende	pierde	prefiere
(nosotros/as)	cerramos	pensamos	entendemos	perdemos	preferimos
(vosotros/as)	cerráis	pensáis	entendéis	perdéis	preferís
(ellos/ellas/ustedes)	cierran	piensan	entienden	pierden	prefieren

➤ A few **-ir** verbs containing -e in the stem change this to -i in the present
simple for all forms <u>APART FROM</u> the **nosotros/nosotras** and **vosotros/
vosotras** forms.

	pedir to ask (for)	servir to serve
(yo)	pido	sirvo
(tú)	pides	sirves
(él/ella/usted)	pide	sirve
(nosotros/as)	pedimos	servimos
(vosotros/as)	pedís	servís
(ellos/ellas/ustedes)	piden	sirven

➤ If you are not sure whether a Spanish verb belongs to this group of <u>radical-
changing verbs</u>, you can look up the **Verb Tables** in the supplement.

⇨ *For more information on **Spelling**, see page 196.*

5 | **Forming the present simple tense of common irregular verbs**

➤ There are many other verbs that do not follow the usual patterns in
Spanish. These include some very common and important verbs such as
tener (meaning *to have*), **hacer** (meaning *to do* or *to make*) and **ir**
(meaning *to go*). These verbs are shown in full on the next page.

➤ Here are the present simple tense endings for **tener**:

	tener	Meaning: *to have*
(yo)	**tengo**	I have
(tú)	**tienes**	you have
(él/ella/usted)	**tiene**	he/she/it has, you have
(nosotros/nosotras)	**tenemos**	we have
(vosotros/vosotras)	**tenéis**	you have
(ellos/ellas/ustedes)	**tienen**	they have, you have

Tengo dos hermanas.	I have two sisters.
No tengo dinero.	I haven't any money.
¿Cuántos sellos tienes?	How many stamps have you got?
Tiene el pelo rubio.	He has blond hair.

➤ Here are the present simple tense endings for **hacer**:

	hacer	Meaning: *to do, to make*
(yo)	**hago**	I do, I make
(tú)	**haces**	you do, you make
(él/ella/usted)	**hace**	he/she/it does, he/she/it makes, you do, you make
(nosotros/nosotras)	**hacemos**	we do, we make
(vosotros/vosotras)	**hacéis**	you do, you make
(ellos/ellas/ustedes)	**hacen**	they do, they make, you do, you make

Hago una tortilla.	I'm making an omelette.
No hago mucho deporte.	I don't do a lot of sport.
¿Qué haces?	What are you doing?
Hace calor.	It's hot.

➤ Here are the present simple tense endings for **ir**:

	ir	Meaning: *to go*
(yo)	**voy**	I go
(tú)	**vas**	you go
(él/ella/usted)	**va**	he/she/it goes, you go
(nosotros/nosotras)	**vamos**	we go
(vosotros/vosotras)	**vais**	you go
(ellos/ellas/ustedes)	**van**	they go, you go

<u>Voy</u> a Salamanca.	I'm going to Salamanca.
¿Adónde <u>vas</u>?	Where are you going?
No <u>va</u> al colegio.	He doesn't go to school.
No <u>van</u> a vender la casa.	They aren't going to sell the house.

⇨ *For other irregular verbs in the present simple tense, see **Verb Tables** in the supplement.*

6 | How to use the present simple tense in Spanish

➤ The present simple tense is often used in Spanish in the same way as it is in English, although there are some differences.

➤ As in English, you use the Spanish present simple to talk about:

- things that are generally true

En verano <u>hace</u> calor.	It's hot in summer.

- things that are true now

<u>Viven</u> en Francia.	They live in France.

- things that happen all the time or at certain intervals or that you do as a habit

Marta <u>lleva</u> gafas.	Marta wears glasses.
Mi tío <u>vende</u> mariscos.	My uncle sells shellfish.

- things that you are planning to do

El domingo <u>jugamos</u> en León.	We're playing in León on Sunday.
Mañana <u>voy</u> a Madrid.	I am going to Madrid tomorrow.

➤ There are some instances when you would use the present simple in Spanish, but you wouldn't use it in English:

- to talk about current projects and activities that may not actually be going on right at this very minute

<u>Construye</u> una casa.	He's building a house.

- when you use certain time expressions in Spanish, especially **desde** (meaning *since*) and **desde hace** (meaning *for*), to talk about activities and states that started in the past and are still going on now

Jaime <u>vive</u> aquí <u>desde hace</u> dos años.	Jaime has been living here for two years.
Daniel <u>vive</u> aquí <u>desde</u> 1999.	Daniel has lived here since 1999.
<u>Llevo</u> horas esperando aquí.	I've been waiting here for hours.

⇨ *For more information on the use of tenses with desde, see page 189.*

ser and estar

➤ In Spanish there are two irregular verbs, **ser** and **estar**, that both mean *to be*, although they are used very differently. In the present simple tense, they follow the patterns shown below.

Pronoun	ser	estar	Meaning: *to be*
(yo)	soy	estoy	I am
(tú)	eres	estás	you are
(él/ella/usted)	es	está	he/she/it is, you are
(nosotros/nosotras)	somos	estamos	we are
(vosotros/vosotras)	sois	estáis	you are
(elllos/ellas/ustedes)	son	están	they/you are

➤ **ser** is used:

- with an adjective when talking about a characteristic or fairly permanent quality, for example, shape, size, height, colour, material, nationality.

Mi hermano <u>es</u> alto.	My brother is tall.
María <u>es</u> inteligente.	María is intelligent.
<u>Es</u> rubia.	She's blonde.
<u>Es</u> muy guapa.	She's very pretty.
<u>Es</u> rojo.	It's red.
<u>Es</u> de algodón.	It's made of cotton.
Sus padres <u>son</u> italianos.	His parents are Italian.
<u>Es</u> joven/viejo.	He's young/old.
<u>Son</u> muy ricos/pobres.	They're very rich/poor.

- with a following noun or pronoun that tells you what someone or something is

Miguel <u>es</u> camarero.	Miguel is a waiter.
<u>Soy</u> yo, Enrique.	It's me, Enrique.
Madrid <u>es</u> la capital de España.	Madrid is the capital of Spain.

- to say that something belongs to someone

La casa <u>es</u> de Javier.	The house belongs to Javier.
<u>Es</u> mío.	It's mine.

- to talk about where someone or something comes from

Yo <u>soy</u> de Escocia.	I'm from Scotland.
Mi mujer <u>es</u> de Granada.	My wife is from Granada.

- to say what time it is or what the date is

  Son las tres y media.   It's half past three.

  Mañana es sábado.   Tomorrow is Saturday.

- in calculations

  Tres y dos son cinco.   Three and two are five.

  ¿Cuánto es? – Son dos euros.   How much is it? It's two euros.

- when followed by an infinitive

  Lo importante es decir la   The important thing is to tell

  verdad.   the truth.

⇨ *For more information on the **Infinitive**, see page 144.*

- to describe actions using the passive (for example *they are made, it is sold*)

  Son fabricados en España.   They are made in Spain.

⇨ *For more information on the **Passive**, see page 122.*

➤ estar is used:

- to talk about where something or someone is

  Estoy en Madrid.   I'm in Madrid.

  ¿Dónde está Burgos?   Where's Burgos?

  Está cerca de aquí.   It's near here.

- with an adjective when there has been a change in the condition of someone or something or to suggest that there is something unexpected about them

  El café está frío.   The coffee's cold.

  ¡Qué guapa estás con este   How pretty you look in that dress!

  vestido!

  Hoy estoy de mal humor.   I'm in a bad mood today.

⇨ *For more information on **Adjectives**, see page 19.*

- with a past participle used as an adjective, to describe the state that something is in

  Las tiendas están cerradas.   The shops are closed.

  No está terminado.   It isn't finished.

  El lavabo está ocupado.   The toilet is engaged.

  Está roto.   It's broken.

⇨ *For more information on **Past participles**, see page 115.*

- when talking about someone's health

¿Cómo **están** ustedes?	How are you?
Estamos todos bien.	We're all well.

- to form continuous tenses such as the present continuous tense

Está comiendo.	He's eating.
Estamos aprendiendo mucho.	We are learning a great deal.

⇨ *For more information on the **Present continuous**, see page 84.*

➤ Both ser and estar can be used with certain adjectives, but the meaning changes depending on which is used.

➤ Use ser to talk about <u>permanent</u> qualities.

Marta <u>es</u> muy joven.	Marta is very young.
<u>Es</u> delgado.	He's slim.
Viajar <u>es</u> cansado.	Travelling is tiring.
La química <u>es</u> aburrida.	Chemistry is boring.

➤ Use estar to talk about <u>temporary</u> states or qualities.

Está muy joven con ese vestido.	She looks very young in that dress.
¡Estás muy delgada!	You're looking very slim!
Hoy <u>estoy</u> cansado.	I'm tired today.
<u>Estoy</u> aburrido.	I'm bored.

➤ ser is used with adjectives such as **importante** (meaning *important*) and **imposible** (meaning *impossible*) when the subject is *it* in English.

<u>Es</u> muy interesante.	It's very interesting.
<u>Es</u> imposible.	It's impossible.
<u>Es</u> fácil.	It's easy.

➤ ser is used in certain set phrases.

<u>Es</u> igual or **<u>Es</u> lo mismo.**	It's all the same.
<u>Es</u> para ti.	It's for you.

➤ estar is also used in some set phrases.

- **estar de pie** — to be standing
  Juan está de pie. — Juan is standing.
- **estar de vacaciones** — to be on holiday
  ¿Estás de vacaciones? — Are you on holiday?
- **estar de viaje** — to be on a trip
  Mi padre está de viaje. — My father's on a trip.
- **estar de moda** — to be in fashion

Las pantallas de plasma están de moda.	Plasma screens are in fashion.
● **estar claro**	to be obvious
Está claro que no entiendes.	It's obvious that you don't understand.

Grammar Extra!

Both ser and estar can be used with past participles.

Use ser and the past participle in passive constructions to describe an action.

> **Son fabricados en España.**   They are made in Spain.

Use estar and the past participle to describe a state.

> **Está terminado.**   It's finished.

⇨ *For more information on **Past participles**, see page 115.*

Key points

✔ ser and estar both mean *to be* in English, but are used very differently.

✔ ser and estar are irregular verbs. You have to learn them.

✔ Use ser with adjectives describing permanent qualities or characteristics; with nouns or pronouns telling you who or what somebody or something is; with time and dates; and to form the passive.

✔ Use estar to talk about location; health; with adjectives describing a change of state; and with past participles used as adjectives to describe states.

✔ estar is also used to form present continuous tenses.

✔ ser and estar can sometimes be used with the same adjectives, but the meaning changes depending on which verb is used.

✔ ser and estar are both used in a number of set phrases.

The present continuous tense

➤ In Spanish, the present continuous tense is used to talk about something that is happening at this very moment.

➤ The Spanish present continuous tense is formed from the <u>present tense</u> of estar and the <u>gerund</u> of the verb. The gerund is the form of the verb that ends in -**ando** (for -**ar** verbs) or -**iendo** (for -**er** and -**ir** verbs) and is the same as the *-ing* form of the verb in English (for example, *walking, swimming*).

<u>**Estoy**</u> trabaj<u>ando</u>	I'm working.
No <u>estamos</u> com<u>iendo</u>.	We aren't eating.
¿<u>**Estás**</u> escrib<u>iendo</u>?	Are you writing?

⤷ *For more information on estar and the **Gerund**, see pages 80 and 125.*

➤ To form the gerund of an -ar verb, take off the -ar ending of the infinitive and add -**ando**:

Infinitive	Meaning	Stem (without -ar)	Gerund	Meaning
hablar	to speak	habl-	habl<u>ando</u>	speaking
trabajar	to work	trabaj-	trabaj<u>ando</u>	working

➤ To form the gerund of an -er or -ir verb, take off the -er or -ir ending of the infinitive and add -**iendo**:

Infinitive	Meaning	Stem (without -er/-ir)	Gerund	Meaning
comer	to eat	com-	com<u>iendo</u>	eating
escribir	to write	escrib-	escrib<u>iendo</u>	writing

Tip

Only use the present continuous to talk about things that are in the middle of happening right now. Use the present simple tense instead to talk about activities which are current but which may not be happening at this minute.

Lydia <u>estudia</u> medicina.	Lydia's studying medicine.

⤷ *For more information on the **Present simple tense**, see page 72.*

Key points
✔ Only use the present continuous in Spanish for actions that are happening right now.
✔ To form the present continuous tense in Spanish, take the present tense of estar and add the gerund of the main verb.

The imperative

> **What is the imperative?**
> An **imperative** is a form of the verb used when giving orders and instructions, for example, *Sit down!; Don't go!; Let's start!*

1   Using the imperative

➤ In Spanish, the form of the imperative that you use for giving instructions depends on:

- whether you are telling someone to do something or not to do something
- whether you are talking to one person or to more than one person
- whether you are on familiar or more formal terms with the person or people

➤ These imperative forms correspond to the familiar **tú** and **vosotros/vosotras** and to the more formal **usted** and **ustedes**, although you don't actually say these pronouns when giving instructions.

⮕ *For more information on **Ways of saying 'you' in Spanish**, see page 44.*

➤ There is also a form of the imperative that corresponds to *let's* in English.

2   Forming the imperative: instructions not to do something

➤ In orders that tell you <u>NOT</u> to do something and that have **no** in front of them in Spanish, the imperative forms for **tú**, **usted**, **nosotros/nosotras**, **vosotros/vosotras** and **ustedes** are all taken from a verb form called the <u>present subjunctive</u>. It's easy to remember because the endings for -**ar** and -**er** verbs are the opposite of what they are in the ordinary present tense.

⮕ *For more information on the **Present tense** and the **Subjunctive**, see pages 69 and 134.*

➤ In regular -**ar** verbs, you take off the -**as**, -**a**, -**amos**, -**áis** and -**an** endings of the present tense and replace them with: -**es**, -**e**, -**emos**, -**éis** and -**en**.

-**ar verb**	trabajar	**to work**
tú **form**	¡no trabajes!	Don't work!
usted **form**	¡no trabaje!	Don't work!
nosotros/as **form**	¡no trabajemos!	Let's not work!
vosotros/as **form**	¡no trabajéis!	Don't work!
ustedes **form**	¡no trabajen!	Don't work!

➤ In regular -er verbs, you take off the -es, -e, -emos, -éis and -en endings of the present tense and replace them with -as, -a, -amos, -áis and -an.

-er verb	comer	to eat
tú form	¡no comas!	Don't eat!
usted form	¡no coma!	Don't eat!
nosotros/as form	¡no comamos!	Let's not eat!
vosotros/as form	¡no comáis!	Don't eat!
ustedes form	¡no coman!	Don't eat!

➤ In regular -ir verbs, you take off the -es, -e, -imos, -ís and -en endings of the present tense and replace them with -as, -a, -amos, -áis and -an.

-ir verb	decidir	to decide
tú form	¡no decidas!	Don't decide!
usted form	¡no decida!	Don't decide!
nosotros/as form	¡no decidamos!	Let's not decide!
vosotros/as form	¡no decidáis!	Don't decide!
ustedes form	¡no decidan!	Don't decide!

➤ A number of irregular verbs also have irregular imperative forms. These are shown in the table below.

	dar to give	decir to say	estar to be	hacer to do/make	ir to go
tú form	¡no des! don't give!	¡no digas! don't say!	¡no estés! don't be!	¡no hagas! don't do/make!	¡no vayas! don't go!
usted form	¡no dé! don't give!	¡no diga! don't say!	¡no esté! don't be!	¡no haga! don't do/make!	¡no vaya! don't go!
nosotros form	¡no demos! let's not give!	¡no digamos! let's not say!	¡no estemos! let's not be!	¡no hagamos! let's not do/make!	¡no vayamos! let's not go!
vosotros form	¡no deis! don't give!	¡no digáis! don't say!	¡no estéis! don't be!	¡no hagáis! don't do/make!	¡no vayáis! don't go!
ustedes form	¡no den! don't give!	¡no digan! don't say!	¡no estén! don't be!	¡no hagan! don't do/make!	¡no vayan! don't go!

	poner to put	salir to leave	ser to be	tener to have	venir to come
tú form	¡no pongas! don't put!	¡no salgas! don't leave!	¡no seas! don't be!	¡no tengas! don't have!	¡no vengas! don't come!
usted form	¡no ponga! don't put!	¡no salga! don't leave!	¡no sea! don't be!	¡no tenga! don't have!	¡no venga! don't come!
nosotros form	¡no pongamos! let's not put!	¡no salgamos! let's not leave!	¡no seamos! let's not be!	¡no tengamos! let's not have!	¡no vengamos! let's not come!
vosotros form	¡no pongáis! don't put!	¡no salgáis! don't leave!	¡no seáis! don't be!	¡no tengáis! don't have!	¡no vengáis! don't come!
ustedes form	¡no pongan! don't put!	¡no salgan! don't leave!	¡no sean! don't be!	¡no tengan! don't have!	¡no vengan! don't come!

i̇ Note that if you take the **yo** form of the present tense, take off the -o and add the endings to this instead for instructions <u>NOT TO DO</u> something, some of these irregular forms will be more predictable.

digo	*I say*	→	negative imperative stem	→	**dig-**
hago	*I do*	→	negative imperative stem	→	**hag-**
pongo	*I put*	→	negative imperative stem	→	**pong-**
salgo	*I leave*	→	negative imperative stem	→	**salg-**
tengo	*I have*	→	negative imperative stem	→	**teng-**
vengo	*I come*	→	negative imperative stem	→	**veng-**

3 | **Forming the imperative: instructions to do something**

➤ In instructions telling you <u>TO DO</u> something, the forms for **usted**, **nosotros** and **ustedes** are exactly the same as they are in negative instructions (instructions telling you not to do something) except that there isn't a **no**.

	trabajar **to work**	comer **to eat**	decidir **to decide**
usted form	¡Trabaje!	¡Coma!	¡Decida!
nosotros/as form	¡Trabajemos!	¡Comamos!	¡Decidamos!
ustedes form	¡Trabajen!	¡Coman!	¡Decidan!

➤ There are special forms of the imperative for **tú** and **vosotros/vosotras** in positive instructions (instructions telling you to do something).

➤ The **tú** form of the imperative is the same as the **tú** form of the ordinary present simple tense, but without the final -s.

trabajar	→	**¡Trabaja!**
to work		Work!
comer	→	**¡Come!**
to eat		Eat!
decidir	→	**¡Decide!**
to decide		Decide!

⇨ *For more information on the **Present simple tense**, see page 72.*

➤ The **vosotros/vosotras** form of the imperative is the same as the infinitive, except that you take off the final -r and add -d instead.

trabajar	→	**Trabajad!**
to work		Work!
comer	→	**Comed!**
to eat		Eat!
decidir	→	**Decidid!**
to decide		Decide!

➤ There are a number of imperative forms that are irregular in Spanish. The irregular imperative forms for **usted**, **nosotros/nosotras** and **ustedes** are the same as the irregular negative imperative forms without the **no**. The **tú** and **vosotros/vosotras** forms are different again.

	dar to give	decir to say	estar to be	hacer to do/make	ir to go
tú form	¡da! give!	¡di! say!	¡está! be!	¡haz! do/make!	¡ve! go!
usted form	¡dé! give!	¡diga! say!	¡esté! be!	¡haga! do/make!	¡vaya! go!
nosotros/as form	¡demos! let's give!	¡digamos! let's say!	¡estemos! let's be!	¡hagamos! let's do/make!	¡vamos! let's go!
vosotros/as form	¡dad! give!	¡decid! say!	¡estad! be!	¡haced! do/make!	¡id! go!
ustedes form	¡den! give!	¡digan! say!	¡estén! be!	¡hagan! do/make!	¡vayan! go!

	poner to put	salir to leave	ser to be	tener to have	venir to come
tú form	¡pon! put!	¡sal! leave!	¡sé! be!	¡ten! have!	¡ven! come!
usted form	¡ponga! put!	¡salga! leave!	¡sea! be!	¡tenga! have!	¡venga! come!
nosotros/as form	¡pongamos! let's put!	¡salgamos! let's leave!	¡seamos! let's be!	¡tengamos! let's have!	¡vengamos! let's come!
vosotros/as form	¡poned! put!	¡salid! leave!	¡sed! be!	¡tened! have!	¡venid! come!
ustedes form	¡pongan! put!	¡salgan! leave!	¡sean! be!	¡tengan! have!	¡vengan! come!

[*i*] Note that the **nosotros/as** form for **ir** in instructions <u>TO DO</u> something is **vamos**; in instructions <u>NOT TO DO</u> something, it is **no vayamos**.

[4] **Position of object pronouns**

➤ An object pronoun is a word like **me** (meaning *me* or *to me*), **la** (meaning *her/it*) or **les** (meaning *to them/to you*) that is used instead of a noun as the object of a sentence. In orders and instructions, the position of these object pronouns in the sentence changes depending on whether you are telling someone <u>TO DO</u> something or <u>NOT TO DO</u> something.

⇨ *For more information on **Object pronouns**, see page 46.*

➤ If you are telling someone <u>NOT TO DO</u> something, the object pronouns go <u>BEFORE</u> the verb.

¡No **me lo** mandes!	Don't send it to me!
¡No **me** molestes!	Don't disturb me!
¡No **los** castigue!	Don't punish them!
¡No **se la** devolvamos!	Let's not give it back to him/her/them!
¡No **las** contestéis!	Don't answer them!

➤ If you are telling someone <u>TO DO</u> something, the object pronouns join on to the <u>END</u> of the verb. An accent is usually added to make sure that the stress in the imperative verb stays the same.

¡**Explícamelo**!	Explain it to me!
¡**Perdóneme**!	Excuse me!
¡**Dígame**!	Tell me!
¡**Esperémosla**!	Let's wait for her/it!

[i] Note that when there are two object pronouns, the indirect object pronoun always goes before the direct object pronoun.

⇨ *For more information on **Stress**, see page 200.*

---

5 | <u>Other ways of giving instructions</u>

➤ For general instructions in instruction leaflets, recipes and so on, use the <u>infinitive</u> form instead of the imperative.

Ver página 9.   See page 9.

➤ **vamos a** with the infinitive is often used to mean *let's*.

Vamos a ver.   Let's see.
Vamos a empezar.   Let's start.

Key points

✔ In Spanish, in instructions <u>not to do</u> something, the endings are taken from the present subjunctive. They are the same as the corresponding endings for -ar and -er verbs in the ordinary present tense, except that the -e endings go on the -ar verbs and the -a endings go on the -er and -ir verbs.

✔ For -ar verbs the forms are: no hables (tú form); no hable (usted form); no hablemos (nosotros/as form); no habléis (vosotros/as form); no hablen (ustedes form)

✔ For -er verbs the forms are: no comas (tú form); no coma (usted form); no comamos (nosotros/as form); no comáis (vosotros/as form); no coman (ustedes form)

✔ For -ir verbs the forms are: no decidas (tú form); no decida (usted form); no decidamos (nosotros/as form); no decidáis (vosotros/as form); no decidan (ustedes form)

✔ In instructions <u>to do</u> something, the forms for usted, nosotros/as and ustedes are the same as they are in instructions not to do something.

✔ The forms for tú and vosotros/as are different:

- the tú form is the same as the corresponding form in the ordinary present tense, but without the final -s: trabaja; come; decide
- the vosotros/as form is the same as the infinitive but with a final -d instead of the -r: trabajad; comed; decidid

✔ A number of verbs have irregular imperative forms.

✔ The object pronouns in imperatives go before the verb when telling someone not to do something; they join onto the end of the verb when telling someone to do something.

Reflexive verbs

What is a reflexive verb?
A **reflexive verb** is one where the subject and object are the same, and where the action 'reflects back' on the subject. It is used with a reflexive pronoun such as *myself*, *yourself* and *herself* in English, for example, *I washed myself.; He shaved himself.*

1 | Using reflexive verbs

➤ In Spanish, reflexive verbs are much more common than in English, and many are used in everyday language. The infinitive form of a reflexive verb has se attached to the end of it, for example, **secarse** (meaning *to dry oneself*). This is the way reflexive verbs are shown in dictionaries. se means *himself, herself, itself, yourself, themselves, yourselves* and *oneself*. se is called a <u>reflexive pronoun</u>.

➤ In Spanish, reflexive verbs are often used to describe things you do to yourself every day or that involve a change of some sort, for example, going to bed, sitting down, getting angry, and so on. Some of the most common reflexive verbs in Spanish are listed here.

acostarse	to go to bed
afeitarse	to shave
bañarse	to have a bath, to have a swim
dormirse	to go to sleep
ducharse	to have a shower
enfadarse	to get angry
lavarse	to wash
levantarse	to get up
llamarse	to be called
secarse	to get dried
sentarse	to sit down
vestirse	to get dressed

<u>Me baño</u> a las siete y media.	I have a bath at half past seven.
¡<u>Duérmete</u>!	Go to sleep!
Mi hermana <u>se ducha</u>.	My sister has a shower.
Mi madre <u>se enfada</u> mucho.	My mother often gets angry.
Mi hermano no <u>se lava</u>.	My brother doesn't wash.
<u>Me levanto</u> a las siete.	I get up at seven o'clock.
¿Cómo <u>te llamas</u>?	What's your name?
¿A qué hora <u>os acostáis</u>?	What time do you go to bed?
¡<u>Sentaos</u>!	Sit down!
<u>Nos vestimos</u>.	We're getting dressed.

[ⁱ] Note that se, me and so on are very rarely translated as *himself, myself*
and so on in English. Instead of *he dresses himself* or *they bath
themselves*, in English, we are more likely to say *he gets dressed* or *they
have a bath*.

➤ Some Spanish verbs can be used both as reflexive verbs and as ordinary
verbs (without the reflexive pronoun). When they are used as ordinary
verbs, the person or thing doing the action is not the same as the person
or thing receiving the action, so the meaning is different.

Me lavo.	I wash (myself).
Lavo la ropa a mano.	I wash the clothes by hand.
Me llamo Antonio.	I'm called Antonio.
¡Llama a la policía!	Call the police!
Me acuesto a las 11.	I go to bed at 11 o'clock.
Acuesta al niño.	He puts the child to bed.

Grammar Extra!

Some verbs mean <u>ALMOST</u> the same in the reflexive as when they are used on their
own.

Duermo.	I sleep.
Me duermo.	I go to sleep.
¿Quieres **ir** al cine?	Do you want to go to the cinema?
Acaba de ir**se**.	He has just left.

2 | Forming the present tense of reflexive verbs

➤ To use a reflexive verb in Spanish, you need to decide which reflexive
pronoun to use. See how the reflexive pronouns in the table on the next
page correspond to the subject pronouns.

Subject pronoun	Reflexive pronoun	Meaning
(yo)	me	myself
(tú)	te	yourself
(él) (ella) (uno) (usted)	se	himself herself oneself itself yourself
(nosotros/nosotras)	nos	ourselves
(vosotros/vosotras)	os	yourselves
(ellos) (ellas) (ustedes)	se	themselves yourselves

(Yo) <u>me</u> levanto temprano.	I get up early.
(Él) <u>se</u> acuesta a las once.	He goes to bed at eleven.
Ellos no <u>se</u> afeitan.	They don't shave.

➤ The present tense forms of a reflexive verb work in just the same way as an ordinary verb, except that the reflexive pronoun is used as well.

➪ *For more information on the **Present tense**, see page 69.*

➤ The following table shows the reflexive verb **lavarse** in full.

Reflexive forms of lavarse	Meaning
(yo) me lavo	I wash (myself)
(tú) te lavas	you wash (yourself)
(él) se lava (ella) se lava (uno) se lava se lava (usted) se lava	he washes (himself) she washes (herself) one washes (oneself) it washes (itself) you wash (yourself)
(nosotros/nosotras) nos lavamos	we wash (ourselves)
(vosotros/vosotras) os laváis	you wash (yourselves)
(ellos) se lavan (ellas) se lavan (ustedes) se lavan	they wash (themselves) they wash (themselves) you wash (yourselves)

➤ Some reflexive verbs, such as **acostarse**, are irregular. Some of these irregular verbs are shown in the **Verb tables** in the supplement.

3   Position of reflexive pronouns

➤ In ordinary tenses such as the present simple, the reflexive pronoun goes UNDERLINE the verb.

> **<u>Me</u> acuesto temprano.**   I go to bed early.
>
> **¿Cómo <u>se</u> llama usted?**   What's your name?

⇨   *For more information on the **Present simple tense**, see page 72.*

➤ When telling someone NOT TO DO something, you also put the reflexive pronoun BEFORE the verb.

> **No <u>te</u> levantes.**   Don't get up.
>
> **¡No <u>os</u> vayáis!**   Don't go away!

➤ When telling someone TO DO something, you join the reflexive pronoun onto the end of the verb.

> **¡Siénten<u>se</u>!**   Sit down!
>
> **¡Cálla<u>te</u>!**   Be quiet!

⇨   *For more information on the **Imperative**, see page 85.*

Típ

When adding reflexive pronouns to the end of the imperative, you drop the final -s of the **nosotros** form and the final -d of the **vosotros** form, before the pronoun.

> **¡Vámo<u>nos</u>!**   Let's go!
>
> **¡Senta<u>os</u>!**   Sit down!

➤ You always join the reflexive pronoun onto the end of infinitives and gerunds (the -**ando** or -**iendo** forms of the verb) unless the infinitive or gerund follows another verb.

> **Hay que relajar<u>se</u> de vez en cuando.**   You have to relax from time to time.
>
> **Acostándo<u>se</u> temprano, se descansa mejor.**   You feel more rested by going to bed early.

➤ Where the infinitive or gerund follows another verb, you can put the reflexive pronoun either at the end of the infinitive or gerund or before the other verb.

> **Quiero bañar<u>me</u>** *or* **<u>Me</u> quiero bañar.**   I want to have a bath.

Tienes que vestir**te** or **Te** tienes que vestir.	You must get dressed.
Está vistiéndo**se** or **Se** está vistiendo.	She's getting dressed.
¿Estás duchándo**te**? or ¿**Te** estás duchando?	Are you having a shower?

⇨ *For more information on **Gerunds**, see page 125.*

[*i*] Note that, when adding pronouns to the ends of verb forms, you will often have to add a written accent to preserve the stress.

⇨ *For more information on **Stress**, see page 200.*

---

4 | **Using reflexive verbs with parts of the body and clothes**

➤ In Spanish, you often talk about actions to do with your body or your clothing using a reflexive verb.

Se está secando **el** pelo.	She's drying her hair.
Nos lavamos **los** dientes.	We clean our teeth.
Se está poniendo **el** abrigo.	He's putting on his coat.

[*i*] Note that in Spanish you do not use a possessive adjective such as *my* and *her* when talking about parts of the body. You use el, la, los and las with a reflexive verb instead.

| **Me** estoy lavando **las** manos. | I'm washing my hands. |

⇨ *For more information on **Articles**, see page 10.*

---

5 | **Other uses of reflexive verbs**

➤ In English we often use a passive construction, for example, *goods <u>are transported</u> all over the world, most of our tea <u>is imported</u> from India and China.* In Spanish, this construction is not used so much. Instead, very often a reflexive verb with se is used.

Aquí <u>se vende</u> café.	Coffee <u>is sold</u> here.
Aquí <u>se venden</u> muchos libros.	Lots of books <u>are sold</u> here.
<u>Se habla</u> inglés.	English <u>is spoken</u> here.
En Suiza <u>se hablan</u> tres idiomas.	Three languages <u>are spoken</u> in Switzerland.

[*i*] Note that the verb has to be singular or plural depending on whether the noun is singular or plural.

⇨ *For more information on the **Passive**, see page 122.*

➤ A reflexive verb with se is also used in some very common expressions.

| ¿Cómo <u>se dice</u> "siesta" en inglés? | How do you say "siesta" in English? |
| ¿Cómo <u>se escribe</u> "Tarragona"? | How do you spell "Tarragona"? |

➤ se is also used in impersonal expressions. In this case, it often corresponds to *one* (or *you*) in English.

| No <u>se puede</u> entrar. | You can't go in. |
| No <u>se permite</u>. | You aren't *or* It isn't allowed. |

⇨ *For more information on **Impersonal verbs**, see page 129.*

➤ nos, os and se are all also used to mean *each other* and *one another*.

<u>Nos</u> escribimos.	We write to one another.
<u>Nos</u> queremos.	We love each other.
Rachel y Julie <u>se</u> odian.	Rachel and Julie hate each other.
No <u>se</u> conocen.	They don't know each other.

Key points

✔ A reflexive verb is made up of a reflexive pronoun and a verb.

✔ The reflexive pronouns are: me, te, se, nos, os, se.

✔ The reflexive pronoun goes before the verb, except when you are telling someone to do something and with infinitives and gerunds.

The future tense

> **What is the future tense?**
> The **future** tense is a verb tense used to talk about something that will
> happen or will be true in the future, for example, *He'll be here soon; I'll
> give you a call; What will you do?; It will be sunny tomorrow.*

1 | Ways of talking about the future

➤ In Spanish, just as in English, you can often use the present tense to refer to
something that is going to happen in the future.

Cogemos el tren de las once.	We're getting the eleven o'clock train.
Mañana voy a Madrid.	I am going to Madrid tomorrow.

➤ In English we often use *going to* with an infinitive to talk about the
immediate future or our future plans. In Spanish, you can use the present
tense of **ir** followed by **a** and an infinitive.

Va a perder el tren.	He's going to miss the train.
Va a llevar una media hora.	It's going to take about half an hour.
Voy a hacerlo mañana.	I'm going to do it tomorrow.

2 | Forming the future tense

➤ In English we can form the future tense by putting *will* or its shortened form
'll before the verb. In Spanish you have to change the verb endings. So, just
as **hablo** means *I speak*, **hablaré** means *I will speak* or *I shall speak*.

➤ To form the future tense of regular -**ar**, -**er** and -**ir** verbs, add the following
endings to the <u>infinitive</u> of the verb: -**é**, -**ás**, -**á**, -**emos**, -**éis**, -**án**.

➤ The following table shows the future tense of three regular verbs: **hablar**
(meaning *to speak*), **comer** (meaning *to eat*) and **vivir** (meaning *to live*).

(yo)	hablaré	comeré	viviré	I'll speak/eat/live
(tú)	hablarás	comerás	vivirás	you'll speak/eat/live
(él) (ella) (usted)	hablará	comerá	vivirá	he'll speak/eat/live she'll speak/eat/live it'll speak/eat/live you'll speak/eat/live
(nosotros/nosotras)	hablaremos	comeremos	viviremos	we'll speak/eat/live
(vosotros/vosotras)	hablaréis	comeréis	viviréis	you'll speak/eat/live
(ellos/ellas/ustedes)	hablarán	comerán	vivirán	they'll/you'll speak/eat/live

Hablaré con ella.	I'll speak to her.
Comeremos en casa de José.	We'll eat at José's.
No volverá.	He won't come back.
¿Lo entenderás?	Will you understand it?

i Note that in the future tense only the **nosotros/nosotras** form doesn't have an accent.

Tip

Remember that Spanish has no direct equivalent of the word *will* in verb forms like *will rain* or *will look* and so on. You change the Spanish verb ending instead to form the future tense.

Grammar Extra!

In English, we sometimes use *will* with the meaning of *be willing to* rather than simply to express the future, for example, *Will you wait for me a moment?* In Spanish you don't use the future tense to say this; you use the verb **querer** (meaning *to want*) instead.

| ¿Me **quieres** esperar un momento, por favor? | Will you wait for me a moment, please? |

---

3 Verbs with irregular stems in the future tense

➤ There are a few verbs that <u>DO NOT</u> use their infinitives as the stem for the future tense. Here are some of the most common.

Verb	Stem	(yo)	(tú)	(él) (ella) (usted)	(nosotros) (nosotras)	(vosotros) (vosotras)	(ellos) (ellas) (ustedes)
decir to say	dir-	diré	dirás	dirá	diremos	diréis	dirán
haber to have	habr-	habré	habrás	habrá	habremos	habréis	habrán
hacer to do/make	har-	haré	harás	hará	haremos	haréis	harán
poder to be able to	podr-	podré	podrás	podrá	podremos	podréis	podrán
poner to put	pondr-	pondré	pondrás	pondrá	pondremos	pondréis	pondrán
querer to want	querr-	querré	querrás	querrá	querremos	querréis	querrán
saber to know	sabr-	sabré	sabrás	sabrá	sabremos	sabréis	sabrán

Verb	Stem	(yo)	(tú)	(él) (ella) (usted)	(nosotros) (nosotras)	(vosotros) (vosotras)	(ellos) (ellas) (ustedes)
salir to leave	saldr-	saldré	saldrás	saldrá	saldremos	saldréis	saldrán
tener to have	tendr-	tendré	tendrás	tendrá	tendremos	tendréis	tendrán
venir to come	vendr-	vendré	vendrás	vendrá	vendremos	vendréis	vendrán

Lo **haré** mañana. — I'll do it tomorrow.
No **podremos** hacerlo. — We won't be able to do it.
Lo **pondré** aquí. — I'll put it here.
Saldrán por la mañana. — They'll leave in the morning.
¿A qué hora **vendrás**? — What time will you come?

[*i*] Note that the verb **haber** is only used when forming other tenses, such as the perfect tense, and in the expression **hay** (meaning *there is* or *there are*).

⇨ *For more information on the **Perfect tense** and on hay, see pages 115 and 130.*

4 **Reflexive verbs in the future tense**

➤ The future tense of reflexive verbs is formed in just the same way as for ordinary verbs, except that you have to remember to give the reflexive pronoun (me, te, se, nos, os, se).

Me leventaré temprano. — I'll get up early.

Key points
✔ You can use a present tense in Spanish to talk about something that will happen or be true, just as in English.
✔ You can use **ir a** with an infinitive to talk about things that will happen in the immediate future.
✔ In Spanish there is no direct equivalent of the word *will* in verb forms like *will rain* and *will look*. You change the verb endings instead.
✔ To form the future tense, add the endings -é, -ás, á, -emos, -éis, -án to the infinitive.
✔ Some verbs have irregular stems in the future tense. It is worth learning these.

The conditional

> **What is the conditional?**
> The **conditional** is a verb form used to talk about things that would
> happen or that would be true under certain conditions, for example, I
> _would_ help you if I could.
> It is also used to say what you would like or need, for example, _Could_ you
> give me the bill?

1 Using the conditional

➤ You can often recognize a conditional in English by the word _would_ or its
shortened form _'d_.

I _would_ be sad if you left.
If you asked him, he_'d_ help you.

➤ You use the conditional for:

- saying what you would like to do
  Me _gustaría_ conocerlo.   I'd like to meet him.
- making suggestions
  Podrías alquilar una bici.   You could hire a bike.
- giving advice
  Deberías hacer más ejercicio.   You should take more exercise.
- saying what you would do
  Le dije que le _ayudaría_.   I said I would help him.

> _Tip_
>
> There is no direct Spanish translation of _would_ in verb forms like
> _would be_, _would like_, _would help_ and so on. You change the Spanish
> verb ending instead.

2 Forming the conditional

➤ To form the conditional of regular -ar, -er, and -ir verbs, add the following
endings to the <u>infinitive</u> of the verb: -ía, -ías, -ía, -íamos, -íais, -ían.

➤ The following table shows the conditional tense of three regular verbs:
hablar (meaning *to speak*), comer (meaning *to eat*) and vivir (meaning
to live).

(yo)	hablaría	comería	viviría	I would speak/eat/live
(tú)	hablarías	comerías	vivirías	you would speak/eat/live
(él) (ella) (usted)	hablaría	comería	viviría	he would speak/eat/live she would speak/eat/live it would speak/eat/live you would speak/eat/live
(nosotros/nosotras)	hablaríamos	comeríamos	viviríamos	we would speak/eat/live
(vosotros/vosotras)	hablaríais	comeríais	viviríais	you would speak/eat/live
(ellos/ellas) (ustedes)	hablarían	comerían	vivirían	they would speak/eat/live you would speak/eat/live

Me <u>gustaría</u> ir a China.	I'd like to go to China.
Dije que <u>hablaría</u> con ella.	I said that I would speak to her.
<u>Debería</u> llamar a mis padres.	I should ring my parents.

Tip

Don't forget to put an accent on the í in the conditional.

ℹ️ Note that the endings in the conditional tense are identical to those of
the <u>imperfect tense</u> for -er and -ir verbs. The only difference is that they
are added to a different stem.

⇨ *For more information on the **Imperfect tense**, see page 110.*

3 Verbs with irregular stems in the conditional

➤ To form the conditional of irregular verbs, use the same stem as for the <u>future tense</u>, then add the usual endings for the conditional. The same verbs that are irregular in the future tense are irregular in the conditional.

Verb	Stem	(yo)	(tú)	(él) (ella) (usted)	(nosotros) (nosotras)	(vosotros) (vosotras)	(ellos) (ellas) (ustedes)
decir to say	dir-	diría	dirías	diría	diríamos	diríais	dirían
haber to have	habr-	habría	habrías	habría	habríamos	habríais	habrían
hacer to do/ make	har-	haría	harías	haría	haríamos	haríais	harían
poder to be able to	podr-	podría	podrías	podría	podríamos	podríais	podrían
poner to put	pondr-	pondría	pondrías	pondría	pondríamos	pondríais	pondrían
querer to want	querr-	querría	querrías	querría	querríamos	querríais	querrían
saber to know	sabr-	sabría	sabrías	sabría	sabríamos	sabríais	sabrían
salir to leave	saldr-	saldría	saldrías	saldría	saldríamos	saldríais	saldrían
tener to have	tendr-	tendría	tendrías	tendría	tendríamos	tendríais	tendrían
venir to come	vendr-	vendría	vendrías	<u>vendría</u>	vendríamos	vendríais	vendrían

⇨ *For more information on the **Future tense**, see page 97.*

¿Qué <u>harías</u> tú en mi lugar?	What would you do if you were me?
¿<u>Podrías</u> ayudarme?	Could you help me?
Yo lo <u>pondría</u> aquí.	I would put it here.

ⓘ Note that the verb **haber** is only used when forming other tenses, such as the perfect tense, and in the expression **hay** (meaning *there is/there are*).

⇨ *For more information on the **Perfect tense** and on **hay**, see pages 115 and 130.*

For further explanation of grammatical terms, please see pages viii-xii.

4 Reflexive verbs in the conditional

➤ The conditional of reflexive verbs is formed in just the same way as for ordinary verbs, except that you have to remember to give the reflexive pronoun (me, te, se, nos, os, se).

Le dije que <u>me levantaría</u> temprano.	I said I would get up early.

Key points

✔ In Spanish, there is no direct equivalent of the word *would* in verb forms like *would go* and *would look* and so on. You change the verb ending instead.

✔ To form the conditional tense, add the endings -ía, ías, -ía, -íamos, -íais, -ían to the infinitive. The conditional uses the same stem as for the future.

✔ Some verbs have irregular stems which are used for both the conditional and the future. It is worth learning these.

The preterite

> **What is the preterite?**
> The **preterite** is a form of the verb that is used to talk about actions that were completed in the past in Spanish. It often corresponds to the simple past in English, as in *I bought a new bike; Mary went to the shops on Friday; I typed two reports yesterday.*

1 Using the preterite

➤ In English, we use the <u>simple past tense</u> to talk about actions:
- that were completed at a certain point in the past
  I <u>bought</u> a dress yesterday.
- that were part of a series of events
  I <u>went</u> to the beach, <u>undressed</u> and <u>put on</u> my swimsuit.
- that went on for a certain amount of time
  The war <u>lasted</u> three years.

➤ In English, we also use the <u>simple past tense</u> to describe actions which happened frequently (*Our parents <u>took</u> us swimming in the holidays*), and to describe settings (*It <u>was</u> a dark and stormy night*).

➤ In Spanish, the <u>preterite</u> is the most common tense for talking about the past. You use the preterite for actions:
- that were completed at a certain point in the past

  Ayer <u>compré</u> un vestido.   I bought a dress yesterday.

- that were part of a series of events

  <u>Fui</u> a la playa, me <u>quité</u> la ropa   I went to the beach, undressed and
  y me <u>puse</u> el bañador.   put on my swimsuit.

- that went on for a certain amount of time

  La guerra <u>duró</u> tres años.   The war lasted for three years.

➤ However, you use the <u>imperfect tense</u> for actions that happened frequently (where you could use *used to* in English) and for descriptions of settings.

⮕ *For more information on the **Imperfect tense**, see page 110.*

2 Forming the preterite of regular verbs

➤ To form the preterite of any regular -**ar** verb, you take off the -**ar** ending to form the stem, and add the endings: -é, -aste, -ó, -amos, -asteis, -aron.

➤ To form the preterite of any regular -er or -ir verb, you also take off the -er or -ir ending to form the stem and add the endings: -í, -iste, -ió, -imos, -isteis, -ieron.

➤ The following table shows the preterite of three regular verbs: **hablar** (meaning *to speak*), **comer** (meaning *to eat*) and **vivir** (meaning *to live*).

(yo)	hablé	comí	viví	I spoke/ate/lived
(tú)	hablaste	comiste	viviste	you spoke/ate/lived
(él) (ella) (usted)	habló	comió	vivió	he spoke/ate/lived she spoke/ate/lived it spoke/ate/lived you spoke/ate/lived
(nosotros/nosotras)	hablamos	comimos	vivimos	we spoke/ate/lived
(vosotros/vosotras)	hablasteis	comisteis	vivisteis	you spoke/ate/lived
(ellos/ellas) (ustedes)	hablaron	comieron	vivieron	they spoke/ate/lived you spoke/ate/lived

Bailé con mi hermana.	I danced with my sister.
No hablé con ella.	I didn't speak to her.
Comimos en un restaurante.	We had lunch in a restaurant.
¿Cerraste la ventana?	Did you close the window?

[*i*] Note that Spanish has no direct translation of *did* or *didn't* in questions or negative sentences. You simply use a past tense and make it a question by making your voice go up at the end or changing the word order; you make it negative by adding **no**.

⟹ *For more information on Questions and Negatives, see pages 160 and 157.*

Tip

Remember the accents on the **yo** and **él/ella/usted** forms of regular verbs in the preterite. Only an accent shows the difference, for example, between **hablo** *I speak* and **habló** *he spoke*.

3 Irregular verbs in the preterite

➤ A number of verbs have very irregular forms in the preterite. The table shows some of the most common.

Verb	(yo)	(tú)	(él) (ella) (usted)	(nosotros) (nosotras)	(vosotros) (vosotras)	(ellos) (ellas) (ustedes)
andar to walk	anduve	anduviste	anduvo	anduvimos	anduvisteis	anduvieron
conducir to drive	conduje	condujiste	condujo	condujimos	condujisteis	condujeron
dar to give	di	diste	dio	dimos	disteis	dieron
decir to say	dije	dijiste	dijo	dijimos	dijisteis	dijeron
estar to be	estuve	estuviste	estuvo	estuvimos	estuvisteis	estuvieron
hacer to do, to make	hice	hiciste	hizo	hicimos	hicisteis	hicieron
ir to go	fui	fuiste	fue	fuimos	fuisteis	fueron
poder to be able to	pude	pudiste	pudo	pudimos	pudisteis	pudieron
poner to put	puse	pusiste	puso	pusimos	pusisteis	pusieron
querer to want	quise	quisiste	quiso	quisimos	quisisteis	quisieron
saber to know	supe	supiste	supo	supimos	supisteis	supieron
ser to be	fui	fuiste	fue	fuimos	fuisteis	fueron
tener to have	tuve	tuviste	tuvo	tuvimos	tuvisteis	tuvieron
traer to bring	traje	trajiste	trajo	trajimos	trajisteis	trajeron
venir to come	vine	viniste	vino	vinimos	vinisteis	vinieron
ver to see	vi	viste	vio	vimos	visteis	vieron

i Note that **hizo** (the **él/ella/usted** form of **hacer**) is spelt with a **z**.

⇨ *For more information on **Spelling**, see page 196.*

Fue a Madrid.	He went to Madrid.
Te **vi** en el parque.	I saw you in the park.
No **vinieron**.	They didn't come.
¿Qué **hizo**?	What did she do?
Se lo **di** a Teresa.	I gave it to Teresa.
Fue en 1999.	It was in 1999.

Tip

The preterite forms of **ser** (meaning *to be*) are the same as the preterite forms of **ir** (meaning *to go*).

➤ Some other verbs are regular <u>EXCEPT FOR</u> the él/ella/usted and ellos/ellas/ustedes forms (*third persons singular and plural*). In these forms the stem vowel changes.

Verb	(yo)	(tú)	(él) (ella) (usted)	(nosotros) (nosotras)	(vosotros) (vosotras)	(ellos) (ellas) (ustedes)
dormir to sleep	dormí	dormiste	d**u**rmió	dormimos	dormisteis	d**u**rmieron
morir to die	morí	moriste	m**u**rió	morimos	moristeis	m**u**rieron
pedir to ask for	pedí	pediste	p**i**dió	pedimos	pedisteis	p**i**dieron
reír to laugh	reí	reíste	r**i**ó	reímos	reísteis	r**i**eron
seguir to follow	seguí	seguiste	siguió	seguimos	seguisteis	siguieron
sentir to feel	sentí	sentiste	s**i**ntió	sentimos	sentisteis	s**i**ntieron

[*i*] Note that **reír** also has an accent in all persons apart from the ellos/ellas/ustedes forms.

Antonio **durmió** diez horas.	Antonio slept for ten hours.
Murió en 1066.	He died in 1066.
Pidió paella.	He asked for paella.
¿Los **siguió**?	Did she follow them?
Sintió un dolor en la pierna.	He felt a pain in his leg.
Nos **reímos** mucho.	We laughed a lot.
Juan no se **rió**.	Juan didn't laugh.

➤ **caer** (meaning *to fall*) and **leer** (meaning *to read*) have an accent in all persons <u>apart from</u> the **ellos/ellas/ustedes** form (*third person plural*). In addition, the vowel changes to **y** in the **él/ella/usted** and **ellos/ellas/ustedes** forms (*third persons singular and plural*).

Verb	(yo)	(tú)	(él) (ella) (usted)	(nosotros) (nosotras)	(vosotros) (vosotras)	(ellos) (ellas) (ustedes)
caer to fall	caí	caíste	cayó	caímos	caísteis	cayeron
construir to build	construí	construiste	construyó	construimos	construisteis	construyeron
leer to read	leí	leíste	leyó	leímos	leísteis	leyeron

i Note that **construir** also changes to **y** in the **él/ella/usted** and **ellos/ellas/ustedes** forms (*third persons singular and plural*), but only has accents in the **yo** and **él/ella/usted** forms.

Se <u>cayó</u> por la ventana.	He fell out of the window.
Ayer <u>leí</u> un artículo muy interesante.	I read a very interesting article yesterday.
<u>Construyeron</u> una nueva autopista.	They built a new motorway.

4 Other spelling changes in the preterite

➤ Spanish verbs that end in **-zar**, **-gar** and **-car** in the infinitive change the **z** to **c**, the **g** to **gu** and the **c** to **qu** in the **yo** form (*first person singular*).

Verb	(yo)	(tú)	(él) (ella) (usted)	(nosotros) (nosotras)	(vosotros) (vosotras)	(ellos) (ellas) (ustedes)
cruzar to cross	cru<u>c</u>é	cruzaste	cruzó	cruzamos	cruzasteis	cruzaron
empezar to begin	empe<u>c</u>é	empezaste	empezó	empezamos	empezasteis	empezaron
pagar to pay for	pa<u>gu</u>é	pagaste	pagó	pagamos	pagasteis	pagaron
sacar to follow	sa<u>qu</u>é	sacaste	sacó	sacamos	sacasteis	sacaron

<u>Crucé</u> el río.	I crossed the river.
<u>Empecé</u> a hacer mis deberes.	I began doing my homework.
No <u>pagué</u> la cuenta.	I didn't pay the bill.
Me <u>saqué</u> las llaves del bolsillo.	I took my keys out of my pocket.

For further explanation of grammatical terms, please see pages viii-xii.

i Note that the change from **g** to **gu** and **c** to **qu** before **e** is to keep the sound hard.

⇨ *For more information on **Spelling**, see page 196.*

5 **Reflexive verbs in the preterite**

➤ The preterite of reflexive verbs is formed in just the same way as for ordinary verbs, except that you have to remember to give the reflexive pronoun (**me**, **te**, **se**, **nos**, **os**, **se**).

<u>Me levanté</u> a las siete.   I got up at seven.

Key points

✔ The preterite is the most common way to talk about the past in Spanish.

✔ To form the preterite of regular -ar verbs, take off the -ar ending and add the endings: -é, -aste, -ó, -amos, -asteis, -aron.

✔ To form the preterite of regular -er and -ir verbs, take off the -er and -ir endings and add the endings: -í, -iste, -ió, -imos, -isteis, -ieron.

✔ There are a number of verbs which are irregular in the preterite. These forms have to be learnt.

✔ With some verbs, the accents and spelling change in certain forms.

The imperfect tense

What is the imperfect tense?

The **imperfect tense** is one of the verb tenses used to talk about the past, especially in descriptions, and to say what was happening or used to happen, for example, *It was sunny at the weekend; We were living in Spain at the time; I used to walk to school.*

---

1 Using the imperfect tense

➤ In Spanish, the imperfect tense is used:

- to describe what things were like and how people felt in the past

Hacía calor.	It was hot.
No **teníamos** mucho dinero.	We didn't have much money.
Tenía hambre.	I was hungry.

- to say what used to happen or what you used to do regularly in the past

Cada día **llamaba** a su madre.	He used to ring his mother every day.

- to describe what was happening or what the situation was when something else took place

Tomábamos café.	We were having coffee.
Me **caí** cuando **cruzaba** la carretera.	I fell over when I was crossing the road.

Grammar Extra!

Sometimes, instead of the ordinary imperfect tense being used to describe what was happening at a given moment in the past when something else occurred interrupting it, the continuous form is used. This is made up of the imperfect tense of **estar** (estaba, estabas and so on), followed by the -ando/-iendo form of the main verb. The other verb – the one that relates the event that occurred – is in the preterite.

Montse **miraba** la televisión *or* Montse **estaba mirando** la televisión cuando sonó el teléfono.	Montse was watching television when the telephone rang.

⇨ *For further information on the **Preterite**, see page 104.*

---

2 Forming the imperfect tense

➤ To form the imperfect of any regular -ar verb, you take off the -ar ending of the infinitive to form the stem and add the endings: -aba, -abas, -aba, -ábamos, -abais, -aban.

➤ The following table shows the imperfect tense of one regular -ar verb: hablar (meaning *to speak*).

(yo)	hab<u>laba</u>	I spoke I was speaking I used to speak
(tú)	hab<u>labas</u>	you spoke you were speaking you used to speak
(él/ella/usted)	hab<u>laba</u>	he/she/it/you spoke he/she/it was speaking, you were speaking he/she/it/you used to speak
(nosotros/nosotras)	hab<u>lábamos</u>	we spoke we were speaking we used to speak
(vosotros/vosotras)	hab<u>labais</u>	you spoke you were speaking you used to speak
(ellos/ellas/ustedes)	hab<u>laban</u>	they/you spoke they/you were speaking they/you used to speak

i Note that in the imperfect tense of -ar verbs, the only accent is on the nosotros/nosotras form

Hablaba francés e italiano.	He spoke French and Italian.
Cuando era joven, mi tío trabajaba mucho.	My uncle worked hard when he was young.
Estudiábamos matemáticas, e inglés.	We were studying maths and English.

➤ To form the imperfect of any regular -er or -ir verb, you take off the -er or -ir ending of the infinitive to form the stem and add the endings: -ía, -ías, -ía, -íamos, -íais, -ían.

➤ The following table shows the imperfect of two regular verbs: **comer** (meaning *to eat*) and **vivir** (meaning *to live*).

(yo)	comía	vivía	I ate/lived I was eating/living I used to eat/live
(tú)	comías	vivías	you ate/lived you were eating/living you used to eat/live
(él/ella/usted)	comía	vivía	he/she/it/you ate/lived he/she/it was eating/living, you were eating/living he/she/it was eating/living, you were eating/living
(nosotros/nosotras)	comíamos	vivíamos	we ate/lived we were eating/living we used to eat/live
(vosotros/vosotras)	comíais	vivíais	you ate/lived you were eating/living you used to eat/live
(ellos/ellas/ustedes)	comían	vivían	they/you ate/lived they/you were eating/living they/you used to eat/live

i Note that in the imperfect tense of **-er** and **-ir** verbs, there's an accent on all the endings.

A veces, <u>comíamos</u> en casa de Pepe.	We sometimes used to eat at Pepe's.
<u>Vivía</u> en un piso en la Avenida de Barcelona.	She lived in a flat in Avenida de Barcelona.
Cuando llegó el médico, ya se <u>sentían</u> mejor.	They were already feeling better when the doctor arrived.

Tip

The imperfect endings for **-er** and **-ir** verbs are the same as the endings used to form the conditional for all verbs. The only difference is that, in the conditional, the endings are added to the future stem.

⤷ *For more information on the **Conditional**, see page 100.*

3 **Irregular verbs in the imperfect tense**

➤ ser, ir and ver are irregular in the imperfect tense.

	ser	Meaning: to be
(yo)	era	I was
(tú)	eras	you were
(él/ella/usted)	era	he/she/it was, you were
(nosotros/nosotras)	éramos	we were
(vosotros/vosotras)	erais	you were
(ellos/ellas/ustedes)	eran	they were/you were

Era un chico muy simpático.   He was a very nice boy.
Mi madre era profesora.   My mother was a teacher.

	ir	Meaning: to go
(yo)	iba	I went/used to go/was going
(tú)	ibas	you went/used to go/were going
(él/ella/usted)	iba	he/she/it went/used to go/was going, you went/used to go/were going
(nosotros/nosotras)	íbamos	we went/used to go/were going
(vosotros/vosotras)	ibais	you went/used to go/were going
(ellos/ellas/ustedes)	iban	they/you went/used to go/were going

Iba a la oficina cada día.   Every day he would go to the office.
¿Adónde iban?   Where were they going?

	ver	Meaning: to see/to watch
(yo)	veía	I saw/used to see I watched/used to watch/was watching
(tú)	veías	you saw/used to see you watched/used to watch/were watching
(él/ella/usted)	veía	he/she/it saw/used to see he/she/it watched/used to watch/was watching you saw/used to see you watched/used to watch/were watching
(nosotros/nosotras)	veíamos	we saw/used to see we watched/used to watch/were watching
(vosotros/vosotras)	veíais	you saw/used to see you watched/used to watch/were watching
(ellos/ellas/ustedes)	veían	they/you saw/used to see they/you watched/used to watch/were watching

| Los sábados, siempre lo <u>veíamos</u>. | We always used to see him on Saturdays. |
| <u>Veía</u> la televisión cuando llegó mi tío. | I was watching television when my uncle arrived. |

4 Reflexive verbs in the imperfect tense

➤ The imperfect of reflexive verbs is formed in just the same way as for ordinary verbs, except that you have to remember to give the reflexive pronoun (me, te, se, nos, os, se).

| Antes <u>se levantaba</u> temprano. | He used to get up early. |

Grammar Extra!

In Spanish, you also use the imperfect tense with certain time expressions, in particular with desde (meaning *since*), desde hacía (meaning *for*) and hacía ... que (meaning *for*) to talk about activities and states that had started previously and were still going on at a particular point in the past:

<u>Estaba</u> enfermo desde 2000.	He had been ill since 2000.
<u>Conducía</u> ese coche desde hacía tres meses.	He had been driving that car for three months.
Hacía mucho tiempo que <u>salían</u> juntos.	They had been going out together for a long time.
Hacía dos años que <u>vivíamos</u> en Madrid.	We had been living in Madrid for two years.

Compare the use of desde, desde hacía and hacía ... que with the imperfect with that of desde, desde hace, and hace ... que with the present.

➪ *For more information on the use of tenses with desde, see page 189.*

Key points

✔ To form the imperfect tense of -ar verbs, take off the -ar ending and add the endings: -aba, -abas, -aba, -ábamos, -abais, -aban.

✔ To form the imperfect tense of -er and -ir verbs, take off the -er and -ir endings and add the endings: -ía, -ías, -ía, -íamos, -íais, -ían.

✔ ser, ir and ver are irregular in the imperfect.

The perfect tense

> **What is the perfect tense?**
> The **perfect** tense is a verb form used to talk about what has or hasn't happened; for example, *I've broken my glasses; We haven't spoken about it.*

1 Using the perfect tense

➤ In English, we use the perfect tense (*have, has* or their shortened forms *'ve* and *'s* followed by a past participle such as *spoken, eaten, lived, been*) to talk about what has or hasn't happened today, this week, this year or in our lives up to now.

➤ The Spanish perfect tense is used in a similar way.

He terminado el libro.	I've finished the book.
¿**Has fregado** el suelo?	Have you washed the floor?
Nunca **ha estado** en Bolivia.	He's never been to Bolivia.
Ha vendido su caballo.	She has sold her horse.
Todavía no **hemos comprado** un ordenador.	We still haven't bought a computer.
Ya se **han ido**.	They've already left.

Grammar Extra!

You may also come across uses of the perfect tense in Spanish to talk about actions completed in the very recent past. In English, we'd use the past simple tense in such cases.

¿Lo **has visto**?	Did you see that?

2 Forming the perfect tense

➤ As in English, the perfect tense in Spanish has two parts to it. These are:

- the <u>present</u> tense of the verb **haber** (meaning *to have*)
- a part of the main verb called the <u>past participle</u>.

3 Forming the past participle

➤ To form the past participle of regular -ar verbs, take off the -ar ending of the infinitive and add -**ado**.

   hablar (*to speak*) → **hablado** (*spoken*)

➤ To form the past participle of regular -er or -ir verbs, take off the -er or -ir ending of the infinitive and add -**ido**.

comer (*to eat*)	→	**comido** (*eaten*)
vivir (*to live*)	→	**vivido** (*lived*)

4 | The perfect tense of some regular verbs

➤ The following table shows how you can combine the present tense of
haber with the past participle of any verb to form the perfect tense.

In this case, the past participles are taken from the following regular verbs:
hablar (meaning *to speak*); trabajar (meaning *to work*); comer (meaning
to eat); vender (meaning *to sell*); vivir (meaning *to live*); decidir (meaning
to decide).

	Present of haber	Past participle	Meaning
(yo)	he	hablado	I have spoken
(tú)	has	trabajado	you have worked
(él/ella/usted)	ha	comido	he/she/it has eaten, you have eaten
(nosotros/nosotras)	hemos	vendido	we have sold
(vosotros/vosotras)	habéis	vivido	you have lived
(ellos/ellas/ustedes)	han	decidido	they/you have decided

Has trabajado mucho.	You've worked hard.
No **he comido** nada.	I haven't eaten anything.

[i] Note that you should not confuse haber with tener. Even though
they both mean *to have*, haber is only used for forming tenses and
in certain impersonal expressions such as hay and había meaning
there is, there are, there was, there were, and so on.

➪ *For further information on* **Impersonal verbs**, *see page 129.*

5 | Verbs with irregular past participles

➤ Some past participles are irregular. There aren't too many, so try to learn
them.

abrir (*to open*)	→	abierto (*opened*)
cubrir (*to cover*)	→	cubierto (*covered*)
decir (*to say*)	→	dicho (*said*)
escribir (*to write*)	→	escrito (*written*)
freír (*to fry*)	→	frito (*fried*)
hacer (*to do, to make*)	→	hecho (*done, made*)
morir (*to die*)	→	muerto (*died*)
oír (*to hear*)	→	oído (*heard*)
poner (*to put*)	→	puesto (*put*)

romper (*to break*)	→	**roto** (*broken*)
ver (*to see*)	→	**visto** (*seen*)
volver (*to return*)	→	**vuelto** (*returned*)

He abierto una cuenta en el banco.	I've opened a bank account.
No **ha dicho** nada.	He hasn't said anything.
Hoy **he hecho** muchas cosas.	I've done a lot today.
Todavía no **he hecho** los deberes.	I haven't done my homework yet.
Han muerto tres personas.	Three people have died.
¿Dónde **has puesto** mis zapatos?	Where have you put my shoes?
Carlos **ha roto** el espejo.	Carlos has broken the mirror.
Jamás **he visto** una cosa parecida.	I've never seen anything like it.
¿**Ha vuelto** Ana?	Has Ana come back?

Tip

he/has/ha and so on must <u>NEVER</u> be separated from the past participle. Any object pronouns go before the form of **haber** being used, and <u>NOT</u> between the form of **haber** and the past participle.

No **lo** he visto.	I haven't seen it.
¿**Lo** has hecho ya?	Have you done it yet?

---

6   **Reflexive verbs in the perfect tense**

➤ The perfect tense of reflexive verbs is formed in the same way as for ordinary verbs. The reflexive pronouns (**me, te, se, nos, os, se**) come before **he, has, ha**, and so on. The table on the next page shows the perfect tense of **lavarse** in full.

(Subject pronoun)	Reflexive pronoun	Present tense of haber	Past Participle	Meaning
(yo)	me	he	lavado	I have washed
(tú)	te	has	lavado	you have washed
(él) (ella) (uno) (usted)	se	ha	lavado	he has washed she has washed one has washed it has washed you have washed
(nosotros) (nosotras)	nos	hemos	lavado	we have washed we have washed
(vosotros) (vosotras)	os	habéis	lavado	you have washed you have washed
(ellos) (ellas) (ustedes)	se	han	lavado	they have washed they have washed you have washed

Grammar Extra!

Don't use the perfect tense with **desde**, **desde hace** and **hace ... que** when talking about how long something has been going on for. Use the <u>present tense</u> instead.

Está enfermo desde julio.	He has been ill since July.
Conduce ese coche desde hace tres meses.	He has been driving that car for three months.
Hace mucho tiempo que <u>salen</u> juntos.	They have been going out together for a long time.

⇨ *For more information on the **Present tense**, see page 72.*

➤ In European Spanish you <u>CAN</u> use the perfect tense in the negative with **desde** and **desde hace**.

No lo **he visto** desde hace mucho tiempo.	I haven't seen him for a long time.

Key points

✔ The Spanish perfect tense is formed using the present tense of **haber** and a past participle.

✔ In Spanish, the perfect tense is used very much as it is in English.

✔ The past participle of regular **-ar** verbs ends in **-ado**, and the past participle of regular **-er** and **-ir** verbs ends in **-ido**.

✔ Make sure you know the following irregular past participle forms: **abierto**, **cubierto**, **dicho**, **escrito**, **frito**, **hecho**, **muerto**, **puesto**, **roto**, **visto**, **vuelto**.

The pluperfect or past perfect tense

> **What is the pluperfect tense?**
> The **pluperfect** is a verb tense that is used to talk about what had happened or had been true at a point in the past, for example, *I'd forgotten to finish my homework.*

1 Using the pluperfect tense

➤ When talking about the past, we sometimes refer to things that had happened previously. In English, we often use *had* followed by a <u>past participle</u> such as *spoken, eaten, lived* or *been* to do this. This tense is known as the <u>pluperfect</u> or <u>past perfect</u> tense.

➤ The Spanish pluperfect tense is used and formed in a similar way.

Ya <u>habíamos comido</u> cuando llegó.	We'd already eaten when he arrived.
Nunca lo <u>había visto</u> antes de aquella noche.	I'd never seen it before that night.

2 Forming the pluperfect tense

➤ Like the perfect tense, the pluperfect tense in Spanish has <u>two</u> parts to it:
- the imperfect tense of the verb **haber** (meaning *to have*)
- the past participle.

⇨ *For more information on the **Imperfect tense** and **Past participles**, see pages 110 and 115.*

➤ The table below shows how you can combine the imperfect tense of **haber** with the past participle of any verb to form the pluperfect tense. Here, the past participles are taken from the following regular verbs: **hablar** (meaning *to speak*); **trabajar** (meaning *to work*); **comer** (meaning *to eat*); **vender** (meaning *to sell*); **vivir** (meaning *to live*); **decidir** (meaning *to decide*).

(Subject pronoun)	Imperfect of <u>haber</u>	Past Participle	Meaning
(yo)	había	hablado	I had spoken
(tú)	habías	trabajado	you had worked
(él/ella/usted)	había	comido	he/she/it/you had eaten
(nosotros/nosotras)	habíamos	vendido	we had sold
(vosotros/vosotras)	habíais	vivido	you had lived
(ellos/ellas/ustedes)	habían	decidido	they/you had decided

No <u>había trabajado</u> antes.	He hadn't worked before.
<u>Había vendido</u> su caballo.	She had sold her horse.

➤ Remember that some very common verbs have irregular past participles.

abrir (to open)	→	abierto (opened)
cubrir (to cover)	→	cubierto (covered)
decir (to say)	→	dicho (said)
escribir (to write)	→	escrito (written)
freír (to fry)	→	frito (fried)
hacer (to do, to make)	→	hecho (done, made)
morir (to die)	→	muerto (died)
oír (to hear)	→	oído (heard)
poner (to put)	→	puesto (put)
romper (to break)	→	roto (broken)
ver (to see)	→	visto (seen)
volver (to return)	→	vuelto (returned)

No <u>había dicho</u> nada.	He hadn't said anything.
Tres personas <u>habían muerto</u>.	Three people had died.

Tip

había/habías/habían and so on must <u>NEVER</u> be separated from the past participle. Any object pronouns go before the form of **haber** being used, and <u>NOT</u> between the form of **haber** and the past participle.

No lo había visto.	I hadn't seen it.

---

3 **Reflexive verbs in the pluperfect tense**

➤ The pluperfect tense of reflexive verbs is formed in the same way as for ordinary verbs. The reflexive pronouns (me, te, se, nos, os, se) come before **había, habías, había,** and so on. The table on the next page shows the pluperfect tense of **lavarse** in full.

(Subject pronoun)	Reflexive pronoun	Imperfect tense of haber	Past Participle	Meaning
(yo)	me	había	lavado	I had washed
(tú)	te	habías	lavado	you had washed
(él) (ella) (uno) (usted)	se	había	lavado	he had washed she had washed one had washed it had washed you had washed
(nosotros) (nosotras)	nos	habíamos	lavado	we had washed we had washed
(vosotros) (vosotras)	os	habíais	lavado	you had washed you had washed
(ellos) (ellas) (ustedes)	se	habían	lavado	they had washed they had washed you had washed

Grammar Extra!

Don't use the pluperfect with desde, desde hacía and hacía ... que when talking about how long something had been going on for. Use the imperfect instead.

<u>Estaba</u> enfermo desde 2000.	He had been ill since 2000.
<u>Conducía</u> ese coche desde hacía tres meses.	He had been driving that car for three months.
Hacía mucho tiempo que <u>salían</u> juntos.	They had been going out together for a long time.

⇨ *For more information on the **Imperfect tense**, see page 110.*

In European Spanish you <u>CAN</u> use the pluperfect tense in the negative with desde and desde hacía.

No lo <u>había visto</u> desde hacía mucho tiempo.	I hadn't seen him for a long time.

Key points

✔ The Spanish pluperfect tense is formed using the imperfect tense of **haber** and a past participle.

✔ In Spanish, the pluperfect tense is used very much as it is in English.

✔ The past participle of regular -ar verbs ends in -ado, while that of regular -er and -ir verbs ends in -ido.

✔ Make sure you know the irregular forms: **abierto, cubierto, dicho, escrito, frito, hecho, muerto, puesto, roto, visto, vuelto.**

The passive

> **What is the passive?**
> The **passive** is a verb form that is used when the subject of the verb is the person or thing that is affected by the action, for example, *Mary is liked by everyone; Two children were hurt in an accident; The house was sold.*

1 | Using the passive

➤ Verbs can be either active or passive.

➤ In a normal or active sentence, the subject of the verb is the person or thing doing the action described by the verb. The object of the verb is the person or thing that the verb most directly affects.

> Peter *(subject)* wrote *(active verb)* a letter *(object)*.
> Ryan *(subject)* hit *(active verb)* me *(object)*.

➤ Provided the verb has an object, in English, as in Spanish, you can turn an active sentence round to make it a passive sentence by using *to be* followed by a past participle. In this case the person or thing directly affected by the action becomes the subject of the verb.

> A letter *(subject)* was written *(passive verb)*.
> I *(subject)* was hit *(passive verb)*.

➤ To show who or what is responsible for the action in a passive construction, in English you use *by*.

> I *(subject)* was hit *(passive verb)* by Ryan.

➤ You use the passive rather than the active when you want to focus attention on the person or thing affected by the action rather than the person or thing that carries it out.

> John was injured in an accident.

➤ You can also use the passive when you don't know who is responsible for the action.

> Several buses were vandalized.

2 | Forming the passive

➤ In English we use the verb *to be* with a past participle (*was painted, were seen, are made*) to form the passive. In Spanish, the passive is formed in exactly the same way, using the verb **ser** (meaning *to be*) and a past participle. When you say who the action is or was done by, you use the preposition **por** (meaning *by*).

⇨ *For more information on the **Past participle**, see page 115.*

Son fabricados en España.	They're made in Spain.
Es hecho a mano.	It's made by hand.
Fue escrito por JK Rowling.	It was written by JK Rowling.
La casa **fue construida** en 1956.	The house was built in 1956.
El cuadro **fue pintado** por mi padre.	The picture was painted by my father.
El colegio va a **ser modernizado**.	The school is going to be modernized.

i Note that the ending of the past participle agrees with the subject of the verb ser in exactly the same way as an adjective would.

⇨ *For more information on **Adjectives**, see page 19.*

➤ Here is the preterite of the -ar verb **enviar** (meaning *to send*) in its passive form.

(Subject pronoun)	Preterite of ser	Past Participle	Meaning
(yo)	fui	**enviado** (masculine) **enviada** (feminine)	I was sent
(tú)	fuiste	**enviado** (masculine) **enviada** (feminine)	you were sent
(él) (ella) (usted)	fue	**enviado** **enviada** **enviado** (masculine) **enviada** (feminine)	he was sent she was sent you were sent
(nosotros) (nosotras)	fuimos fuimos	**enviados** **enviadas**	we were sent we were sent
(vosotros) (vosotras)	fuisteis	**enviados** **enviadas**	you were sent you were sent
(ellos) (ellas) (ustedes)	fueron	**enviados** **enviadas** **enviados** (masculine) **enviadas** (feminine)	they were sent they were sent you were sent you were sent

➤ You can form other tenses in the passive by changing the tense of the verb ser.

Future: **serán enviados** they will be sent.
Perfect: **han sido enviados** they have been sent.

➤ Irregular past participles are the same as they are in the perfect tense.

⇨ *For more information on **Irregular past participles**, see page 116.*

3 **Avoiding the passive**

➤ Passives are not as common in Spanish as they are in English. Spanish native speakers usually prefer to avoid using the passive by:

- using the active construction instead of the passive

La policía <u>interrogó</u> al sospechoso.	The suspect was interrogated by the police.
Su madre le <u>regaló</u> un libro.	He was given a book by his mother.

- using an active verb in the third person plural

<u>Ponen</u> demasiados anuncios en la televisión.	Too many adverts are shown on television.

- using a reflexive construction (as long as you don't need to say who the action is done by)

<u>Se fabrican</u> en España.	They're made in Spain.
<u>Se hace</u> a mano.	It's made by hand.
La casa <u>se construyó</u> en 1956.	The house was built in 1956.
Todos los libros <u>se han vendido</u>.	All the books have been sold.

⇨ *For more information on **Reflexive verbs**, see page 91.*

- using an impersonal se construction

<u>Se</u> cree que va a morir.	It is thought he will die.

⇨ *For more information on the impersonal se construction, see page 133.*

> *Típ*
>
> Active verbs often have both a direct object and an indirect object.
> He gave me (*indirect object*) a book (*direct object*).
> In English, both of these objects can be made the subject of a passive verb; *I was given a book*. or *A book was given to me*.
> In Spanish, an indirect object can <u>NEVER</u> become the subject of a passive verb.

Key points

✔ The passive is formed using **ser** + past participle, sometimes followed by **por** (meaning *by*).

✔ The past participle must agree with the subject of **ser**.

✔ Passive constructions are not as common as they are in English. You can often avoid the passive by using the third person plural of the active verb or by using a reflexive construction.

For further explanation of grammatical terms, please see pages viii-xii.

The gerund

> **What is a gerund?**
> The **gerund** is a verb form ending in *-ing* which is used to form verb tenses, and which in English may also be used as an adjective and a noun, for example, *What are you <u>doing</u>?; the <u>setting</u> sun; <u>Swimming</u> is easy!*

1   Using the gerund

➤ In Spanish, the gerund is a form of the verb that usually ends in **-ando** or **-iendo** and is used to form continuous tenses.

Estoy traba<u>jando</u>.	I'm work<u>ing</u>.
Estamos com<u>iendo</u>.	We are eat<u>ing</u>.

➤ It is used with **estar** to form continuous tenses such as:

* the present continuous

<u>Está fregando</u> los platos.	He's washing the dishes.
<u>Estoy escribiendo</u> una carta.	I'm writing a letter.

⇨ *For more information on the **Present continuous**, see page 84.*

* the imperfect continuous

<u>Estaba reparando</u> el coche.	She was fixing the car.
<u>Estaban esperándo</u>nos.	They were waiting for us.

ℹ️ Note that continuous tenses should only be used in Spanish to describe action that is or was happening at the precise moment you are talking about.

Grammar Extra!

Sometimes another verb, such as **ir** or **venir** is used instead of estar with a gerund in continuous tenses. These verbs emphasize the gradualness or the slowness of the process.

<u>Iba anocheciendo</u>.	It was getting dark.
Eso lo <u>vengo diciendo</u> desde hace tiempo.	That's what I've been saying all along.

➤ The gerund is also used after certain other verbs:

* **seguir haciendo algo** and **continuar haciendo algo** are both used with the meaning of *to go on doing something* or *to continue doing something*.

Siguió cantando *or* **Continuó cantando.**	He went on singing *or* He continued singing.
Siguieron leyendo *or* **Continuaron leyendo.**	They went on reading *or* They continued reading.

- **llevar** with a time expression followed by the gerund is used to talk about how long someone has been doing something:

Lleva dos años estudiando inglés.	He's heen studying English for two years.
Llevo una hora esperando aquí.	I've been waiting here for an hour.

[i] Note that the present tense of **llevar** followed by a gerund means the same as the English *have/has been + -ing*.

➤ **pasar(se)** with a time expression followed by the gerund is used to talk about how long you've spent doing something.

Pasé or **Me pasé el fin de semana estudiando.**	I spent the weekend studying.
Pasamos or **Nos pasamos el día leyendo.**	We spent the day reading.

➤ Verbs of movement, such as **salir** (meaning *to come out* or *to go out*), **entrar** (meaning *to come in* or *to go in*), and **irse** (meaning *to leave*) are sometimes followed by a gerund such as **corriendo** (meaning *running*) or **cojeando** (meaning *limping*). The English equivalent of **salir corriendo**, **entrar corriendo** or **irse cojeando**, would be *to run out*, *to run in* or *to limp off* in such cases.

Salió corriendo.	He ran out.
Se fue cojeando.	He limped off.

Tip

Use a past participle not a gerund to talk about physical position.

Estaba <u>tumbado</u> en el sofá.	He was lying on the sofa.
Estaba <u>sentada</u>.	She was sitting down.
Lo encontré <u>tendido</u> en el suelo.	I found him lying on the floor.
La escalera estaba <u>apoyada</u> contra la pared.	The ladder was leaning against the wall.

⇨ *For more information on the **Past participles**, see page 115.*

➤ You will also come across the gerund used in other ways. For example:

Los vimos jugando al fútbol.	We saw them playing football.
Estudiando, aprobarás.	By studying, *or* If you study, you'll pass.

2 Forming the gerund of regular verbs

➤ To form the gerund of regular -ar verbs, take off the -ar ending of the infinitive to form the stem, and add -ando.

Infinitive	Stem	Gerund
hablar	habl-	hablando
trabajar	trabaj-	trabajando

➤ To form the gerund of regular -er and -ir verbs, take off the -er and -ir ending of the infinitive to form the stem, and add -iendo.

Infinitive	Stem	Gerund
comer	com-	comiendo
vivir	viv-	viviendo

3 The gerund of irregular verbs

➤ Some verbs have an irregular gerund form. You have to learn these.

Infinitives	Meaning	Gerund	Meaning
decir	to say	diciendo	saying
dormir	to sleep	durmiendo	sleeping
freír	to fry	friendo	frying
morir	to die	muriendo	dying
pedir	to ask for	pidiendo	asking for
poder	to be able to	pudiendo	being able to
reír	to laugh	riendo	laughing
seguir	to follow	siguiendo	following
sentir	to feel	sintiendo	feeling
venir	to come	viniendo	coming
vestir	to dress	vistiendo	dressing

➤ In the next group of verbs there is a y rather than the normal i.

Infinitives	Meaning	Gerund	Meaning
caer	to fall	cayendo	falling
creer	to believe	creyendo	believing
leer	to read	leyendo	reading
oír	to hear	oyendo	hearing
traer	to bring	trayendo	bringing
ir	to go	yendo	going

Tip

In English, we often use *-ing* forms as adjectives, for example, *running water, shining eyes, the following day*. In Spanish, you cannot use the **-ando** and **-iendo** forms like this.

Instead, there are sometimes corresponding forms ending in **-ante** and **-iente** that can be used as adjectives.

agua <u>corriente</u>	running water
ojos <u>brillantes</u>	shining eyes
Al día <u>siguiente</u>, visitamos Toledo.	The following day we visited Toledo.

Similarly, in English, we often use the *-ing* forms as nouns. In Spanish you have to use the <u>infinitive</u> instead.

<u>Fumar</u> es malo para la salud.	<u>Smoking</u> is bad for you.

---

4 | **Position of pronouns with the gerund**

➤ Object pronouns and reflexive pronouns are usually attached to the end of the gerund, although you can also often put them before **estar** in continuous tenses.

Estoy hablándo<u>te</u> or **<u>Te</u> estoy hablando.**	I'm talking to you.
Está vistiéndo<u>se</u> or **<u>Se</u> está vistiendo.**	He's getting dressed.
Estaban mostrándo<u>selo</u> *or* **<u>Se lo</u> estaban mostrando.**	They were showing it to him/her/them/you.

i Note that you will always have to add an accent to keep the stress in the same place when adding pronouns to the end of a gerund.

⟹ *For more information on **Stress**, see page 200.*

Key points

✔ Use the gerund in continuous tenses with **estar** as well as after **seguir** and **continuar**.

✔ Gerunds for **-ar** verbs add **-ando** to the stem of the verb.

✔ Gerunds for **-er** and **-ir** verbs usually add **-iendo** to the stem of the verb.

✔ **-ando** and **-iendo** gerunds <u>cannot</u> be used as adjectives or nouns.

✔ You can attach pronouns to the end of the gerund, or sometimes put them before the previous verb.

For further explanation of grammatical terms, please see pages viii-xii.

Impersonal verbs

> **What is an impersonal verb?**
> An **impersonal verb** is a verb whose subject is *it*, but this '*it*' does not refer to any specific thing; for example, *It's going to rain; It's nine o'clock.*

1 Verbs that are always used impersonally

➤ There are some verbs such as **llover** (meaning *to rain*) and **nevar** (meaning *to snow*), that are only used in the '*it*' form, the infinitive, and as a gerund (the -*ing* form of the verb). These are called <u>impersonal verbs</u> because there is no person, animal or thing performing the action.

Llueve.	It's raining.
Está lloviendo.	It's raining.
Va a llover.	It's going to rain.
Nieva.	It's snowing.
Está nevando.	It's snowing.
Nevaba.	It was snowing.
Estaba nevando.	It was snowing.
Mañana nevará.	It will snow tomorrow.

2 Verbs that are sometimes used impersonally

➤ There are also some other very common verbs that are sometimes used as impersonal verbs, for example **hacer**, **haber** and **ser**.

➤ **hacer** is used in a number of impersonal expressions relating to the weather:

<u>Hace</u> **frío/calor.**	It's cold/hot.
Ayer <u>hacía</u> **mucho frío/calor.**	It was very cold/hot yesterday.
<u>Hace</u> **sol/viento.**	It's sunny/windy.
Va a <u>hacer</u> **sol/viento.**	It's going to be sunny/windy.
<u>Hace</u> **un tiempo estupendo/horrible.**	It's a lovely/horrible day.

➤ **hacer** is also used in combination with **que** and **desde** in impersonal time expressions, to talk about how long something has been going on for or how long it is since something happened.

<u>Hace</u> **seis meses** <u>que</u> **vivo aquí.** *or* **Vivo aquí** <u>desde hace</u> **seis meses.**	I've been living here for six months.

Hace tres años **que** estudio español *or* Estudio español **desde hace** tres años.	I've been studying Spanish for three years.
Hace mucho tiempo **que** no la veo *or* No la veo **desde hace** mucho tiempo.	I haven't seen her for ages *or* It is ages since I saw her.
Hace varias semanas **que** no voy por allí *or* No voy por allí **desde hace** varias semanas.	I haven't been there for several weeks *or* It is several weeks since I went there.

i Note the use of the <u>present simple</u> in Spanish in the above examples where in English we'd use the perfect tense or the past tense.

➤ hacer is also used impersonally in the expression (**me/te/le**) **hace falta**, which means *it is necessary* (*for me/you/him*).

Si **hace falta**, voy.	I'll go if necessary.
No **hace falta** llamar.	We/You/I needn't call.
Me **hace falta** otro vaso más.	I need another glass.
No **hace falta** ser un experto.	You don't need to be an expert.
No **hacía falta**.	It wasn't necessary.

i Note that not all impersonal expressions in Spanish are translated into English using impersonal expressions.

➤ haber too can be used impersonally with the meaning *there is/there are, there was/there were, there will be,* and so on. It has the special form hay in the present. For the other tenses, you take the third person singular (the '*it*' form) of haber in the appropriate tense.

Hay un cine cerca de aquí.	There's a cinema near here.
Hay dos supermercados.	There are two supermarkets.
No **hay** bares.	There are no bars.
Había mucho ruido.	There was a lot of noise.
Había muchos coches.	There were a lot of cars
Hubo un accidente.	There was an accident.
Hubo varios problemas.	There were several problems.
¿**Habrá** tiempo?	Will there be time?
¿**Habrá** suficientes sillas?	Will there be enough chairs?

i Note that you should <u>ALWAYS</u> use the singular form (never the plural), no matter how many things there are.

➤ **haber** is used in the construction **hay que** with an infinitive to talk about actions that need to be taken.

<u>Hay que</u> trabajar más.	We/You need to work harder.
<u>Hay que</u> ser respetuoso.	You/We/One must be respectful.
<u>Habrá</u> que decírselo.	We'll/You'll have to tell him.

➤ **ser** can be used in certain impersonal constructions with adjectives, for example:

- es/era/fue + adjective + infinitive

<u>Es</u> importante ahorrar dinero.	It's important to save money.
<u>Fue</u> torpe hacer eso.	It was silly to do that.
<u>Sería</u> mejor esperar.	It would be better to wait.

- es/era/fue + adjective + que + verb

<u>Es cierto que</u> tengo problemas.	It's true that I've got problems.
<u>Es verdad que</u> trabaja mucho.	It's true that he works hard.

i Note that when they are used in the negative (**no es cierto que...**; **no es verdad que...**), these expressions have to be followed by the subjunctive.

⇨ *For more information on the Subjunctive, see page 134.*

Grammar Extra!

When impersonal expressions that don't state facts are followed by **que** (meaning *that*) and a verb, this verb must be in the <u>subjunctive</u>.

For this reason, the following non-factual impersonal expressions are all followed by the subjunctive:

- **Es posible que...**
  Es posible que ganen.

  It's possible that ... / ...might...
  They might win.

- **Es imposible que...**
  Es imposible que lo sepan.

  It's impossible that... / ...can't possibly...
  They can't possibly know.

- **Es necesario que...**
  No es necesario que vengas.

  It's necessary that.../ ...need to...
  You don't need to come.

- **Es mejor que...**
  Es mejor que lo pongas aquí.

  ... be better to ...
  You'd be better to put it here.

⇨ *For more information on the Subjunctive, see page 134.*

➤ ser is also used impersonally with de día and de noche to say whether it's day or night.

Era de noche cuando llegamos.	It was night when we arrived.
Todavía es de día allí.	It's still day there.

⇨ *For other time expressions with ser, see page 80.*

➤ basta con is used impersonally:

- with a following <u>infinitive</u> to mean *it's enough to/all you need do is*

Basta con telefonear para reservar un asiento.	All you need do is to phone to reserve a seat.
Basta con dar una vuelta por la ciudad para...	You only need to take a walk round the city to ...

- with a <u>noun</u> or <u>pronoun</u> to mean *all you need is* or *all it takes is*

Basta con un error para que todo se estropee.	All it takes is one mistake to ruin everything.

➤ (me) parece que is used to give opinions.

Parece que va a llover.	It looks as if it's going to rain.
Me parece que estás equivocado.	I think that you are wrong.

[*i*] Note that when **(me) parece que** is used in the negative, the following verb has to be in the <u>subjunctive</u>.

⇨ *For more information on the **Subjunctive**, see page 134.*

➤ vale la pena is used to talk about what's worth doing.

Vale la pena.	It's worth it.
No vale la pena.	It's not worth it.
Vale la pena hacer el esfuerzo.	It's worth making the effort.
No vale la pena gastar tanto dinero.	It's not worth spending so much money.

Grammar Extra!

se is often used in impersonal expressions, especially with the verbs **creer, decir, poder,** and **tratar.** In such cases it often corresponds to *it, one* or *you* in English.

- **Se cree que...**   It is thought *or* People think
                                        that...

  Se cree que es un mito.   It is thought to be a myth.

- **Se dice que...**   It is said *or* People say that...

  Se dice que es rico.   He is said to be rich.

- **Se puede...**   One can.../People can.../You can...

  Aquí se puede aparcar.   One can park here.

- **Se trata de...**   It's a question of .../It's about ...

  No se trata de dinero.   It isn't a question of money.

  Se trata de resolverlo.   We must solve it.

⟱ *For more information on **Reflexive verbs**, see page 91.*

Key points

- ✔ Impersonal verbs and expressions can only be used in the *'it'* form, the infinitive and the gerund.
- ✔ Impersonal expressions relating to the weather are very common.
- ✔ Although in English we use *there is* or *there are* depending on the number of people or things that there are, in Spanish **hay, había, hubo** and so on are used in the singular form only.
- ✔ Some very common ordinary verbs are also used as impersonal verbs.

The subjunctive

> **What is the subjunctive?**
> The **subjunctive** is a verb form that is used in certain circumstances especially when expressing some sort of feeling or when there is doubt about whether something will happen or whether something is true. It is only used occasionally in modern English, for example, *If I _were_ you, ...; So be it.; I wish you _were_ here.*

1 Using the subjunctive

➤ Although you may not know it, you will already be familiar with many of the forms of the present subjunctive, as it is used when giving orders and instructions not to do something as well as in the **usted**, **ustedes** and **nosotros** forms of instructions to do something. For example, if you phone someone in Spain, they will probably answer with ¡**diga**! or ¡**dígame**!, an imperative form taken from the present subjunctive of **decir**.

⇨ *For more information on **Imperatives**, see page 85.*

➤ In Spanish the subjunctive is used after certain verbs and conjunctions when two parts of a sentence have different subjects.

Tengo miedo de que le ocurra algo.   I'm afraid <u>something</u> may (*subjunctive*) happen to him.

(The subject of the first part of the sentence is *I*; the subject of the second part of the sentence is *something*.).

➤ In English, in a sentence like *We want him/José to be happy*, we use an infinitive (*to be*) for the second verb even though *want* and *be happy* have different subjects (*we* and *him/José*).

➤ In Spanish you cannot do this. You have to use the <u>subjunctive</u> for the second verb.

Queremos que él sea feliz.   We want that he (*subjunctive*) be happy.

Queremos que José sea feliz. We want that José (*subjunctive*) be happy.

➤ You <u>CAN</u> use an infinitive for the second verb in Spanish when the subject of both verbs is the same.

Queremos ser felices.   We want to be happy.

2 Coming across the subjunctive

➤ The subjunctive has several tenses, the main ones being the <u>present subjunctive</u> and the <u>imperfect subjunctive</u>. The tense used for the subjunctive verb depends on the tense of the previous verb.

➪ *For more information on **Tenses with the subjunctive**, see page 139.*

➤ In sentences containing two verbs with different subjects, you will find that the second verb is in the subjunctive when the first verb:

- expresses a wish

Quiero que <u>vengan</u>.	I want them to come.
Quiero que se <u>vaya</u>.	I want him/her to go away.
Deseamos que <u>tengan</u> éxito.	We want them to be successful.

- expresses an emotion

Siento mucho que no <u>puedas</u> venir.	I'm very sorry that you can't come.
Espero que <u>venga</u>.	I hope he comes.
Me sorprende que no <u>esté</u> aquí.	I'm surprised that he isn't here.
Me alegro de que te <u>gusten</u>.	I'm pleased that you like them.

➤ If the subject of both verbs is the <u>same</u>, an infinitive is used as the second verb instead of a subjunctive.

➤ Compare the following examples. In the examples on the left, both the verb expressing the wish or emotion and the second verb have the same subject, so the second verb is an <u>infinitive</u>. In the examples on the right, each verb has a different subject, so the second verb is in the <u>subjunctive</u>.

Infinitive construction	Subjunctive construction
Quiero <u>estudiar</u>. I want to study.	**Quiero que José <u>estudie</u>.** I want José to study.
Maite quiere <u>irse</u>. Maite wants to leave.	**Maite quiere que me <u>vaya</u>.** Maite wants me to leave.
Siento no <u>poder</u> venir. I'm sorry I can't come.	**Siento que no <u>puedas</u> venir.** I'm sorry that you can't come.
Me alegro de <u>poder</u> ayudar. I'm pleased to be able to help.	**Me alegro de que <u>puedas</u> ayudar.** I'm pleased you can help.

➤ You will also come across the verb + que + subjunctive construction (often with a personal object such as me, te and so on) when the first verb is one you use to ask or advise somebody to do something.

Sólo te pido que <u>tengas</u> cuidado.	I'm only asking you to be careful.
Te aconsejo que no <u>llegues</u> tarde.	I'd advise you not to be late.

➤ You will also come across the subjunctive in the following cases:

- after verbs expressing doubt or uncertainty, and verbs saying what you think about something that are used with **no**

Dudo que <u>tenga</u> tiempo.	I doubt I'll have time.
No creo que <u>venga</u>.	I don't think she'll come.
No pienso que <u>esté</u> bien.	I don't think it's right.

- in impersonal constructions that show a need to do something

¿Hace falta que <u>vaya</u> Jaime?	Does Jaime need to go?
No es necesario que <u>vengas</u>.	You don't need to come.

- in impersonal constructions that do not express facts

Es posible que <u>tengan</u> razón.	They may be right.

⇨ *For more information on **Impersonal verbs**, see page 129.*

Grammar Extra!

Use the <u>indicative</u> (that is, any verb form that isn't subjunctive) after impersonal expressions that state facts provided they are <u>NOT</u> in the negative.

Es verdad que <u>es</u> interesante.	It's true that it's interesting.
Es cierto que me <u>gusta</u> el café.	It's true I like coffee.
Parece que se <u>va</u> a ir.	It seems that he's going to go.

➤ The subjunctive is used after **que** to express wishes.

¡Que lo <u>pases</u> bien!	Have a good time!
¡Que te <u>diviertas</u>!	Have fun!

➤ The subjunctive is also used after certain conjunctions linking two parts of a sentence which each have different subjects.

- **antes de que**   before

¿Quieres decirle algo antes de que se <u>vaya</u>?	Do you want to say anything to him before he goes?

- **para que**   so that

Es para que te <u>acuerdes</u> de mí.	It's so that you'll remember me.

- **sin que**   without

Salimos sin que nos <u>vieran</u>.	We left without them seeing us.

⇨ *For more information on **Conjunctions**, see page 192.*

Típ

Use **para**, **sin** and **antes de** with the <u>infinitive</u> when the subject of both verbs is the <u>same</u>.

Fue en taxi para no <u>llegar</u> tarde.	He went by taxi so that he wouldn't be late.
Pedro se ha ido sin <u>esperarnos</u>.	Pedro's gone without waiting for us.
Cenamos antes de <u>ir</u> al teatro.	We had dinner before we went to the theatre.

3 Forming the present subjunctive

➤ To form the present subjunctive of most verbs, take off the -o ending of the **yo** form of the <u>present simple</u>, and add a fixed set of endings.

➤ For -ar verbs, the endings are: -e, -es, -e, -emos, -éis, -en.

➤ For both -er and -ir verbs, the endings are: -a, -as, -a, -amos, -áis, -an.

➤ The following table shows the present subjunctive of three regular verbs: **hablar** (meaning *to speak*), **comer** (meaning *to eat*) and **vivir** (meaning *to live*).

Infinitive	(yo)	(tú)	(él) (ella) (usted)	(nosotros) (nosotras)	(vosotros) (vosotras)	(ellos) (ellas) (ustedes)
hablar to speak	habl<u>e</u>	habl<u>es</u>	habl<u>e</u>	habl<u>emos</u>	habl<u>éis</u>	habl<u>en</u>
comer to eat	com<u>a</u>	com<u>as</u>	com<u>a</u>	com<u>amos</u>	com<u>áis</u>	com<u>an</u>
vivir to live	viv<u>a</u>	viv<u>as</u>	viv<u>a</u>	viv<u>amos</u>	viv<u>áis</u>	viv<u>an</u>

Quiero que <u>comas</u> algo.	I want you to eat something.
Me sorprende que no <u>hable</u> inglés.	I'm surprised he doesn't speak English.
No es verdad que <u>trabajen</u> aquí.	It isn't true that they work here.

➤ Some verbs have very irregular yo forms in the ordinary present tense and these irregular forms are reflected in the stem for the present subjunctive.

Infinitive	(yo)	(tú)	(él) (ella) (usted)	(nosotros) (nosotras)	(vosotros) (vosotras)	(ellos) (ellas) (ustedes)
decir to say	diga	digas	diga	digamos	digáis	digan
hacer to do/make	haga	hagas	haga	hagamos	hagáis	hagan
poner to put	ponga	pongas	ponga	pongamos	pongáis	pongan
salir to leave	salga	salgas	salga	salgamos	salgáis	salgan
tener to have	tenga	tengas	tenga	tengamos	tengáis	tengan
venir to come	venga	vengas	venga	vengamos	vengáis	vengan

Voy a limpiar la casa antes de que <u>vengan</u>.	I'm going to clean the house before they come.

[*i*] Note that only the vosotros form has an accent.

> *Típ*
> The present subjunctive endings are the opposite of what you'd expect, as -ar verbs have endings starting with -e, and -er and -ir verbs have endings starting with -a.

[4] **Forming the present subjunctive of irregular verbs**

➤ The following verbs have irregular subjunctive forms:

Infinitive	(yo)	(tú)	(él) (ella) (usted)	(nosotros) (nosotras)	(vosotros) (vosotras)	(ellos) (ellas) (ustedes)
dar to give	dé	des	dé	demos	deis	den
estar to be	esté	estés	esté	estemos	estéis	estén
haber to have	haya	hayas	haya	hayamos	hayáis	hayan
ir to go	vaya	vayas	vaya	vayamos	vayáis	vayan
saber to know	sepa	sepas	sepa	sepamos	sepáis	sepan
ser to be	sea	seas	sea	seamos	seáis	sean

No quiero que te <u>vayas</u>.	I don't want you to go.
Dudo que <u>esté</u> aquí.	I doubt if it's here.
No piensan que <u>sea</u> él.	They don't think it's him.
Es posible que <u>haya</u> problemas.	There may be problems.

For further explanation of grammatical terms, please see pages viii–xii.

➤ Verbs that change their stems (<u>radical-changing verbs</u>) in the ordinary present usually change them in the same way in the present subjunctive.

⤵ *For more information on **radical-changing verbs**, see page 76.*

Infinitive	(yo)	(tú)	(él) (ella) (usted)	(nosotros) (nosotras)	(vosotros) (vosotras)	(ellos) (ellas) (ustedes)
pensar to think	piense	pienses	piense	pensemos	penséis	piensen
entender to understand	entienda	entiendas	entienda	entendamos	entendáis	entiendan
poder to be able	pueda	puedas	pueda	podamos	podáis	puedan
querer to want	quiera	quieras	quiera	queramos	queráis	quieran
volver to return	vuelva	vuelvas	vuelva	volvamos	volváis	vuelvan

> **No hace falta que <u>vuelvas</u>.**　There's no need for you to come back.
>
> **Es para que lo <u>entiendas</u>.**　It's so that you understand.
>
> **Me alegro de que <u>puedas</u> venir.**　I'm pleased you can come.

➤ Sometimes the stem of the **nosotros** and **vosotros** forms isn't the same as it is in the ordinary present tense.

Infinitive	(yo)	(tú)	(él) (ella) (usted)	(nosotros) (nosotras)	(vosotros) (vosotras)	(ellos) (ellas) (ustedes)
dormir to sleep	duerma	duermas	duerma	<u>durmamos</u>	<u>durmáis</u>	duerman
morir to die	muera	mueras	muera	<u>muramos</u>	<u>muráis</u>	mueran
pedir to ask for	pida	pidas	pida	<u>pidamos</u>	<u>pidáis</u>	pidan
seguir to follow	siga	sigas	siga	<u>sigamos</u>	<u>sigáis</u>	sigan
sentir to feel	sienta	sientas	sienta	<u>sintamos</u>	<u>sintáis</u>	sientan

> **Queremos hacerlo antes de que nos <u>muramos</u>.**　We want to do it before we die.
>
> **Vendré a veros cuando os <u>sintáis</u> mejor.**　I'll come and see you when you feel better.

5 | **Tenses with the subjunctive**

➤ If the verb in the first part of the sentence is in the <u>present, future</u> or <u>imperative</u>, the second verb will usually be in the <u>present subjunctive</u>.

> **Quiero** *(present)* **que lo hagas** *(present subjunctive)*.
> I want you to do it.
>
> **Iremos** *(future)* **por aquí para que no nos vean** *(present subjunctive)*.
> We'll go this way so that they won't see us.

➤ If the verb in the first part of the sentence is in the <u>conditional</u> or a <u>past tense</u>, the second verb will usually be in the <u>imperfect subjunctive</u>.

Me gustaría *(conditional)* que llegaras *(imperfect subjunctive)* temprano.
I'd like you to arrive early.

Les pedí *(preterite)* que me esperaran *(imperfect subjunctive)*.
I asked them to wait for me.

6 | Indicative or subjunctive?

➤ Many expressions are followed by the <u>indicative</u> (the ordinary form of the verb) when they state facts, and by the <u>subjunctive</u> when they refer to possible or intended future events and outcomes.

➤ Certain conjunctions relating to time such as **cuando** (meaning *when*), **hasta que** (meaning *until*), **en cuanto** (meaning *as soon as*) and **mientras** (meaning *while*) are used with the <u>indicative</u> when the action has happened or when talking about what happens regularly.

¿Qué dijo cuando te <u>vio</u>?	What did he say when he saw you?
Siempre lo compro cuando <u>voy</u> a España.	I always buy it when I go to Spain.
Me quedé allí hasta que <u>volvió</u> Antonio.	I stayed there until Antonio came back.

➤ The same conjunctions are followed by the <u>subjunctive</u> when talking about a vague future time.

¿Qué quieres hacer cuando <u>seas</u> mayor?	What do you want to do when you grow up? *(but you're not grown up yet)*
¿Por qué no te quedas aquí hasta que <u>vuelva</u> Antonio?	Why don't you stay here until Antonio comes back? *(but Antonio hasn't come back yet)*
Lo haré en cuanto <u>pueda</u> *or* **tan pronto como <u>pueda</u>.**	I'll do it as soon as I can. *(but I'm not able to yet)*

Grammar Extra!

aunque is used with the <u>indicative</u> (the ordinary verb forms) when it means *although* or *even though*. In this case, the second part of the sentence is stating a fact.

Me gusta el francés aunque <u>prefiero</u> el alemán.	I like French although I prefer German.
Seguí andando aunque me <u>dolía</u> la pierna.	I went on walking even though my leg hurt.

aunque is used with the <u>subjunctive</u> when it means *even if*. Here, the second part of the sentence is not yet a fact.

Te llamaré cuando vuelva aunque <u>sea</u> tarde.	I'll ring you when I get back, even if it's late.

For further explanation of grammatical terms, please see pages viii-xii.

7 | Forming the imperfect subjunctive

➤ For all verbs, there are two imperfect subjunctive forms that are exactly the same in meaning.

➤ The stem for both imperfect subjunctive forms is the same: you take off the -aron or -ieron ending of the ellos form of the preterite and add a fixed set of endings to what is left.

⇨ *For more information on the Preterite, see page 104.*

➤ For -ar verbs, the endings are: -ara, -aras, -ara, -áramos, -arais, -aran or -ase, -ases, -ase, -ásemos, -aseis, -asen. The first form is more common.

➤ For -er and -ir verbs, the endings are: -iera, -ieras, -iera, -iéramos, -ierais, -ieran or -iese, -ieses, -iese, -iésemos, -ieseis, -iesen. The first form is more common.

➤ The following table shows the subjunctive of three regular verbs: hablar (meaning *to speak*), comer (meaning *to eat*) and vivir (meaning *to live*).

Infinitive	(yo)	(tú)	(él) (ella) (usted)	(nosotros) (nosotras)	(vosotros) (vosotras)	(ellos) (ellas) (ustedes)
hablar to speak	hablara	hablaras	hablara	habláramos	hablarais	hablaran
	hablase	hablases	hablase	hablásemos	hablaseis	hablasen
comer to eat	comiera	comieras	comiera	comiéramos	comierais	comieran
	comiese	comieses	comiese	comiésemos	comieseis	comiesen
vivir to live	viviera	vivieras	viviera	viviéramos	vivierais	vivieran
	viviese	vivieses	viviese	viviésemos	vivieseis	viviesen

➤ Many verbs have irregular preterite forms which are reflected in the stem for the imperfect subjunctive. For example:

Infinitive	(yo)	(tú)	(él) (ella) (usted)	(nosotros) (nosotras)	(vosotros) (vosotras)	(ellos) (ellas) (ustedes)
dar to give	diera	dieras	diera	diéramos	dierais	dieran
	diese	dieses	diese	diésemos	dieseis	diesen
estar to be	estuviera	estuvieras	estuviera	estuviéramos	estuvierais	estuvieran
	estuviese	estuvieses	estuviese	estuviésemos	estuvieseis	estuviesen
hacer to do/ make	hiciera	hicieras	hiciera	hiciéramos	hicierais	hicieran
	hiciese	hicieses	hiciese	hiciésemos	hicieseis	hiciesen
poner to put	pusiera	pusieras	pusiera	pusiéramos	pusierais	pusieran
	pusiese	pusieses	pusiese	pusiésemos	pusieseis	pusiesen
tener to have	tuviera	tuvieras	tuviera	tuviéramos	tuvierais	tuvieran
	tuviese	tuvieses	tuviese	tuviésemos	tuvieseis	tuviesen
ser to be	fuera	fueras	fuera	fuéramos	fuerais	fueran
	fuese	fueses	fuese	fuésemos	fueseis	fuesen
venir to come	viniera	vinieras	viniera	viniéramos	vinierais	vinieran
	viniese	vinieses	viniese	viniésemos	vinieseis	viniesen

8 | Forming the imperfect subjunctive of some irregular -ir verbs

➤ In some irregular -ir verbs – the ones that don't have an i in the ellos form of the preterite – -era, -eras, -era, -éramos, -erais, -eran or -ese, -eses, -ese, -ésemos, -eseis, -esen are added to the preterite stem instead of -iera and -iese and so on.

➪ *For more information on the **Preterite**, see page 104.*

Infinitive	(yo)	(tú)	(él) (ella) (usted)	(nosotros) (nosotras)	(vosotros) (vosotras)	(ellos) (ellas) (ustedes)
decir to say	dijera	dijeras	dijera	dijéramos	dijerais	dijeran
	dijese	dijeses	dijese	dijésemos	dijeseis	dijesen
ir to go	fuera	fueras	fuera	fuéramos	fuerais	fueran
	fuese	fueses	fuese	fuésemos	fueseis	fuesen

i Note that the imperfect subjunctive forms of **ir** and **ser** are identical.

Teníamos miedo de que se fuera. We were afraid he might leave.
No era verdad que fueran ellos. It wasn't true that it was them.

9 **Present indicative or imperfect subjunctive after si**

➤ Like some other conjunctions, si (meaning *if*) is sometimes followed by the ordinary present tense (the <u>present indicative</u>) and sometimes by the <u>imperfect subjunctive</u>.

➤ si is followed by the <u>present indicative</u> when talking about likely possibilities.

Si <u>quieres</u>, te dejo el coche.	If you like, I'll lend you the car. *(and you may well want to borrow the car)*
Compraré un bolígrafo si <u>tienen</u>.	I'll buy a pen if they have any. *(and there may well be some pens)*

➤ si is followed by the <u>imperfect subjunctive</u> when talking about unlikely or impossible conditions.

Si <u>tuviera</u> más dinero, me lo compraría.	If I had more money, I'd buy it. *(but I haven't got more money)*
Si yo <u>fuera</u> tú, lo compraría.	If I were you, I'd buy it. *(but I'm not you)*

Tip

You probably need the imperfect subjunctive in Spanish after si if the English sentence has *would* in it.

Key points

✔ After certain verbs you have to use a subjunctive in Spanish when there is a different subject in the two parts of the sentence.

✔ A subjunctive is also found after impersonal expressions, as well as after certain conjunctions.

✔ Structures with the subjunctive can often be avoided if the subject of both verbs is the same. An infinitive can often be used instead.

✔ The endings of the present subjunctive in regular -ar verbs are: -e, -es, -e, -emos, -éis, -en.

✔ The endings of the present subjunctive in regular -er and -ir verbs are: -a, -as, -a, -amos, -áis, -an.

✔ The endings of the imperfect subjunctive in regular -ar verbs are: -ara, -aras, -ara, -áramos, -arais, -aran or -ase, -ases, -ase, -ásemos, -aseis, -asen.

✔ The endings of the imperfect subjunctive in regular -er and -ir verbs are: -iera, -ieras, -iera, -iéramos, -ierais, -ieran or -iese, -ieses, -iese, -iésemos, -ieseis, -iesen.

✔ Some verbs have irregular subjunctive forms.

The Infinitive

What is the infinitive?
The **infinitive** is a form of the verb that hasn't had any endings added to it and doesn't relate to any particular tense. In English, the infinitive is usually shown with *to*, as in *to speak, to eat, to live*.

1 Using the infinitive

➤ In English, the infinitive is usually thought of as being made up of two words, for example, *to speak*. In Spanish, the infinitive consists of one word and is the verb form that ends in **-ar**, **-er** or **-ir**, for example, **hablar, comer, vivir**.

➤ When you look up a verb in the dictionary, you will find that information is usually listed under the infinitive form.

➤ In Spanish, the infinitive is often used in the following ways:

- after a preposition such as **antes de** (meaning *before*), **después de** (meaning *after*)

Después de comer, fuimos a casa de Pepe.	<u>After eating</u>, we went round to Pepe's.
Salió <u>sin hacer</u> ruido.	She went out <u>without making</u> a noise.
Siempre veo la tele <u>antes de acostarme</u>.	I always watch TV <u>before going to bed</u>.

i Note that in English we always use the *-ing* form of the verb after a preposition, for example, *before <u>going</u>*. In Spanish you have to use the <u>infinitive</u> form after a preposition.

- in set phrases, particularly after adjectives or nouns

Estoy <u>encantada de poder</u> ayudarte.	I'm delighted to be able to help you.
Está <u>contento de vivir</u> aquí.	He's happy living here.
<u>Tengo ganas de salir</u>.	I feel like going out.
No <u>hace falta comprar</u> leche.	We/You don't need to buy any milk.
<u>Me dio</u> mucha <u>alegría verla</u>.	I was very pleased to see her.
<u>Me da miedo cruzar</u> la carretera.	I'm afraid of crossing the road.

- after another verb, sometimes as the object of it

Debo llamar a casa.	I must phone home.
Prefiero esquiar.	I prefer skiing.
Me gusta escuchar música.	I like listening to music.
Nos encanta nadar.	We love swimming.
¿Te apetece ir al cine?	Do you fancy going to the cinema?

[*i*] Note that, when it comes after another verb, the Spanish infinitive often corresponds to the *-ing* form in English.

- in instructions that are aimed at the general public – for example in cookery books or on signs

Cocer a fuego lento.	Cook on a low heat.
Prohibido <u>pisar</u> el césped.	Don't walk on the grass.

- as a noun, where in English we would use the *-ing* form of the verb

Lo importante es <u>intentarlo</u>.	Trying is the important thing.

[*i*] Note that, when the infinitive is the subject of another verb, it may have the article el before it, particularly if it starts the sentence.

El viajar tanto me resulta cansado.	I find so much travelling tiring.

Tip

Be especially careful when translating the English *-ing* form. It is often translated by the infinitive in Spanish.

---

2 **Linking two verbs together**

➤ There are three ways that verbs can be linked together when the second verb is an infinitive:

- with no linking word in between

¿Quieres venir?	Do you want to come?
Necesito hablar contigo.	I need to talk to you.

- with a preposition:

ir <u>a</u> hacer algo	to be going to do something
aprender <u>a</u> hacer algo	to learn to do something
dejar <u>de</u> hacer algo	to stop doing something
Voy <u>a</u> **comprarme un móvil.**	I'm going to buy a mobile.
Aprendimos <u>a</u> **esquiar.**	We learnt to ski.
Quiere dejar <u>de</u> **fumar.**	He wants to stop smoking.

[*i*] Note that you have to learn the preposition required for each verb.

- in set structures

tener que hacer algo	to have to do something
Tengo que salir.	I've got to go out.
Tendrías que comer más.	You should eat more.
Tuvo que devolver el dinero.	He had to pay back the money.

3 Verbs followed by the infinitive with no preposition

➤ Some Spanish verbs and groups of verbs can be followed by an infinitive with no preposition:

- **poder** (meaning *to be able to, can, may*), **saber** (meaning *to know how to, can*), **querer** (meaning *to want*) and **deber** (meaning *to have to, must*)

No <u>puede venir</u>.	He can't come.
¿<u>Sabes esquiar</u>?	Can you ski?
<u>Quiere estudiar</u> medicina.	He wants to study medicine.
<u>Debes hacerlo</u>.	You must do it.

- verbs like **gustar**, **encantar** and **apetecer,** where the infinitive is the subject of the verb

<u>Me gusta estudiar</u>.	I like studying.
<u>Nos encanta bailar</u>.	We love dancing.
¿<u>Te apetece ir</u> al cine?	Do you fancy going to the cinema?

- verbs that relate to seeing or hearing, such as **ver** (meaning *to see*) and **oír** (meaning *to hear*)

Nos <u>ha visto llegar</u>.	He saw us arrive.
Te <u>he oído cantar</u>.	I heard you singing.

- the verbs **hacer** (meaning *to make*) and **dejar** (meaning *to let*)

¡No me <u>hagas reír</u>!	Don't make me laugh!
Mis padres no me <u>dejan salir</u> por la noche.	My parents don't let me go out at night.

- the following common verbs

decidir	to decide
desear	to wish, want
esperar	to hope
evitar	to avoid
necesitar	to need
odiar	to hate
olvidar	to forget
pensar	to think
preferir	to prefer
recordar	to remember
sentir	to regret

Han <u>decidido comprarse</u> una casa.	They've decided to buy a house.
No <u>desea tener</u> más hijos.	She doesn't want to have any more children.
<u>Espero poder</u> ir.	I hope to be able to go.
<u>Evita gastar</u> demasiado dinero.	He avoids spending too much money.
<u>Necesito salir</u> un momento.	I need to go out for a moment.
<u>Olvidó dejar</u> su dirección.	She forgot to leave her address.
<u>Pienso hacer</u> una paella.	I'm thinking of making a paella.
<u>Siento molestarte</u>.	I'm sorry to bother you.

➤ Some of these verbs combine with infinitives to make set phrases with a special meaning:

- **querer decir** to mean
  ¿Qué <u>quiere decir</u> eso? What does that mean?
- **dejar caer** to drop
  <u>Dejó caer</u> la bandeja. She dropped the tray.

4	**Verbs followed by the preposition a and the infinitive**

➤ The following verbs are the most common ones that can be followed by **a** and the infinitive:

- verbs relating to movement such as **ir** (meaning *to go*) and **venir** (meaning *to come*)
  Se va <u>a</u> comprar un caballo. He's going to buy a horse.
  Viene <u>a</u> vernos. He's coming to see us.

● the following common verbs

aprender **a** hacer algo	to learn to do something
comenzar **a** hacer algo	to begin to do something
decidirse **a** hacer algo	to decide to do something
empezar **a** hacer algo	to begin to do something
llegar **a** hacer algo	to manage to do something
llegar **a** ser algo	to become something
probar **a** hacer algo	to try to do something
volver **a** hacer algo	to do something again

Me gustaría aprender a nadar.	I'd like to learn to swim.
No llegó a terminar la carrera.	He didn't manage to finish his degree course.
Llegó a ser primer ministro.	He became prime minister.
No vuelvas a hacerlo nunca más.	Don't ever do it again.

➤ The following verbs can be followed by a and a person's name or else by a and a noun or pronoun referring to a person, and then by another a and an infinitive.

ayudar **a** alguien **a** hacer algo	to help someone to do something
enseñar **a** alguien **a** hacer algo	to teach someone to do something
invitar **a** alguien **a** hacer algo	to invite someone to do something

¿Le podrías ayudar a Antonia a fregar los platos?	Could you help Antonia do the dishes?
Le enseñó a su hermano a nadar.	He taught his brother to swim.
Los he invitado a tomar unas copas en casa.	I've invited them over for drinks.

---

5   Verbs followed by the preposition de and the infinitive

➤ The following verbs are the most common ones that can be followed by de and the infinitive:

aburrirse **de** hacer algo	to get bored with doing something
acabar **de** hacer algo	to have just done something
acordarse **de** haber hecho/**de** hacer algo	to remember having done/doing something
alegrarse **de** hacer algo	to be glad to do something
dejar **de** hacer algo	to stop doing something
tener ganas **de** hacer algo	to want to do something
tratar **de** hacer algo	to try to do something

Me aburría <u>de</u> no poder salir de casa.	I was getting bored with not being able to leave the house.
Acabo <u>de</u> comprar un móvil.	I've just bought a mobile.
Acababan <u>de</u> llegar cuando...	They had just arrived when...
Me alegro <u>de</u> verte.	I'm glad to see you.
¿Quieres dejar <u>de</u> hablar?	Will you stop talking?
Tengo ganas <u>de</u> volver a España.	I want to go back to Spain.

6   Verbs followed by the preposition con and the infinitive

➤ The following verbs are the most common ones that can be followed by con and the infinitive:

amenazar <u>con</u> hacer algo	to threaten to do someting
soñar <u>con</u> hacer algo	to dream about doing something
Amenazó <u>con</u> denunciarlos.	He threatened to report them.
Sueño <u>con</u> vivir en España.	I dream about living in Spain.

7   Verbs followed by the preposition en and the infinitive

➤ The verb quedar is the most common one that can be followed by en and the infinitive:

quedar <u>en</u> hacer algo	to agree to do something
Habíamos quedado <u>en</u> encontrarnos a las ocho.	We had agreed to meet at eight.

Key points

✔ Infinitives are found after prepositions, set phrases and in instructions to the general public.

✔ They can also function as the subject or object of a verb, when the infinitive corresponds to the -ing form in English.

✔ Many Spanish verbs can be followed by another verb in the infinitive.

✔ The two verbs may be linked by nothing at all, or by a, de or another preposition.

✔ The construction in Spanish does not always match the English. It's best to learn these constructions when you learn a new verb.

Prepositions after verbs

➤ In English, there are some phrases which are made up of verbs and prepositions, for example, to _accuse_ somebody _of_ something, to _look forward to_ something and to _rely on_ something.

➤ In Spanish there are also lots of set phrases made up of verbs and prepositions. Often the prepositions in Spanish are not the same as they are in English, so you will need to learn them. Listed below are phrases using verbs and some common Spanish prepositions.

⇨ _For more information on verbs used with a preposition and the infinitive, see page 147._

1 **Verbs followed by a**

➤ **a** is often the equivalent of the English word _to_ when it is used with an indirect object after verbs like **enviar** (meaning _to send_), **dar** (meaning _to give_) and **decir** (meaning _to say_).

dar algo <u>a</u> alguien	to give something to someone
decir algo <u>a</u> alguien	to say something to someone
enviar algo <u>a</u> alguien	to send something to someone
escribir algo <u>a</u> alguien	to write something to someone
mostrar algo <u>a</u> alguien	to show something to someone

⇨ _For more information on **Indirect objects**, see page 49._

Tip

There is an important difference between Spanish and English with this type of verb. In English, you can say either _to give something to someone_ or _to give someone something_.
You can <u>NEVER</u> miss out **a** in Spanish in the way that you can sometimes miss out _to_ in English.

➤ Here are some verbs taking **a** in Spanish that have a different construction in English.

asistir <u>a</u> algo	to attend something, to be at something
dirigirse <u>a</u> (un lugar)	to head for (a place)
dirigirse a alguien	to address somebody
jugar <u>a</u> algo	to play something _(sports/games)_
llegar <u>a</u> (un lugar)	to arrive at (a place)

oler <u>a</u> algo	to smell of something
parecerse <u>a</u> alguien/algo	to look like somebody/something
subir(se) <u>a</u> un autobús/un coche	to get on a bus/into a car
subir(se) <u>a</u> un árbol	to climb a tree
tener miedo <u>a</u> alguien	to be afraid of somebody

Este perfume huele <u>a</u> jazmín.	This perfume smells of jasmine.
¡De prisa, sube <u>al</u> coche!	Get into the car, quick!
Nunca tuvieron miedo <u>a</u> su padre.	They were never afraid of their father.

⇨ *For verbs such as **gustar**, **encantar** and **faltar**, see **Verbal idioms** on page 154.*

---

2 | **Verbs followed by de**

➤ Here are some verbs taking **de** in Spanish that have a different construction in English:

acordarse <u>de</u> algo/alguien	to remember something/somebody
alegrarse <u>de</u> algo	to be glad about something
bajarse <u>de</u> un autobús/un coche	to get off a bus/out of a car
darse cuenta <u>de</u> algo	to realize something
depender <u>de</u> algo/alguien	to depend on something/somebody
despedirse <u>de</u> alguien	to say goodbye to somebody
preocuparse <u>de</u> algo/alguien	to worry about something/somebody
quejarse <u>de</u> algo	to complain about something
reírse <u>de</u> algo/alguien	to laugh at something/somebody
salir <u>de</u> (un cuarto/un edificio)	to leave (a room/a building)
tener ganas <u>de</u> algo	to want something
tener miedo <u>de</u> algo	to be afraid of something
trabajar <u>de</u> (camarero/secretario)	to work as (a waiter/secretary)
tratarse <u>de</u> algo/alguien	to be a question of something/to be about somebody

Nos acordamos muy bien <u>de</u> aquellas vacaciones.	We remember that holiday very well.
Se bajó <u>del</u> coche.	He got out of the car.
No depende <u>de</u> mí.	It doesn't depend on me.
Se preocupa mucho <u>de</u> su apariencia.	He worries a lot about his appearance.

3 **Verbs followed by con**

➤ Here are some verbs taking con in Spanish that have a different construction in English:

comparar algo/a alguien <u>con</u> algo/alguien	to compare something/somebody with something/somebody
contar <u>con</u> alguien/algo	to rely on somebody/something
encontrarse <u>con</u> alguien	to meet somebody (*by chance*)
enfadarse <u>con</u> alguien	to get annoyed with somebody
estar de acuerdo <u>con</u> alguien/algo	to agree with somebody/something
hablar <u>con</u> alguien	to talk to somebody
soñar <u>con</u> alguien/algo	to dream about somebody/something
Cuento <u>contigo</u>.	I'm relying on you.
Me encontré <u>con</u> ella al entrar en el banco.	I met her as I was going into the bank.
¿Puedo hablar <u>con</u> usted un momento?	May I talk to you for a moment?

4 **Verbs followed by en**

➤ Here are some verbs taking en in Spanish that have a different construction in English:

entrar <u>en</u> (un edificio/un cuarto)	to enter, go into (a building/a room)
pensar <u>en</u> algo/alguien	to think about something/somebody
trabajar <u>en</u> (una oficina/una fábrica)	to work in (an office/a factory)
No quiero pensar <u>en</u> eso.	I don't want to think about that.

5 **Verbs followed by por**

➤ Here are some verbs taking por in Spanish that have a different construction in English:

interesarse <u>por</u> algo/alguien	to ask about something/somebody
preguntar <u>por</u> alguien	to ask for/about somebody
preocuparse <u>por</u> algo/alguien	to worry about something/somebody

Me interesaba mucho <u>por</u> la arqueología.	I was very interested in archaeology.
Se preocupa mucho <u>por</u> su apariencia.	He worries a lot about his appearance.

6 | Verbs taking a direct object in Spanish but not in English

➤ In English there are a few verbs that are followed by *at*, *for* or *to* which, in Spanish, are not followed by any preposition other than the personal **a**.

⇨ *For more information on **Personal** a, see page 182.*

mirar algo/a alguien	to look at something/somebody
escuchar algo/a alguien	to listen to something/somebody
buscar algo/a alguien	to look for something/somebody
pedir algo	to ask for something
esperar algo/a alguien	to wait for something/somebody
pagar algo	to pay for something
Mira esta foto.	Look at this photo.
Me gusta escuchar música.	I like listening to music.
Estoy buscando las gafas.	I'm looking for my glasses.
Pidió una taza de té.	He asked for a cup of tea.
Estamos esperando el tren.	We're waiting for the train.
Ya he pagado el billete.	I've already paid for my ticket.
Estoy buscando a mi hermano.	I'm looking for my brother.

Key points

✔ The prepositions used with Spanish verbs are often very different from those used in English, so make sure you learn common expressions involving prepositions in Spanish.

✔ The most common prepositions used with verbs in Spanish are **a**, **de**, **con**, **en** and **por**.

✔ Some Spanish verbs are not followed by a preposition, but are used with a preposition in English.

Verbal Idioms

1 Present tense of gustar

➤ You will probably already have come across the phrase **me gusta...** meaning *I like...* . Actually, **gustar** means literally *to please*, and if you remember this, you will be able to use **gustar** much more easily.

Me <u>gusta</u> el chocolate.	I like chocolate. (*literally: chocolate pleases me*)
Me <u>gustan</u> los animales.	I like animals. (*literally: animals please me*)
Nos <u>gusta</u> el español.	We like Spanish. (*literally: Spanish pleases us*)
Nos <u>gustan</u> los españoles.	We like Spanish people. (*literally: Spanish people please us*)

➤ Even though **chocolate**, **animales**, and so on, come after **gustar**, they are the <u>subject</u> of the verb (the person or thing performing the action) and therefore the endings of **gustar** change to agree with them.

➤ When the thing that you like is <u>singular</u>, you use **gusta** (*third person singular*), and when the thing that you like is <u>plural</u>, you use **gustan** (*third person plural*).

Le <u>gusta</u> Francia.	He/She likes France. (*literally: France pleases him/her*)
Le <u>gustan</u> los caramelos.	He/She likes sweets. (*literally: Sweets please him/her*)

[*i*] Note that **me, te, le, nos, os** and **les**, which are used with **gustar**, are indirect object pronouns.

➪ *For more information on **Indirect object pronouns**, see page 49.*

2 Other tenses of gustar

➤ You can use **gustar** in other tenses in Spanish.

Les <u>gustó</u> la fiesta.	They liked the party.
Les <u>gustaron</u> los fuegos artificiales.	They liked the fireworks.
Te <u>va a gustar</u> la película.	You'll like the film.
Te <u>van a gustar</u> las fotos.	You'll like the photos.
Les <u>ha gustado</u> mucho el museo.	They liked the museum a lot
Les <u>han gustado</u> mucho los cuadros.	They liked the paintings a lot.

For further explanation of grammatical terms, please see pages viii-xii.

➤ You can also use **más** with **gustar** to say what you prefer.

A mí me <u>gusta más</u> el rojo.	I prefer the red one. (*literally: the red one* <u>*pleases*</u> *me* <u>*more*</u>)
A mí me <u>gustan más</u> los rojos.	I prefer the red ones. (*literally: the red ones* <u>*please*</u> *me* <u>*more*</u>)

3 Other verbs like gustar

➤ There are several other verbs which behave in the same way as **gustar**:

- encantar

Me <u>encanta</u> el flamenco.	I love flamenco.
Me <u>encantan</u> los animales.	I love animals.

- faltar

Le <u>faltaba</u> un botón.	He had a button missing.
Le <u>faltaban</u> tres dientes.	He had three teeth missing.

- quedar

No les <u>queda</u> nada.	They have nothing left.
Sólo nos <u>quedan</u> dos kilómetros.	We've only got two kilometres left.

- doler

Le <u>dolía</u> la cabeza.	His head hurt.
Le <u>dolían</u> las muelas.	His teeth hurt.

- interesar

Te <u>interesará</u> el libro.	The book will interest you.
Te <u>interesarán</u> sus noticias.	His news will interest you.

- importar

No me <u>importa</u> la lluvia.	The rain doesn't matter to me. *or* I don't mind the rain.
Me <u>importan</u> mucho mis estudios.	My studies matter to me a lot.

- hacer falta

Nos <u>hace</u> falta un ordenador.	We need a computer.
Nos <u>hacen</u> falta libros.	We need books.

Grammar Extra!

All the examples given above are in the third persons singular and plural as these are by far the most common. However, it is also possible to use these verbs in other forms.

Creo que le <u>gustas</u>.	I think he likes you. (*literally: I think you please him*)

---

4 Verbal idioms used with another verb

➤ In English you can say *I like playing football, we love swimming* and so on, and in Spanish you can also use another verb with most of the verbs like gustar. However, the verb form you use for the second verb in Spanish is the <u>infinitive</u>.

Le <u>gusta jugar</u> al fútbol.	He/She likes playing football.
No me <u>gusta bailar</u>.	I don't like dancing.
Nos <u>encanta estudiar</u>.	We love studying.
No me <u>importa tener</u> que esperar.	I don't mind having to wait.

⮕ *For more information on the **Infinitive**, see page 144.*

Key points

✔ There are a number of common verbs in Spanish which are used in the opposite way to English, for example, **gustar**, **encantar**, **hacer falta**, and so on. With all these verbs, the object of the English verb is the subject of the Spanish verb.

✔ The endings of these verbs change according to whether the thing liked or needed and so on is singular or plural.

✔ All these verbs can be followed by another verb in the infinitive.

NEGATIVES

What is a negative?
A **negative** question or statement is one which contains a word such as *not*, *never* or *nothing* and is used to say that something is not happening, is not true or is absent.

1   <u>no</u>

➤ In English, we often make sentences negative by adding *don't, doesn't* or *didn't* before the verb. In Spanish you simply add **no** (meaning *not*) before the main verb.

Positive			**Negative**	
Trabaja.	He works.	→	<u>No</u> trabaja.	He doesn't work.
Comen.	They eat.	→	<u>No</u> comen.	They don't eat.
Salió.	She went out.	→	<u>No</u> salió.	She didn't go out.
Lo he visto.	I've seen it.	→	<u>No</u> lo he visto.	I haven't seen it.
Sabe nadar.	He can swim.	→	<u>No</u> sabe nadar.	He can't swim.

Típ
<u>NEVER</u> translate *don't, doesn't, didn't* using **hacer**.

➤ Where there is a subject (the person doing the action) in the sentence, put **no** between the subject and the verb.

Juan <u>no</u> vive aquí.	Juan doesn't live here.
Mi hermana <u>no</u> lee mucho.	My sister doesn't read much.
Mis padres <u>no</u> han llamado.	My parents haven't called.
Él <u>no</u> lo comprenderá.	He won't understand.

[i] Note that the Spanish word **no** also means *no* in answer to a question.

➤ Where the subject is only shown by the verb ending, **no** goes before the verb.

<u>No</u> tenemos tiempo.	We haven't got time.
Todavía <u>no</u> ha llegado.	He hasn't arrived yet.
<u>No</u> hemos comido.	We haven't eaten.
<u>No</u> llevará mucho tiempo.	It won't take long.

➤ If there are any object pronouns (for example, **me, te, lo, los, le** *and so on*) before the verb, **no** goes <u>BEFORE</u> them.

<u>No</u> lo he visto.	I didn't see it.
<u>No</u> me gusta el fútbol.	I don't like football.

➤ In phrases consisting only of *not* and another word, such as *not now* or *not me*, the Spanish **no** usually goes <u>AFTER</u> the other word.

Ahora <u>no</u>.	Not now.
Yo <u>no</u>.	Not me.
Todavía <u>no</u>.	Not yet.

➤ Some phrases have a special construction in Spanish.

Espero que sí.	I hope so.	→	**Espero que no.**	I hope not.
Creo que sí.	I think so.	→	**Creo que no.**	I don't think so.

2 | Other negative words

➤ In Spanish, you can form negatives using pairs and groups of words, as you can in English.

* **no ... nunca**   never *or* not ... ever
  <u>No</u> la veo <u>nunca</u>.   I never see her *or*
                                              I don't ever see her.

* **no ... jamás**   never *or* not ... ever
  <u>No</u> la veo <u>jamás</u>.   I never see her *or*
                                              I don't ever see her.

* **no ... nada**   nothing *or* not ... anything
  <u>No</u> ha dicho <u>nada</u>.   He has said nothing *or*
                                              He hasn't said anything.

* **no ... nadie**   nobody *or* not ... anybody
  <u>No</u> hablaron con <u>nadie</u>.   They spoke to nobody *or*
                                              They didn't speak to anybody.

* **no ... tampoco**   not ... either
  Yo <u>no</u> la vi. – Yo <u>tampoco</u>.   I didn't see her. – Neither did I.
                                              or I didn't either. *or* Nor did I.

  A él <u>no</u> le gusta el café y a mí   He doesn't like coffee and neither
  <u>tampoco</u>.   do I.

* **no ... ni ... ni**   neither ... nor
  <u>No</u> vinieron <u>ni</u> Carlos <u>ni</u> Ana.   Neither Carlos nor Ana came.

* **no ... más**   no longer *or* not .. any more
  <u>No</u> te veré <u>más</u>.   I won't see you any more.

* **no ... ningún/ninguna** + *noun*   no *or* not ... any
  <u>No</u> tiene <u>ningún</u> interés en ir.   She has no interest in going.

➤ Most of these negative words can also be used without **no** provided they come before any verb.

Nunca or **Jamás** la veo.	I never see her.
Nadie vino.	No one came.
Ni Pedro **ni** Pablo fuman.	Neither Pedro nor Pablo smokes.
¿Quién te ha dicho eso? – **Nadie**.	Who told you that? - No one.
¿Qué has hecho? – **Nada**.	What have you done? – Nothing.

➤ Sometimes negative expressions combine with each other.

Nunca hacen **nada**.	They never do anything.
Nunca viene **nadie**.	No one ever comes.
No lo haré **nunca más**.	I'll never do it again.
No veo **nunca** a **nadie**.	I never see anyone.

3   Word order with negatives

➤ In English you can put words like *never* and *ever* between *have/has/had* and the past participle, for example, *We <u>have</u> never <u>been</u> to Argentina*. You should <u>NEVER</u> separate **he, has, ha, había** and so on from the past participle of the verb in Spanish.

Nunca hemos estado en Argentina.	We have never been to Argentina.
Nunca había visto **nada** así.	I had never seen anything like this.
Ninguno de nosotros había esquiado **nunca**.	None of us had ever skied.

⇨ *For more information on **Past participles**, see page 115.*

> **Key points**
> ✔ The Spanish word **no** is equivalent to both *no* and *not* in English.
> ✔ You can make sentences negative by putting **no** before the verb (and before any object pronouns that are in front of the verb).
> ✔ Other negative words also exist, such as **nunca, nadie** and **nada**. Use them in combination with **no**, with the verb sandwiched in between. Most of them also work on their own provided they go <u>before</u> any verb.
> ✔ Never insert negative words, or anything else, between **he, has, ha, había** and so on and the past participle.

QUESTIONS

What is a question?
A **question** is a sentence which is used to ask someone about something and which often has the verb in front of the subject. Questions often include a question word such as *why*, *where*, *who*, *which* or *how*.

Asking questions in Spanish

There are three main ways of asking questions in Spanish:

- by making your voice go up at the end of the sentence
- by changing normal word order
- by using a question word

> *Tip*
> Don't forget the opening question mark in Spanish. It goes at the beginning of the question or of the question part of the sentence.
>
> **¿No quieres tomar algo?**   Wouldn't you like something to eat or drink?
>
> **Eres inglés, ¿verdad?**   You're English, aren't you?

1   Asking a question by making your voice go up

➤ If you are expecting the answer *yes* or *no*, there is a very simple way of asking a question. You keep the word order exactly as it would be in a normal sentence but you turn it into a question by making your voice go up at the end.

¿Hablas español?	Do you speak Spanish?
¿Es profesor?	Is he a teacher?
¿Hay leche?	Is there any milk?
¿Te gusta la música?	Do you like music?

➤ When the subject (the person or thing doing the action) of the verb is a noun, pronoun or name it can be given before the verb, just as in an ordinary sentence. But you turn the statement into a question by making your voice go up at the end.

¿Tu hermana ha comprado pan?	Did your sister buy any bread?
¿Tú lo has hecho?	Did you do it?
¿Tu padre te ha visto?	Did your father see you?
¿El diccionario está aquí?	Is the dictionary here?

For further explanation of grammatical terms, please see pages viii-xii.

2 | Asking a question by changing word order

➤ When the subject of the verb is specified, another even more common way of asking questions is to change the word order so that the verb comes <u>BEFORE</u> the subject instead of after it.

¿Lo has hecho tú?	Did you do it?
¿Te ha visto tu padre?	Did your father see you?
¿Está el diccionario aquí?	Is the dictionary here?

[i] Note that the position of object pronouns is not affected.

➯ *For more information on **Word order with object pronouns**, see pages 47, 50 and 52.*

Grammar Extra!

If the verb has an object, such as *any bread* in *Did your sister buy any bread?*, the subject comes <u>AFTER</u> the object, provided the object is short.

¿Ha compado <u>pan</u> tu hermana?	Did your sister buy any bread?
¿Vio <u>la película</u> tu novio?	Did your boyfriend see the film?

If the object is made up of several words, the subject goes <u>BEFORE</u> it.

Se han comprado tus padres <u>aquella casa de que me hablaste</u>?	Have your parents bought that house you told me about?

When there is an adverbial phrase (*to the party*, *in Barcelona*) after the verb, the subject can go <u>BEFORE OR AFTER</u> the adverbial phrase.

¿Viene <u>a la fiesta</u> Andrés? *or* **¿Viene Andrés <u>a la fiesta</u>?**	Is Andrés coming to the party?

---

3 | Asking a question by using a question word

➤ Question words are words like *when, what, who, which, where* and *how* that are used to ask for information. In Spanish, <u>ALL</u> question words have an accent on them.

¿adónde?	where ... to?
¿cómo?	how?
¿cuál/cuáles?	which
¿cuándo?	when?
¿cuánto/cuánta?	how much?
¿cuántos/cuántas?	how many?
¿dónde?	where?
¿para qué?	what for?
¿por qué?	why?
¿qué?	what?, which?
¿quién?	who?

> *Típ*
>
> Be careful not to mix up **por qué** (meaning *why*) with **porque** (meaning *because*).

¿**Cuándo** se fue?	When did he go?
¿**Qué** te pasa?	What's the matter?
¿**Qué** chaqueta te vas a poner?	Which jacket are you going to wear?
¿**Cuál** de los dos quieres?	Which do you want?
¿**Cuánto** azúcar quieres?	How much sugar do you want?
¿**Cuánto** tiempo llevas esperando?	How long have you been waiting?

⇨ *For more information on question words, see **Interrogative adjectives** on page 32 and **Interrogative pronouns** on page 65.*

➤ When the question starts with a question word that isn't the subject of the verb, the noun or pronoun (if given) that is the subject of the verb goes <u>AFTER</u> it.

¿De qué color es <u>la moqueta</u>?	What colour's the carpet?
¿A qué hora comienza <u>el concierto</u>?	What time does the concert start?
¿Dónde están <u>tus pantalones</u>?	Where are your trousers?
¿Adónde iba <u>tu padre</u>?	Where was your father going?
¿Cómo están <u>tus padres</u>?	How are your parents?
¿Cuándo volverán <u>ustedes</u>?	When will you come back?

4   Which question word to use?

➤ **qué** or **cuál** or **cuáles** can be used to mean *which*:
* always use **qué** before a noun

¿**Qué chaqueta** te vas a poner?	<u>Which jacket</u> are you going to wear?

* otherwise use **cuál** (*singular*) or **cuáles** (*plural*)

¿**Cuál** quieres?	<u>Which (one)</u> do you want?
¿**Cuáles** quieres?	<u>Which (ones)</u> do you want?

➤ **quién** or **quiénes** can be used to mean *who*:
* use **quién** when asking about one person

¿**Quién** ganó?	<u>Who</u> won?

* use **quiénes** when asking about more than one person

¿**Quiénes** estaban?	<u>Who</u> was there?

[*i*] Note that you need to put the personal **a** before **quién** and **quiénes** when it acts as an object.

¿A quién viste?	<u>Who</u> did you see?

⇨ *For more information on **Personal a**, see page 182.*

➤ **de quién** or **de quiénes** can be used to mean *whose*:

- use **de quién** when there is likely to be one owner

¿De quién es este abrigo?	<u>Whose</u> coat is this?

- use **de quiénes** when there is likely to be more than one owner

¿De quiénes son estos abrigos?	<u>Whose</u> coats are these?

[*i*] Note that the structure in Spanish is the equivalent of *Whose <u>is</u> this coat?/Whose <u>are</u> these coats?* Don't try putting **¿de quién?** or **¿de quiénes?** immediately before a noun.

➤ **qué**, **cómo**, **cuál** and **cuáles** can all be used to mean *what* although **qué** is the most common translation:

- use **cómo** not **qué** when asking someone to repeat something that you didn't hear properly

¿Cómo (has dicho)?	<u>What</u> (did you say)?

- use **¿cuál es ... ?** and **¿cuáles son ... ?** to mean *what is ... ?* and *what/are ... ?* when you aren't asking for a definition

¿Cuál es la capital de Francia?	<u>What's</u> the capital of France?
¿Cuál es su número de teléfono?	<u>What's</u> his telephone number?

- use **¿qué es ... ?** and **¿qué son ... ?** to mean *what is ... ?* and *what are ... ?* when you are asking for a definition

¿Qué son los genes?	<u>What are</u> genes?

- always use **qué** to mean *what* before another noun

¿Qué hora es?	<u>What time</u> is it?
¿Qué asignaturas estudias?	<u>What subjects</u> are you studying?

Tip

You can finish an English question (or sentence) with a preposition such as *about*, for example, *Who did you write to?; What are you talking about?* You can <u>NEVER</u> end a Spanish question or sentence with a preposition.

¿Con quién hablaste?	Who did you speak <u>to</u>?

Grammar Extra!

All the questions we have looked at so far have been straight questions, otherwise known as <u>direct questions</u>. However, sometimes instead of asking directly, for example, *Where is it?* or *Why did you do it?*, we ask the question in a more roundabout way, for example, *Can you tell me where it is?* or *Please tell me why you did it.* These are called <u>indirect questions.</u>

In indirect questions in English we say *where <u>it is</u>* instead of *where <u>is it</u>* and *why <u>you did it</u>* instead of *why <u>did you do it</u>*, but in Spanish you still put the subject <u>AFTER</u> the verb.

¿Sabes adónde <u>iba tu padre</u>?	Do you know where your father was going?
¿Puedes decirme para qué <u>sirven los diccionarios</u>?	Can you tell me what dictionaries are for?

The subject also goes <u>AFTER</u> the verb in Spanish when you report a question in indirect speech.

Quería saber adónde <u>iba mi padre</u>.	He wanted to know where my father was going.

<u>*i*</u> Note that you still put accents on question words in Spanish even when they are in indirect and reported questions or when they come after expressions of uncertainty:

No sé <u>qué</u> hacer.	I don't know what to do.
No sabemos <u>por qué</u> se fue.	We don't know why he left.

---

5 Negative questions

➤ When you want to make a negative question, put **no** before the verb in the same way that you do in statements (non-questions).

¿<u>No</u> vienes?	Aren't you coming?
¿<u>No</u> lo has visto?	Didn't you see it?

➤ You can also use **o no** at the end of a question in the same way that we can ask *or not* in English.

¿Vienes <u>o no</u>?	Are you coming <u>or not</u>?
¿Lo quieres <u>o no</u>?	Do you want it <u>or not</u>?

6 Short questions

➤ In English we sometimes check whether our facts and beliefs are correct by putting *isn't it?*, *don't they?*, *are they?* and so on at the end of a comment. In Spanish, you can add **¿verdad?** in the same way.

Hace calor, <u>¿verdad?</u>	It's hot, <u>isn't it</u>?
Te gusta, <u>¿verdad?</u>	You like it, <u>don't you</u>?

For further explanation of grammatical terms, please see pages viii–xii.

| No te olvidarás, ¿verdad? | You won't forget, <u>will you</u>? |
| No vino, ¿verdad? | He didn't come, <u>did he</u>? |

➤ You can also use ¿no?, especially after positive comments.

| Hace calor, ¿no? | It's hot, <u>isn't it</u>? |
| Te gusta, ¿no? | You like it, <u>don't you</u>? |

7 | Answering questions

➤ To answer a question which requires a *yes* or *no* answer, just use sí or no.

¿Te gusta? – Sí/No.	Do you like it? – Yes, I do/No, I don't.
¿Está aquí? – Sí/No.	Is he here? – Yes he is/No, he isn't.
¿Tienes prisa? – Sí/No.	Are you in a hurry? – Yes, I am/ No, I'm not.
No lo has hecho, ¿verdad? – Sí/No.	You haven't done it, have you? - Yes, I have/No, I haven't.

➤ You can also often answer sí or no followed by the verb in question. In negative answers this may mean that you say no twice.

| Quieres acompañarme? – Sí, quiero. | Would you like to come with me? – Yes, I would. |
| ¿Vas a ir a la fiesta? – No, no voy. | Are you going to the party? – No, I'm not. |

Key points

✔ You ask a question in Spanish by making your voice go up at the end of the sentence, by changing normal word order, and by using question words.

✔ Question words always have an accent on them.

✔ To make a negative question, add no before the verb.

✔ You can add ¿verdad? to check whether your facts or beliefs are correct.

ADVERBS

What is an adverb?
An **adverb** is a word usually used with verbs, adjectives or other adverbs that gives more information about when, how, where, or in what circumstances something happens, or to what degree something is true, for example, *quickly, happily, now, extremely, very.*

How adverbs are used

➤ In general, adverbs are used together with verbs, adjectives and other adverbs, for example, *act <u>quickly</u>; smile <u>cheerfully</u>; <u>rather</u> ill; <u>a lot</u> happier; <u>really</u> slowly; <u>very</u> well.*

➤ Adverbs can also relate to the whole sentence. In this case they often tell you what the speaker is thinking or feeling.

<u>Fortunately</u>, Jan had already left.

How adverbs are formed

1 The basic rules

➤ In English, adverbs that tell you how something happened are often formed by adding *-ly* to an adjective, for example, *sweet → sweetly*. In Spanish, you form this kind of adverb by adding **-mente** to the feminine singular form of the adjective.

Masculine adjective	Feminine adjective	Adverb	Meaning
lento	lenta	lentamente	slowly
normal	normal	normalmente	normally

Habla muy lenta<u>mente</u>.	He speaks very slowly.
¡Hazlo inmediata<u>mente</u>!	Do it immediately!
Normal<u>mente</u> llego a las nueve.	I normally arrive at nine o'clock.

i Note that adverbs <u>NEVER</u> change their endings in Spanish to agree with anything.

> *Tip*
> You don't have to worry about adding or removing accents on the adjective when you add **-mente**; they stay as they are.
> **fácil** easy   →   **fácilmente** easily

For further explanation of grammatical terms, please see pages viii-xii.

Grammar Extra!

When there are two or more adverbs joined by a conjunction such as **y** (meaning *and*) or **pero** (meaning *but*), leave out the **-mente** ending on all but the last adverb.

> **Lo hicieron lenta pero eficazmente.** They did it slowly but efficiently.

Use the form **recién** rather than **recientemente** (meaning *recently*) before a past participle (the form of the verb ending in **-ado** and **-ido** in regular verbs).

> **El comedor está recién pintado.** The dining room has just been painted.

⇨ *For more information on **Past participles**, see page 115.*

In Spanish, adverbs ending in **-mente** are not as common as adverbs ending in *-ly* in English. For this reason, you will come across other ways of expressing an adverb in Spanish, for example, **con** used with a noun or **de manera** used with an adjective.

> **Conduce con cuidado.** Drive carefully.
> **Todos estos cambios ocurren** All these changes happen naturally.
> **de manera natural.**

---

2 | **Irregular adverbs**

➤ The adverb that comes from **bueno** (meaning *good*) is **bien** (meaning *well*). The adverb that comes from **malo** (meaning *bad*) is **mal** (meaning *badly*).

> **Habla bien el español.** He speaks Spanish well.
> **Está muy mal escrito.** It's very badly written.

➤ Additionally, there are some other adverbs in Spanish which are exactly the same as the related masculine singular adjective:

- **alto** (adjective: *high, loud*; adverb: *high, loudly*)
  > **El avión volaba alto sobre las** The plane flew high over the
  > **montañas.** mountains.
  > **Pepe habla muy alto.** Pepe talks very loudly.

- **bajo** (adjective: *low, quiet*; adverb: *low, quietly*)
  > **El avión volaba muy bajo.** The plane was flying very low.
  > **¡Habla bajo!** Speak quietly.

- **barato** (adjective: *cheap*; adverb: *cheaply*)
  > **Aquí se come muy barato.** You can eat really cheaply here.

- **claro** (adjective: *clear*; adverb: *clearly*)
  > **Lo oí muy claro.** I heard it very clearly.

- **derecho** (adjective: *right, straight*; adverb: *straight*)
  > **Vino derecho hacia mí.** He came straight towards me.

- **fuerte** (adjective: *loud, hard*; adverb: *loudly, hard*)

Habla muy <u>fuerte</u>.	He talks very <u>loudly</u>.
No lo golpees tan <u>fuerte</u>.	Don't hit it so <u>hard</u>.

- **rápido** (adjective: *fast, quick*; adverb: *fast, quickly*)

Conduces demasiado <u>rápido</u>.	You drive too <u>fast</u>.
Lo hice tan <u>rápido</u> como pude.	I did it as <u>quickly</u> as I could.

[*i*] Note that, when used as adverbs, these words do <u>NOT</u> agree with anything.

⇨ *For more information on words which can be both adjectives and adverbs, see page 175.*

Grammar Extra!

Sometimes an <u>adjective</u> is used in Spanish where in English we would use an <u>adverb</u>.

Esperaban <u>impacientes</u>.	They were waiting <u>impatiently</u>.
Vivieron muy <u>felices</u>.	They lived very <u>happily</u>.

[*i*] Note that these Spanish <u>adjectives</u> describe the person or thing being talked about and therefore <u>MUST</u> agree with them.

Often you could equally well use an adverb or an adverbial expression in Spanish.

Esperaban <u>impacientemente</u> *or*	
con impaciencia.	They were waiting <u>impatiently</u>.

Key points

✔ To form adverbs that tell you how something happens, you can usually add -mente to the feminine singular adjective in Spanish.

✔ Adverbs don't agree with anything.

✔ Some Spanish adverbs are irregular, as in English.

✔ Some Spanish adverbs are identical in form to their corresponding adjectives; when used as adverbs, they never agree with anything.

Comparatives and superlatives of adverbs

1 **Comparative adverbs**

> **What is a comparative adverb?**
> A **comparative adverb** is one which, in English, has -er on the end of it or *more* or *less* in front of it, for example, *earlier, later, more/less often.*

➤ Adverbs can be used to make comparisons in Spanish, just as they can in English. The comparative of adverbs (*more often, more efficiently, faster*) is formed using the same phrases as for adjectives:

- **más ... (que)**   more ... (than)
  más rápido (que)   faster (than), more quickly (than)
  Corre más rápido que tú.   He runs faster than you do.

- **menos ... (que)**   less ... (than)
  menos rápido (que)   less fast (than), less quickly (than)
  Conduce menos rápido tú.   He drives less fast than you do.

2 **Superlative adverbs**

> **What is a superlative adverb?**
> A **superlative adverb** is one which, in English, has -est on the end of it or *most* or *least* in front of it, for example, *soonest, most/least often.*

➤ The superlative of adverbs (*the most often, the most efficiently, the fastest*) is formed in the same way in Spanish as the comparative, using más and menos. In this case they mean *the most* and *the least*.

María es la que corre más rápido.	Maria is the one who runs (the) fastest.
la chica que sabe más	the girl who knows (the) most
la chica que sabe menos	the girl who knows (the) least
El que llegó menos tarde fue Miguel.	Miguel was the one who arrived least late.

i Note that even though comparative and superlative adverbs are usually identical in Spanish, you can tell which one is meant by the rest of the sentence.

3 **Irregular comparative and superlative adverbs**

➤ Some common Spanish adverbs have irregular comparatives and superlatives.

Adverb	Meaning	Comparative	Meaning	Superlative	Meaning
bien	well	**mejor**	better	**mejor**	(the) best
mal	badly	**peor**	worse	**peor**	(the) worst
mucho	a lot	**más**	more	**más**	(the) most
poco	little	**menos**	less	**menos**	(the) least

La conozco mejor que tú.	I know her <u>better</u> than you do.
¿Quién lo hace mejor?	Who does it (the) <u>best</u>?
Ahora salgo más/menos.	I go out <u>more/less</u> these days.

Tip

When saying *more than*, *less than* or *fewer than* followed by a number, use **más** and **menos** <u>de</u> rather than **más** and **menos** **que**.

más/menos <u>de</u> veinte cajas   more/fewer than twenty boxes

---

[*i*] Note that in phrases like *it's the least one can expect* or *it's the least I can do*, where the adverb is qualified by further information, in Spanish you have to put **lo** before the adverb.

Es <u>lo menos que</u> se puede esperar.   It's the least one can expect.

4 Other ways of making comparisons

➤ There are other ways of making comparisons in Spanish:

- **tanto como**   as much as

  No lee <u>tanto como</u> tú.   He doesn't read <u>as much as</u> you.

- **tan ... como**   as ... as

  Vine <u>tan</u> pronto <u>como</u> pude.   I came <u>as</u> fast <u>as</u> I could.

Key points

✔ **más** + adverb (+ **que**) = *more* + adverb + (*than*)
✔ **menos** + adverb (+ **que**) = *less* + adverb + (*than*)
✔ **más** + adverb = (*the*) *most* + adverb
✔ **menos** + adverb = (*the*) *least* + adverb
✔ There are a few irregular comparative and superlative adverbs.
✔ There are other ways of making comparisons in Spanish: **tanto como**, **tan ... como**.

For further explanation of grammatical terms, please see pages viii-xii.

Common adverbs

1 One-word adverbs not ending in -mente

➤ There are some common adverbs that do not end in **-mente**, most of which give more information about when or where something happens or to what degree something is true.

- **ahí** there
  ¡**Ahí** están! — <u>There</u> they are!

- **ahora** now
  ¿Dónde vamos <u>ahora</u>? — Where are we going <u>now</u>?

- **allá** there
  allá arriba — up <u>there</u>

- **allí** there
  Allí está. — <u>There</u> it is.

- **anoche** last night
  Anoche llovió. — It rained <u>last night</u>.

- **anteanoche** the night before last
  Anteanoche nevó. — It snowed <u>the night before last</u>.

- **anteayer** the day before yesterday
  Anteayer hubo tormenta. — There was a storm <u>the day before yesterday</u>.

- **antes** before
  Esta película ya la he visto <u>antes</u>. — I've seen this film <u>before</u>.

- **apenas** hardly
  Apenas podía levantarse. — He could <u>hardly</u> stand up.

- **aquí** here
  Aquí está el informe. — <u>Here</u>'s the report.

- **arriba** above, upstairs
  Visto desde arriba parece más pequeño. — Seen from above it looks smaller.
  Arriba están los dormitorios. — The bedrooms are <u>upstairs</u>.

- atrás   behind

  Yo me quedé <u>atrás</u>.   I stayed <u>behind</u>.

- aun   even

  **<u>Aun</u> sentado me duele la   <u>Even</u> when I'm sitting down, my
  pierna.**   leg hurts.

- aún   still, yet

  ¿<u>Aún</u> te duele?   Does it <u>still</u> hurt?

Típ

The following mnemonic (memory jogger) should help you
remember when to use **aun** and when to use **aún**:
<u>Even</u> **aun** doesn't have an accent.
aún <u>still</u> has an accent.
aún hasn't lost its accent <u>yet</u>.

- ayer   yesterday

  <u>Ayer</u> me compré un bolso.   I bought a handbag <u>yesterday</u>.

- casi   almost

  Son <u>casi</u> las cinco.   It's <u>almost</u> five o'clock.

- cerca   near

  El colegio está muy <u>cerca</u>.   The school is very <u>near</u>.

- claro   clearly

  Lo oí muy <u>claro</u>.   I heard it very <u>clearly</u>.

- debajo   underneath

  Miré <u>debajo</u>.   I looked <u>underneath</u>.

- dentro   inside

  ¿Qué hay <u>dentro</u>?   What's <u>inside</u>?

- despacio   slowly

  Conduce <u>despacio</u>.   Drive <u>slowly</u>.

- después   afterwards

  **<u>Después</u> estábamos muy   We were very tired <u>afterwards</u>.
  cansados.**

- detrás   behind

  Vienen <u>detrás</u>.   They're coming along <u>behind</u>.

For further explanation of grammatical terms, please see pages viii-xii.

- enfrente   opposite
  la casa de <u>enfrente</u>   the house <u>opposite</u>

- enseguida   straightaway
  La ambulancia llegó <u>enseguida</u>.   The ambulance arrived <u>straightaway</u>.

- entonces   then
  ¿Qué hiciste <u>entonces</u>?   What did you do <u>then</u>?

- hasta   even
  Estudia <u>hasta</u> cuando está de   He studies <u>even</u> when he's on
  vacaciones.   holiday.

- hoy   today
  <u>Hoy</u> no tenemos clase.   We haven't any lessons <u>today</u>.

- jamás   never
  <u>Jamás</u> he visto nada parecido.   I've <u>never</u> seen anything like it.

- lejos   far
  ¿Está <u>lejos</u>?   Is it <u>far</u>?

- luego   then, later
  <u>Luego</u> fuimos al cine.   <u>Then</u> we went to the cinema.

- muy   very
  Estoy <u>muy</u> cansada.   I'm <u>very</u> tired.

- no   no, not
  <u>No</u>, no me gusta.   <u>No</u>. I don't like it.

- nunca   never
  No viene <u>nunca</u>.   He <u>never</u> comes.
  '¿Has estado alguna vez en   'Have you ever been to Argentina?'
  Argentina?' – 'No, <u>nunca</u>.'   – 'No, <u>never</u>.'

- pronto   soon, early
  Llegarán <u>pronto</u>.   They'll be here <u>soon</u>.
  ¿Por qué has llegado tan   Why have you arrived so early?
  <u>pronto</u>?

- quizás   perhaps
  <u>Quizás</u> está cansado.   <u>Perhaps</u> he's tired.

[*i*] Note that you use the present subjunctive after **quizás** if referring to the future.

> **Quizás venga mañana.**   <u>Perhaps</u> he'll come tomorrow.

⇨ *For more information on the Subjunctive, see page 134.*

- sí   yes

  > **¿Te apetece un café? –**   Do you fancy a coffee? – <u>Yes</u>,
  > **Sí, gracias.**   please.

- siempre   always

  > **Siempre dicen lo mismo.**   They <u>always</u> say the same thing.

- sólo   only

  > **Sólo cuesta tres euros.**   It <u>only</u> costs three euros.

- también   also, too

  > **A mí también me gusta.**   I like it <u>too</u>.

- tampoco   either, neither

  > **Yo tampoco lo compré.**   I didn't buy it <u>either</u>.
  > **Yo no la vi. – Yo tampoco.**   I didn't see her. – <u>Neither</u> did I.

- tan   as, so

  > **Vine tan pronto como pude.**   I came as fast as I could.
  > **Habla tan deprisa que no**   She speaks so fast that I can't
  > **la entiendo.**   understand her.

- tarde   late

  > **Se está haciendo tarde.**   It's getting <u>late</u>.

- temprano   early

  > **Tengo que levantarme**   I've got to get up <u>early</u>.
  > **temprano.**

- todavía   still, yet, even

  > **Todavía tengo dos.**   I've <u>still</u> got two.
  > **Todavía no han llegado.**   They haven't arrived <u>yet</u>.
  > **mejor todavía**   <u>even</u> better

- <u>ya</u>   already

  > **Ya lo he hecho.**   I've <u>already</u> done it.

2   **Words which are used both as adjectives and adverbs**

➤ bastante, demasiado, tanto, mucho and poco can be used both as
adjectives and as adverbs. When they are <u>adjectives</u>, their endings change
in the feminine and plural to agree with what they describe. When they are
<u>adverbs</u>, the endings don't change.

	Adjective use	Adverb use
bastante enough; quite a lot; quite	Hay <u>bastantes</u> libros. There are enough books.	Ya has comido <u>bastante</u>. You've had enough to eat. Son <u>bastante</u> ricos. They are quite rich.
demasiado too much (*plural*: too many); too	<u>demasiada</u> mantequilla too much butter <u>demasiados</u> libros too many books	He comido <u>demasiado</u>. I've eaten too much. Llegamos <u>demasiado</u> tarde. We arrived too late.
tanto as much (*plural*: as many); as often	Ahora no bebo <u>tanta</u> leche. I don't drink as much milk these days. Tengo <u>tantas</u> cosas que hacer. I've so many things to do.	Se preocupa <u>tanto</u> que no puede dormir. He worries so much that he can't sleep. Ahora no la veo <u>tanto.</u> I don't see her so often now.
mucho a lot (of), much (*plural*: many)	Había <u>mucha</u> gente. There were a lot of people. <u>muchas</u> cosas a lot of things	¿Lees <u>mucho</u>? Do you read a lot? ¿Está <u>mucho</u> más lejos? Is it much further?
poco little, not much, (*plural*: few, not many); not very	Hay <u>poca</u> leche. There isn't much milk. Tiene <u>pocos</u> amigos. He hasn't got many friends.	Habla muy <u>poco</u>. He speaks very little. Es <u>poco</u> sociable. He's not very sociable.

Tip

Don't confuse **poco**, which means *little, not much* or *not very*, with
un poco, which means *a little* or *a bit*.

   Come <u>poco</u>.   He eats <u>little</u>.
   ¿Me das un <u>poco</u>?   Can I have <u>a bit</u>?

➤ más and menos can also be used both as adjectives and adverbs. However, they <u>NEVER</u> change their endings, even when used as adjectives.

	Adjective use	Adverb use
más more	No tengo <u>más</u> dinero. I haven't any more money. <u>más</u> libros more books	Es <u>más</u> inteligente que yo. He's more intelligent than I am. Mi hermano trabaja <u>más</u> ahora. My brother works more now.
menos less; fewer	<u>menos</u> mantequilla less butter Había <u>menos</u> gente que ayer. There were fewer people than yesterday.	Estoy <u>menos</u> sorprendida que tú. I'm less surprised than you are. Trabaja <u>menos</u> que yo. He doesn't work as hard as I do.

3 | Adverbs made up of more than one word

➤ Just as in English, some Spanish adverbs are made up of two or more words instead of just one.

a veces	sometimes
a menudo	often
de vez en cuando	from time to time
todo el tiempo	all the time
hoy en día	nowadays
en seguida	immediately

> **Key points**
> ✔ There are a number of common adverbs in Spanish which do not end in -mente.
> ✔ bastante, demasiado, tanto, mucho and poco can be used both as adjectives and as adverbs. Their endings change in the feminine and plural when they are adjectives, but when they are adverbs their endings <u>do not</u> change.
> ✔ más and menos can be both adjectives and adverbs – their endings <u>never</u> change.
> ✔ A number of Spanish adverbs are made up of more than one word.

Position of adverbs

1   Adverbs with verbs

➤ In English, adverbs can come in various places in a sentence, at the beginning, in the middle or at the end.

> I'm <u>never</u> coming back.
> See you <u>soon</u>!
> <u>Suddenly</u>, the phone rang.
> I'd <u>really</u> like to come.

➤ In Spanish, the rules for the position of adverbs in a sentence are more fixed. The adverb can either go immediately <u>AFTER</u> the verb or <u>BEFORE</u> it for emphasis.

No conocemos <u>todavía</u> al nuevo médico.	We still haven't met the new doctor.
<u>Todavía</u> estoy esperando.	I'm still waiting.
<u>Siempre</u> le regalaban flores.	They always gave her flowers.

➤ When the adverb goes with a verb in the perfect tense or in the pluperfect, you can <u>NEVER</u> put the adverb between **haber** and the past participle.

Lo he hecho <u>ya</u>.	I've already done it.
No ha estado <u>nunca</u> en Italia.	She's never been to Italy.

⇨   *For more information on the **Perfect tense**, see page 115.*

2   Adverbs with adjectives and adverbs

➤ The adverb normally goes <u>BEFORE</u> any adjective or adverb it is used with.

un sombrero <u>muy</u> bonito	a very nice hat
hablar <u>demasiado</u> alto	to talk too loudly

> **Key points**
> ✔ Adverbs follow the verb in most cases.
> ✔ Adverbs can go before verbs for emphasis.
> ✔ You can <u>never</u> separate **haber, he, ha** and so on from the following past participle (the **-ado/-ido** form of regular verbs).
> ✔ Adverbs generally come just before an adjective or another adverb.

PREPOSITIONS

What is a preposition?
A **preposition** is a word such as *at*, *for*, *with*, *into* or *from*, which is usually followed by a noun, pronoun or, in English, a word ending in *-ing*. Prepositions show how people and things relate to the rest of the sentence, for example, *She's at home.*; *a tool for cutting grass*; *It's from David.*

Using prepositions

➤ Prepositions are used in front of nouns and pronouns (such as *people*, *the man*, *me*, *him* and so on), and show the relationship between the noun or pronoun and the rest of the sentence. Although prepositions can be used before verb forms ending in *-ing* in English, in Spanish, they're followed by the <u>infinitive</u> – the form of the verb ending in **-ar**, **-er**, or **-ir**.

Le enseñé el billete <u>a</u> la revisora.	I showed my ticket <u>to</u> the ticket inspector.
Ven <u>con</u> nosotros.	Come <u>with</u> us.
Sirve <u>para</u> limpiar zapatos.	It's <u>for</u> cleaning shoes.

➪ *For more information on **Nouns, Pronouns** and **Infinitives**, see pages 1, 41 and 144.*

➤ Prepositions are also used after certain adjectives and verbs and link them to the rest of the sentence.

Estoy muy contento <u>con</u> tu trabajo.	I'm very happy <u>with</u> your work.
Estamos hartos <u>de</u> repetirlo.	We're fed up <u>with</u> repeating it.
¿Te gusta jugar <u>al</u> fútbol?	Do you like playing football?

➤ As in English, Spanish prepositions can be made up of several words instead of just one.

delante de	in front of
antes de	before

➤ In English we can end a sentence with a preposition such as *for*, *with* or *into*, even though some people think this is not good grammar. You can <u>NEVER</u> end a Spanish sentence with a preposition.

¿<u>Para</u> qué es?	What's it <u>for</u>?
la chica <u>con</u> la que hablaste	the girl you spoke <u>to</u>

Tip

The choice of preposition in Spanish is not always what we might expect, coming from English. It is often difficult to give just one English equivalent for a particular Spanish preposition, since prepositions are used so differently in the two languages. This means that you need to learn how they are used and look up set phrases involving prepositions (such as *to be fond <u>of</u> somebody* or *dressed <u>in</u> white*) in a dictionary in order to find an equivalent expression in Spanish.

a, de, en, para and por

1   a

> **Tip**
>
> When a is followed by el, the two words merge to become al.

➤ a can mean *to* with places and destinations.

Voy <u>a</u> Madrid.	I'm going <u>to</u> Madrid.
Voy <u>al</u> cine.	I'm going <u>to the</u> cinema.

> **Tip**
>
> de is also used with a to mean *from ... to ...*
>
> | | |
> |---|---|
> | <u>de</u> la mañana <u>a</u> la noche | <u>from</u> morning <u>to</u> night |
> | <u>de</u> 10 <u>a</u> 12 | <u>from</u> 10 <u>to</u> 12 |

➤ a can mean *to* with indirect objects.

Se lo dio <u>a</u> María.	He gave it <u>to</u> María.

➤ a can mean *to* after ir when talking about what someone is *going to* do.

Voy <u>a</u> verlo mañana.	I'm going <u>to</u> see him tomorrow.

➤ a can mean *at* with times.

<u>a</u> las cinco	<u>at</u> five o'clock
<u>a</u> las dos y cuarto	<u>at</u> quarter past two
<u>a</u> medianoche	<u>at</u> midnight

➤ a can mean *at* with prices and rates.

<u>a</u> dos euros el kilo	(<u>at</u>) two euros a kilo
<u>a</u> 100 km por hora	<u>at</u> 100 km per hour

➤ a can mean *at* with ages.

<u>a</u> los 18 años	<u>at</u> the age of 18

➤ a can mean *at* with places, but generally only after verbs suggesting movement.

Te voy a buscar <u>a</u> la estación.	I'll meet you <u>at</u> the station.
cuando llegó <u>al</u> aeropuerto	when he arrived <u>at</u> the airport

Tip

You can't use **a** to mean *at* when talking about a building, area, or village where someone is. Use **en** instead.

Está en casa. He's *at* home.

➤ **a** can mean *onto*.

Se cayó al suelo. He fell <u>onto</u> the floor.

➤ **a** can mean *into*.

pegar una foto al álbum to stick a photo <u>into</u> the album

➤ **a** is also used to talk about distance.

a 8 km de aquí (at a distance of) 8 km from here

➤ **a** is also used after certain adjectives and verbs.

parecido a esto similar to this

➤ **a** can mean *from* after certain verbs.

Se lo compré a mi hermano. I bought it <u>from</u> my brother.
Les robaba dinero a sus He was stealing money <u>from</u> his
compañeros de clase. classmates.

⇨ *For more information on **Prepositions after verbs**, see page 150.*

➤ **a** is used in set phrases.

<u>a</u> final/finales/fines de mes	at the end of the month
<u>a</u> veces	at times
<u>a</u> menudo	often
<u>a</u> la puerta	at the door
<u>a</u> mano	by hand
<u>a</u> caballo	on horseback
<u>a</u> pie	on foot
<u>a</u> tiempo	on time
<u>al</u> sol	in the sun
<u>a</u> la sombra	in the shade

Grammar Extra!

a is often used to talk about the manner in which something is done.

a la inglesa	in the English manner
a paso lento	slowly
poco a poco	little by little

The Spanish equivalent of the English construction *on* with a verb ending in *-ing* is **al** followed by the <u>infinitive</u>.

al levantarse	on getting up
al abrir la puerta	on opening the door

2 | **Personal a**

➤ When the direct object of a verb is a specific person or pet animal, **a** is placed immediately before it.

Querían mucho a sus hijos.	They loved their children dearly.
Cuido a mi hermana pequeña.	I look after my little sister.

[i] Note that personal a is <u>NOT</u> used after the verb **tener**.

Tienen dos hijos.	They have two children.

⇨ *For more information on **Direct objects**, see page 46.*

3 | **de**

Tip

When **de** is followed by **el**, the two words merge to become **del**.

➤ **de** can mean *from*.

Soy de Londres.	I'm <u>from</u> London.
un médico de Valencia	a doctor <u>from</u> Valencia

Tip

de is also used with **a** to mean *from ... to ...*

de la mañana a la noche	<u>from</u> morning <u>to</u> night
de 10 a 12	<u>from</u> 10 <u>to</u> 12

➤ de can mean *of*.

el presidente de Francia	the president of France
dos litros de leche	two litres of milk

➤ de shows who or what something belongs to.

el sombrero de mi padre	my father's hat (*literally*: the hat of my father)
la oficina del presidente	the president's office (*literally*: the office of the president)

➤ de can indicate what something is made of, what it contains or what it is used for.

un vestido de seda	a silk dress
una caja de cerillas	a box of matches
una taza de té	a cup of tea *or* a teacup
una silla de cocina	a kitchen chair
un traje de baño	a swimming costume

➤ de is used in comparisons when a number is mentioned.

Había más/menos de 100 **personas.**	There were more/fewer than 100 people.

[*i*] Note that you do NOT use que with más or menos when there is a number involved.

➤ de can mean *in* after superlatives (*the most..., the biggest, the least...*).

la ciudad más/menos **contaminada del mundo**	the most/least polluted city in the world

⇨ *For more information on **Superlative adjectives**, see page 26.*

➤ de is used after certain adjectives and verbs.

contento de ver	pleased to see
Es fácil/difícil de entender.	It's easy/difficult to understand.
Es capaz de olvidarlo.	He's quite capable of forgetting it.

⇨ *For more information on **Prepositions after verbs**, see page 150.*

Grammar Extra!

de is often used in descriptions.

la mujer del sombrero verde	the woman in the green hat
un chico de ojos azules	a boy with blue eyes

---

4 **en**

➤ **en** can mean *in* with places.

en el campo	in the country
en Londres	in London
en la cama	in bed
con un libro en la mano	with a book in his hand

➤ **en** can mean *at*.

en casa	at home
en el colegio	at school
en el aeropuerto	at the airport
en la parada de autobús	at the bus stop
en Navidad	at Christmas

➤ **en** can mean *in* with months, years and seasons and when saying how long something takes or took.

en marzo	in March
en 2005	in 2005
Nació en invierno.	He was born in winter.
Lo hice en dos días.	I did it in two days.

[i] Note the following time phrase which does not use *in* in English.

en este momento	at this moment

> ## Típ
>
> There are two ways of talking about a length of time in Spanish which translate the same in English, but have very different meanings.
>
> **Lo haré dentro de una semana** I'll do it in a week.
> **Lo haré en una semana.** I'll do it in a week.
>
> Though both can be translated in the same way, the first sentence means that you'll do it in a week's time; the second means that it will take you a week to do it.

➤ **en** can mean *in* with languages and in set phrases.

Está escrito en español.	It's written in Spanish.
en voz baja	in a low voice

➤ en can mean *on*.

sentado <u>en</u> una silla	sitting <u>on</u> a chair
<u>en</u> la planta baja	<u>on</u> the ground floor
Hay dos cuadros <u>en</u> la pared.	There are two pictures <u>on</u> the wall.

➤ en can mean *by* with most methods of transport.

<u>en</u> coche	<u>by</u> car
<u>en</u> avión	<u>by</u> plane
<u>en</u> tren	<u>by</u> train

➤ en can mean *into*.

No entremos <u>en</u> la casa.	Let's not go <u>into</u> the house.
Metió la mano <u>en</u> su bolso.	She put her hand <u>into</u> her handbag.

➤ en is also used after certain adjectives and verbs.

Es muy buena/mala <u>en</u> geografía.	She is very good/bad at geography.
Fueron los primeros/últimos/ únicos <u>en</u> llegar.	They were the first/last/only ones to arrive.

⇨ *For more information on **Prepositions after verbs**, see page 150.*

5	**para**

➤ para can mean *for* with a person, destination or purpose.

<u>Para</u> mí un zumo de naranja.	An orange juice <u>for</u> me.
Salen <u>para</u> Cádiz.	They are leaving <u>for</u> Cádiz.
¿<u>Para</u> qué lo quieres?	What do you want it <u>for</u>?

[i] Note that you cannot end a sentence in Spanish with a preposition as you can in English.

➤ para can mean *for* with time.

Es <u>para</u> mañana.	It's <u>for</u> tomorrow.
una habitación <u>para</u> dos noches	a room <u>for</u> two nights

➤ para is also used with an infinitive with the meaning of *(in order) to*.

Lo hace <u>para</u> ganar dinero.	He does it <u>to</u> earn money.
Lo hice <u>para</u> ayudarte.	I did it <u>to</u> help you.

Tip

para mí can be used to mean *in my opinion*.
Para mí, es estupendo.   In my opinion, it's great.

6   **por**

➤ por can mean *for* when it means *for the benefit of* or *because of*.

Lo hice por mis padres.	I did it <u>for</u> my parents.
Lo hago por ellos.	I'm doing it <u>for</u> them.
por la misma razón	<u>for</u> the same reason

➤ por can mean *for* when it means *in exchange for*.

¿Cuánto me darán por este libro?	How much will they give me <u>for</u> this book?
Te lo cambio por éste.	I'll swap you it <u>for</u> this one.

➤ por can mean *by* in passive constructions.

descubierto por unos niños	discovered <u>by</u> some children
odiado por sus enemigos	hated <u>by</u> his enemies

⇨ *For more information on the* **Passive**, *see page 122.*

➤ por can mean *by* with means of transport when talking about <u>freight</u>.

por barco	<u>by</u> boat
por tren	<u>by</u> train
por avión	<u>by</u> airmail
por correo aéreo	<u>by</u> airmail

➤ por can mean *along*.

Vaya por ese camino.	Go <u>along</u> that path.

➤ por can mean *through*.

por el túnel	<u>through</u> the tunnel

➤ por can mean *around*.

pasear por el campo	to walk <u>around</u> the countryside

➤ por is used to talk vaguely about where something or someone is.

Tiene que estar por aquí.	It's got to be around here somewhere.
Lo busqué por todas partes.	I looked for him everywhere.

➤ por is used to talk about time.

por la mañana	in the morning
por la tarde	in the afternoon/evening
por la noche	at night

➤ por is used to talk about rates.

90 km por hora	90 km an hour
un cinco por ciento	five per cent
Ganaron por 3 a 0.	They won by 3 to 0.

➤ por is used in certain phrases which talk about the reason for something.

¿por qué?	why?, for what reason?
por todo eso	because of all that
por lo que he oído	judging by what I've heard

➤ por is used to talk about how something is done.

llamar por teléfono	to telephone
Lo oí por la radio.	I heard it on the radio.

Grammar Extra!

por is often combined with other Spanish prepositions and words, usually to show movement.

Saltó por encima de la mesa.	She jumped over the table.
Nadamos por debajo del puente.	We swam under the bridge.
Pasaron por delante de Correos.	They went past the post office.

Key points

✔ a, de, en, para and por are very frequently used prepositions which you will need to study carefully.

✔ Each of them has several possible meanings, which depend on the context they are used in.

Some other common prepositions

➤ The following prepositions are also frequently used in Spanish.

- antes de   before

  antes de las 5   before 5 o'clock

i Note that, like many other prepositions, **antes de** is used before
infinitives in Spanish where in English we'd usually use the
-*ing* form of the verb.

  Antes de abrir el paquete,   Before opening the packet, read
  lea las instrucciones.   the instructions.

- bajo   below, under

  un grado bajo cero   one degree below zero
  bajo la cama   under the bed

i Note that **debajo de** is more common than **bajo** when talking about
the actual position of something.

  debajo de la cama   under the bed

- con   with

  Vino con su amigo.   She came with her friend.

i Note that **con** can be used after certain adjectives as well as in a few
very common phrases.

  enfadado con ellos   angry with them
  un café con leche   a white coffee
  un té con limón   a (cup of) tea with a slice of lemon

- contra   against

  Estaba apoyado contra   He was leaning against the wall.
  la pared.
  El domingo jugamos contra   We play against Malaga on Sunday.
  el Málaga.

- debajo de   under

  debajo de la cama   under the bed

- delante de   in front of

  Iba delante de mí.   He was walking in front of me.

- desde   from, since

Desde aquí se puede ver.	You can see it <u>from</u> here.
Llamaron **desde** España.	They phoned <u>from</u> Spain.
desde otro punto de vista	<u>from</u> a different point of view
desde entonces	<u>from</u> then onwards
desde la una **hasta** las siete	<u>from</u> one o'clock <u>to</u> seven
desde la boda	<u>since</u> the wedding

Típ

Spanish uses the <u>present tense</u> with **desde** (meaning *since*) and the expressions **desde hace** and **hace ... que** (meaning *for*) to talk about actions that started in the past and are still going on.

Estoy aquí desde las diez.	I've been here since ten o'clock.
Estoy aquí desde hace dos horas. *or* Hace dos horas que **estoy** aquí.	I've been here for two hours.

If you are saying how long something has NOT happened for, in European Spanish you can use the <u>perfect tense</u> with **desde** and **desde hace**.

No <u>ha trabajado</u> desde el accidente.	He hasn't worked since the accident.
No <u>ha trabajado</u> desde hace dos meses.	He hasn't worked for two months.

⇨ *For more information on the **Present tense** and the **Perfect tense**, see pages 69 and 115.*

- después de   after

después del partido	<u>after</u> the match

[i] Note that, like many other prepositions, **después de** is used before infinitives in Spanish where in English we'd usually use the *-ing* form of the verb.

Después de ver la televisión me fui a la cama.	<u>After watching</u> television I went to bed.

- detrás de   behind

Están **detrás de** la puerta.	They are <u>behind</u> the door.

- durante   during, for

durante la guerra	<u>during</u> the war
Anduvieron **durante** 3 días.	They walked <u>for</u> 3 days.

- **entre**   between, among
  entre 8 y 10   between 8 and 10
  Hablaban **entre** sí.   They were talking among
                                                          themselves.

- **hacia**   towards, around
  Van **hacia** ese edificio.   They're going towards that building.
  hacia las tres   at around three (o'clock)
  hacia finales de enero   around the end of January

Grammar Extra!

hacia can also combine with some adverbs to show movement in a particular direction.

hacia arriba	upwards
hacia abajo	downwards
hacia adelante	forwards
hacia atrás	backwards

- **hasta**   until, as far as, to, up to
  hasta la noche   until night
  Fueron en coche **hasta** Sevilla.   They drove as far as Seville.
  desde la una **hasta** las tres   from one o'clock to three
  Hasta ahora no ha llamado   No one has called up to now.
  nadie.

[*i*] Note that there are some very common ways of saying goodbye using
hasta.

  ¡**Hasta** luego!   See you!
  ¡**Hasta** mañana!   See you tomorrow!

- **sin**   without
  sin agua/dinero   without any water/money
  sin mi marido   without my husband

Tip

Whereas in English we say *without a doubt*, *without a hat* and
so on, in Spanish the indefinite article isn't given after **sin**.

  sin duda   without a doubt
  sin sombrero   without a hat

⇨ *For more information on **Articles**, see page 10.*

---

i Note that sin is used before infinitives in Spanish where in English we would use the -ing form of the verb.

Se fue <u>sin decir</u> nada.	He left <u>without saying</u> anything.

- sobre   on, about

<u>sobre</u> la cama	<u>on</u> the bed
Ponlo <u>sobre</u> la mesa.	Put it <u>on</u> the table.
un libro <u>sobre</u> Shakespeare	a book <u>on</u> or <u>about</u> Shakespeare
Madrid tiene <u>sobre</u> 4 millones de habitantes.	Madrid has <u>about</u> 4 million inhabitants.
Vendré <u>sobre</u> las cuatro.	I'll come <u>about</u> four o'clock.

➤ Spanish prepositions can be made up of more than one word, for example, antes de, detrás de. Here are some more common prepositions made up of two or more words:

- a causa de   because of

No salimos <u>a causa de</u> la lluvia.	We didn't go out <u>because of</u> the rain.

- al lado de   beside, next to

<u>al lado de</u> la tele	<u>beside</u> the TV

- cerca de   near, close to

Está <u>cerca de</u> la iglesia.	It's <u>near</u> the church.

- encima de   on, on top of

Ponlo <u>encima de</u> la mesa.	Put it <u>on</u> the table.

- por encima de   above, over

Saltó <u>por encima de</u> la mesa.	He jumped <u>over</u> the table.

- en medio de   in the middle of

Está <u>en medio de</u> la plaza.	It's <u>in the middle of</u> the square.

- junto a   by

Está <u>junto al</u> cine.	It's <u>by</u> the cinema.

- junto con   together with

Fue detenido <u>junto con</u> su hijo.	He was arrested <u>together with</u> his son.

- lejos de   far from

No está <u>lejos de</u> aquí.	It isn't <u>far from</u> here.

CONJUNCTIONS

What is a conjunction?
A **conjunction** is a word such as *and*, *but*, *or*, *so*, *if* and *because*, that links two words or phrases of a similar type, or two parts of a sentence, for example, *Diane and I have been friends for years.; I left because I was bored.*

y, o, pero, porque and si

➤ y, o, pero, porque and si are the most common conjunctions that you need to know in Spanish:

- y   and

  el coche y la casa   the car and the house

[*i*] Note that you use e instead of y before words beginning with i or hi (but not hie).

  Diana e Isabel   Diana and Isabel
  madre e hija   mother and daughter
  BUT
  árboles y hierba   trees and grass

- o   or

  patatas fritas o arroz   chips or rice

[*i*] Note that you use u instead of o before words beginning with o or ho.

  diez u once   ten or eleven
  minutos u horas   minutes or hours

[*i*] Note that you use ó instead of o between numerals to avoid confusion with zero.

  37 ó 38   37 or 38

⇨ *For more information on **Numbers**, see page 206.*

- pero   but

  Me gustaría ir, pero estoy muy   I'd like to go, but I am very tired.
  cansado.

[*i*] Note that you use sino in direct contrasts after a negative.

  No es escocesa, sino irlandesa.   She's not Scottish but Irish.

For further explanation of grammatical terms, please see pages viii-xii.

- **porque** because

  Ha llamado <u>porque</u> necesita un libro.   He called <u>because</u> he needs a book.

[*i*] Note that you don't use **porque** at the beginning of a sentence; you should use **como** instead.

  <u>Como</u> está lloviendo no podemos salir.   <u>Because</u> or <u>As</u> it's raining, we can't go out.

> **Típ**
>
> Be careful not to mix up **porque** (meaning *because*) and **por qué** (meaning *why*).

- **que** that

  Dice <u>que</u> me quiere.   He says <u>that</u> he loves me.
  Dicen <u>que</u> te han visto.   They say <u>that</u> they've seen you.
  Sabe <u>que</u> estamos aquí.   He knows <u>that</u> we are here.

➡ *For more information on* **que** *followed by the subjunctive and* **que** *(meaning than) in comparisons, see pages 136 and 26.*

> **Típ**
>
> In English we can say both *He says he loves me* and *He says <u>that</u> he loves me*, or *She knows you're here* and *She knows <u>that</u> you're here*. You can <u>NEVER</u> leave out **que** in Spanish in the way that you can leave out *that* in English.

- **si** if, whether

  <u>Si</u> no estudias, no aprobarás.   <u>If</u> you don't study, you won't pass.
  ¿Sabes <u>si</u> nos han pagado ya?   Do you know <u>if</u> or <u>whether</u> we've been paid yet?
  Avisadme <u>si</u> no podéis venir.   Let me know <u>if</u> you can't come.

➡ *For information on* **si** *followed by the subjunctive, see page 143.*

> **Típ**
>
> There is no accent on **si** when it means *if*. Be careful not to confuse **si** (meaning *if*) with **sí** (meaning *yes* or *himself/herself/yourself/ themselves/yourselves*).

Some other common conjunctions

➤ Here are some other common Spanish conjunctions:

- como   as

Como es domingo, puedes quedarte en la cama.	<u>As</u> it's Sunday, you can stay in bed.

- cuando   when

Cuando entré estaba leyendo.	She was reading <u>when</u> I came in.

➯ *For information on* cuando *followed by the subjunctive, see page 140.*

- pues   then, well

Tengo sueño. – ¡Pues, vete a la cama!	I'm tired. – <u>Then</u> go to bed!
Pues, no lo sabía.	<u>Well</u>, I didn't know.
Pues, como te iba contando ...	<u>Well</u>, as I was saying ...

- mientras   while (*referring to time*)

Lava tú mientras yo seco.	You wash <u>while</u> I dry.
Él leía mientras yo cocinaba.	He would read <u>while</u> I cooked.

➯ *For information on* mientras *followed by the subjunctive, see page 140.*

- mientras que   whereas

Isabel es muy dinámica mientras que Ana es más tranquila.	Isabel is very dynamic <u>whereas</u> Ana is more laid-back.

- aunque   although, even though

Me gusta el francés, aunque prefiero el alemán.	I like French <u>although</u> I prefer German.
Seguí andando aunque me dolía mucho la pierna.	I went on walking <u>even though</u> my leg hurt a lot.

Grammar Extra!

aunque is also used to mean *even if*. In this case, it is followed by the subjunctive.

➯ *For more information on the* **Subjunctive**, *see page 134.*

Split conjunctions

In English we have conjunctions which are made up of two parts (*both … and,
neither … nor*). Spanish also has conjunctions which have more than one part,
the commonest of which are probably **ni … ni** (meaning *neither … nor*) and **o
… o** (meaning *either … or*):

- **ni … ni**   neither … nor

  Ni Carlos ni Sofía vinieron. *or*   <u>Neither</u> Carlos <u>nor</u> Sofía came.
  No vinieron ni Carlos ni Sofía.

i Note that if you're putting **ni … ni** after the verb you must put **no**
before the verb.

  No tengo ni hermanos ni   I have <u>neither</u> brothers <u>nor</u>
  hermanas.   sisters.

- **o … o**   either … or

  Puedes tomar o helado o yogur. You can have <u>either</u> ice cream <u>or</u>
  yoghurt.

Key points

✔ **y, o, pero, porque** and **si** are the most common conjunctions
  that you need to know in Spanish.
✔ Use **e** rather than **y** before words beginning with **i** or **hi** (but not
  with **hie**).
✔ Use **u** rather than **o** before words beginning with **o** or **ho**.
✔ **que** very often means *that*. *That* is often missed out in English,
  but **que** can never be left out in Spanish.
✔ Some conjunctions such as **ni … ni** and **o … o** consist of two
  parts.

SPELLING

1   <u>Sounds that are spelled differently depending on the letter that follows</u>

➤ Certain sounds are spelled differently in Spanish depending on what letter follows them. For example, the hard [k] sound heard in the English word *car* is usually spelled:
- c before a, o and u
- qu before e and i

➤ This means that the Spanish word for *singer* is spelled c**a**ntante (pronounced [*kan-tan-tay*]); the word for *coast* is spelled c**o**sta (pronounced [*ko-sta*]); and the word for *cure* is spelled c**u**ra (pronounced [*koo-ra*]).

➤ However, the Spanish word for cheese is spelled qu**e**so (pronounced [*kay-so*]) and the word for *chemistry* is spelled qu**í**mica (pronounced [*kee-mee-ka*]).

i   Note that although the letter k is not much used in Spanish, it is found in words relating to *kilos*, *kilometres* and *kilograms*; for example **un kilo** (meaning *a kilo*); **un kilogramo** (meaning *a kilogram*); **un kilómetro** (meaning *a kilometre*).

➤ Similarly, the [g] sound heard in the English word *gone* is spelled:
- g before a, o and u
- gu before e and i

➤ This means that the Spanish word for *cat* is spelled g**a**to (pronounced [*ga-toe*]); the word for *goal* is spelled g**o**l (pronounced [*gol*]); and the word for *worm* is spelled g**u**sano (pronounced [*goo-sa-no*]).

➤ However, the Spanish word for *war* is spelled gu**e**rra (pronounced [*gair-ra*]) and the word for *guitar* is spelled gu**i**tarra (pronounced [*ghee-tar-ra*]).

For further explanation of grammatical terms, please see pages viii-xii.

2 | **Letters that are pronounced differently depending on what follows**

➤ Certain letters are pronounced differently depending on what follows them. As we have seen, when c comes before a, o or u, it is pronounced like a [k]. When it comes before e or i, in European Spanish it is pronounced like the [th] in the English word *pith* and in Latin American Spanish it is pronounced like the [s] in *sing*.

➤ This means that casa (meaning *house*) is pronounced [ka-sa], but centro (meaning *centre*) is pronounced [then-tro] in European Spanish and [sen-tro] in Latin American Spanish. Similarly, cita (meaning *date*) is pronounced [the-ta] in European Spanish and [see-ta] in Latin American Spanish.

➤ In the same way, when g comes before a, o or u, it is pronounced like the [g] in *gone*. When it comes before e or i, however, it is pronounced like the [ch] in *loch*, as it is pronounced in Scotland.

➤ This means that gas (meaning *gas*) is pronounced [gas] but gente (meaning *people*) is pronounced [chen-tay]. Similarly, gimnasio (meaning *gym*) is pronounced [cheem-na-see-o].

3 | **Spelling changes that are needed in verbs to reflect the pronunciation**

➤ Because c sounds like [k] before a, o and u, and like [th] or [s] before e and i, you sometimes have to alter the spelling of a verb when adding a particular ending to ensure the word reads as it is pronounced:

● In verbs ending in -car (which is pronounced [kar]), you have to change the c to qu before endings starting with an e to keep the hard [k] pronunciation. So the yo form of the preterite tense of sacar (meaning to take out) is spelled saqué. This spelling change affects the preterite and the present subjunctive of verbs ending in -car.

● In verbs ending in -cer and -cir (which are pronounced [ther] and [thir] or [ser] and [sir]), you have to change the c to z before endings starting with a or o to keep the soft [th/s] pronunciation. So while the yo form of the preterite tense of hacer is spelled hice, the él/ella/usted form is spelled hizo. This spelling change affects the ordinary present tense as well as the present subjunctive of verbs ending in -cer or -cir.

➤ Because **g** sounds like the [g] of *gone* before **a**, **o** and **u**, and like the [ch] of *loch* before **e** and **i**, you also sometimes have to alter the spelling of a verb when adding a particular ending to ensure the verb still reads as it is pronounced:

- In verbs ending in **-gar** (which is pronounced [gar]), you have to change the **g** to **gu** before endings starting with an **e** or an **i** to keep the hard [g] pronunciation. So the **yo** form of the preterite tense of **pagar** (meaning *to pay*) is spelled **pagué**. This spelling change affects the preterite and the present subjunctive of verbs ending in **-gar**.

- In verbs ending in **-ger** and **-gir** (which are pronounced [cher] and [chir]), you have to change the **g** to **j** before endings starting with **a** or **o** to keep the soft [ch] pronunciation. So while the **él/ella/usted** form of the present tense of **coger** (meaning *to take* or *to catch*) is spelled **coge**, the **yo** form is spelled **cojo**. This spelling change affects the ordinary present tense as well as the present subjunctive of verbs ending in **-ger** or **-gir**.

➤ Because **gui** sounds like [ghee] in verbs ending in **-guir**, but **gua** and **guo** sound like [gwa] and [gwo], you have to drop the **u** before **a** and **o** in verbs ending in **-guir**. So while the **él/ella/usted** form of the present tense of **seguir** (meaning *to follow*) is spelled **sigue**, the **yo** form is spelled **sigo**. This spelling change affects the ordinary present tense as well as the present subjunctive of verbs ending in **-guir**.

➤ Finally, although **z** is always pronounced [th] in European Spanish and [s] in Latin American Spanish, in verbs ending in **-zar** the **z** spelling is changed to **c** before **e**. So, while the **él/ella/usted** form of the preterite tense of **cruzar** is spelled **cruzó**, the **yo** form is spelled **crucé**. This spelling change affects the preterite and the present subjunctive of verbs ending in **-zar**.

<h2>4   <u>Spelling changes that are needed when making nouns and adjectives plural</u></h2>

➤ In the same way that you have to make some spelling changes when modifying the endings of certain verbs, you sometimes have to change the spelling of nouns and adjectives when making them plural.

➤ This affects nouns and adjectives ending in **-z**. When adding the **-es** ending of the plural, you have to change the **z** to **c**.

una vez	once, one time	→	**dos veces**	twice, two times
una luz	a light	→	**unas luces**	some lights
capaz	capable (*singular*)	→	**capaces**	capable (*plural*)

➤ The following table shows the usual spelling of the various sounds discussed above:

	Usual spelling				
	before a	before o	before u	before e	before i
[k] sound (as in *cap*)	ca: casa house	co: cosa thing	cu: cubo bucket	que: queso cheese	qui: química chemistry
[g] sound (as in *gap*)	ga: gato cat	go: gordo fat	gu: gusto taste	gue: guerra war	gui: guitarra guitar
[th] sound (as in *pith*) (pronounced [s] in Latin America)	za: zapato shoe	zo: zorro fox	zu: zumo juice	ce: cero zero	ci: cinta ribbon
[ch] sound (as in *loch*)	ja: jardín garden	jo: joven young	ju: jugar to play	ge: gente people	gi: gigante giant

[*i*] Note that because **j** is still pronounced [*ch*] even when it comes before **e** or **i**, there are quite a number of words that contain **je** or **ji**; for example,

el **jefe**/la **jefa**	the boss
el **jerez**	sherry
el **jersey**	jersey
el **jinete**	jockey
la **jirafa**	giraffe
el e**jemplo**	the example
di**je**/di**jiste**	I said/you said
de**jé**	I left

Similarly, because **z** is also pronounced [*th*] or [*s*] even when it comes before **i** or **e**, there are one or two exceptions to the spelling rules described above; for example, el **zigzag** (meaning *zigzag*) and la **zeta** (the name of the letter *z* in Spanish).

STRESS

Which syllable to stress

➤ Most words can be broken up into <u>syllables</u>. These are the different sounds that words are broken up into. They are shown in this section by | and the stressed syllable is underlined.

➤ There are some very simple rules to help you remember which part of the word to stress in Spanish, and when to write an accent. 重音

➤ Words <u>DON'T</u> have a written acute accent if they follow the normal stress rules for Spanish. If they do not follow the normal stress rules, they <u>DO</u> need an accent.

> ### Tip
> The accent that shows stress is always an <u>acute</u> accent in Spanish (´). To remember which way an acute accents slopes try thinking of this saying:
> *It's low on the left, with the height on the right.*

1 <u>Words ending in a vowel or -n or -s</u>

➤ Words ending in a vowel (*a, e, i, o* or *u*) or **-n** or **-s** are normally stressed on the <u>last syllable but one</u>. If this is the case, they do <u>NOT</u> have any written accents.

<u>ca</u>|sa	house	<u>ca</u>|sas	houses
pa|<u>la</u>|bra	word	pa|<u>la</u>|bras	words
<u>tar</u>|de	afternoon	<u>tar</u>|des	afternoons
<u>ha</u>|bla	he/she speaks	<u>ha</u>|blan	they speak
<u>co</u>|rre	he/she runs	<u>co</u>|rren	they run

➤ Whenever words ending in a vowel or **-n** or **-s** are <u>NOT</u> stressed on the last syllable but one, they have a written accent on the vowel that is stressed.

<u>úl</u>|ti|mo	last
<u>jó</u>|ve|nes	young people
<u>crí</u>|me|nes	crimes

2 | **Words ending in a consonant other than -n or -s**

➤ Words ending in a consonant (a letter that isn't a vowel) other than -n or -s
are normally stressed on the <u>last syllable</u>. If this is the case, they do <u>NOT</u>
have an accent.

re|<u>loj</u>	clock, watch
ver|<u>dad</u>	truth
trac|<u>tor</u>	tractor

➤ Whenever words ending in a consonant other than -n or -s are <u>NOT</u>
stressed on the last syllable, they have an accent.

ca|<u>rác</u>|ter	character
di|<u>fí</u>|cil	difficult
<u>fá</u>|cil	easy

3 | **Accents on feminine and plural forms**

➤ The same syllable is stressed in the plural form of adjectives and nouns as in
the singular. To show this, you need to:

- add an accent in the plural in the case of unaccented nouns and
adjectives of more than one syllable ending in -n

<u>or</u>|den	order	<u>ór</u>|de|nes	orders
e|<u>xa</u>|men	exam	e|<u>xá</u>|me|nes	exams
BUT: **tren**	train	**tre**|**nes**	trains

i Note that in the case of one-syllable words ending in -n or -s, such as
tren above, no accent is needed in the plural, since the stress falls
naturally on the last syllable but one thanks to the plural -s ending.

- drop the accent in the plural form of nouns and adjectives ending in -n
or -s which have an accent on the last syllable in the singular

au|to|<u>bús</u>	bus	au|to|<u>bu</u>|ses	buses
re|vo|lu|<u>ción</u>	revolution	re|vo|lu|<u>cio</u>|nes	revolutions

➤ The feminine forms of nouns or adjectives whose masculine form ends in an
accented vowel followed by -n or -s do <u>NOT</u> have an accent.

un franc<u>é</u>s	a Frenchman
una franc<u>e</u>sa	a French woman

> ### Tip
>
> Just because a word has a written accent in the singular does not necessarily mean it has one in the plural, and vice versa.
>
> **jo|ven**
> *Ends in n, so rule is to stress last syllable but one; follows rule, so <u>no</u> accent needed in singular*
>
> **jó|ve|nes**
> *Ends in s, so rule is to stress last syllable but one; breaks rule, so accent <u>is</u> needed in plural to keep stress on jo-*
>
> **lec|<u>ción</u>**
> *Ends in n, so rule is to stress last syllable but one; breaks rule, so accent <u>is</u> needed in singular*
>
> **lec|<u>cio</u>|nes**
> *Ends in s, so rule is to stress last syllable but one; follows rule, so <u>no</u> accent needed in plural to keep stress on -cio-*

---

4   **<u>Which vowel to stress in vowel combinations</u>**

➤ The vowels **i** and **u** are considered to be <u>weak</u>. The vowels **a**, **e** and **o** are considered to be <u>strong</u>.

➤ When a weak vowel (**i** or **u**) combines with a strong one (**a**, **e** or **o**), they form <u>ONE</u> sound that is part of the <u>SAME</u> syllable. Technically speaking, this is called a <u>diphthong</u>. The strong vowel is emphasized more.

b<u>ai</u>|le	dance
c<u>ie</u>|rra	he/she/it closes
b<u>oi</u>|na	beret
p<u>ei</u>|ne	comb
c<u>au</u>|sa	cause

> ### Tip
>
> To remember which are the weak vowels, try thinking of this saying: *U and I are weaklings and always lose out to other vowels!*

➤ When **i** is combined with **u** or **u** with **i** (the two weak vowels), they also form <u>ONE</u> sound within the <u>SAME</u> syllable; there is more emphasis on the second vowel.

ci<u>u</u>dad	city, town
fu<u>i</u>	I went

➤ When you combine two strong vowels (**a**, **e** or **o**), they form <u>TWO</u> separate sounds and are part of <u>DIFFERENT</u> syllables.

ca|er	to fall
ca|os	chaos
fe|o	ugly

For further explanation of grammatical terms, please see pages viii-xii.

5 | Adding accents to some verb forms

➤ When object pronouns are added to the end of certain verb forms, an accent is often required to show that the syllable stressed in the verb form does not change. These verb forms are:

- the <u>gerund</u> whenever one or more pronouns are added

comprando	buying
compr**á**ndo(se)lo	buying it (for him/her/them)

- the <u>infinitive</u>, when followed by two pronouns

vender	to sell
vend**é**rselas	to sell them to him/her/them

- <u>imperative</u> forms

compra	buy
c**ó**mpralo	buy it
hagan	do
h**á**ganselo	do it for him/her/them
BUT:	
comprad	buy
compradlo	buy it

⇨ *For more information on* **Gerunds, Infinitives** *and the* **Imperative**, *see pages 125, 144 and 85.*

6 | Accents on adjectives and adverbs

➤ Adjectives ending in **-ísimo** always have an accent on **-ísimo**. This means that any other accents are dropped.

caro	→	**carísimo**
expensive		very expensive
difícil	→	**dificilísimo**
difficult		very difficult

➤ Accents on adjectives are <u>NOT</u> affected when you add **-mente** to turn them into adverbs.

fácil	→	**fácilmente**
easy		easily

The acute accent used to show meaning

➤ The acute accent is often used to distinguish between the written forms of
some words which are pronounced the same but have a different meaning
or function.

Without an accent		With an accent	
mi	my	mí	me
tu	your	tú	you
te	you	té	tea
si	if	sí	yes; himself
el	the	él	he
de	of	dé	give
solo	alone; by oneself	sólo	only
mas	but	más	more

Han robado <u>mi</u> coche.	They've stolen my car.
A <u>mí</u> no me vio.	He didn't see me.
¿Te gusta <u>tu</u> trabajo?	Do you like your job?
<u>Tú</u>, ¿qué opinas?	What do you think?
...<u>si</u> no viene	...if he doesn't come
<u>Sí</u> que lo sabe.	Yes, he does know.
<u>El</u> puerto está cerca.	The harbour's nearby.
<u>Él</u> lo hará.	He'll do it.
Vino <u>solo</u>.	He came alone or by himself.
<u>Sólo</u> lo sabe él.	Only he knows.

➤ The acute accent is often used on the <u>demonstrative pronouns</u> (éste/ésta,
aquél/aquélla, ése/ésa and so on) to distinguish them from the
<u>demonstrative adjectives</u> (este/esta, aquel/aquella, ese/esa and so on).

Me gusta <u>esta</u> casa. (= *adjective*)	I like this house.
Me quedo con <u>ésta</u>. (= *pronoun*)	I'll take this one.
¿Ves <u>aquellos</u> edificios? (= *adjective*)	Can you see those buildings?
<u>Aquéllos</u> son más bonitos. (= *pronoun*)	Those are prettier.

[*i*] Note that no accent is given on the neuter pronouns esto, eso and
aquello since there is no adjective form with which they might be
confused.

⇨ *For more information on **Demonstrative adjectives** and **Demonstrative**
pronouns, see pages 30 and 67.*

➤ An accent is needed on question words in direct and indirect questions as well as after expressions of uncertainty.

¿**Cómo** estás?	How are you?
Dime **cómo** estás.	Tell me how you are.
Me preguntó **cómo** estaba.	He asked me how I was.
¿Con **quién** viajaste?	Who did you travel with?
¿**Dónde** encontraste eso?	Where did you find that?
No sé **dónde** está.	I don't know where it is.

⇨ *For more information on* **Questions**, *see page 160.*

➤ An accent is also needed on exclamation words.

¡**Qué** asco!	How revolting!
¡**Qué** horror!	How awful!
¡**Qué** raro!	How strange!
¡**Cuánta** gente!	What a lot of people!

Key points

✔ When deciding whether or not to write an accent on a word, think about how it sounds and what letter it ends in, as there are certain rules to say when an accent should be used.

✔ The vowels i and u are considered to be weak. The vowels a, e and o are considered to be strong. They can combine in a number of ways.

✔ Accents are added to written forms of words which are pronounced the same but have a different meaning, for example, mi/mí, tu/tú and so on.

✔ Accents are also added to most demonstrative pronouns so that they are not confused with demonstrative adjectives.

✔ Adjectives ending in -ísimo always have an accent on -ísimo, but no accent is added when adverbs are formed by adding -mente to adjectives.

✔ Question words used in direct and indirect questions as well as exclamation words always have an acute accent.

NUMBERS

1	uno (un, una)	31	treinta y uno (un, una)
2	dos	40	cuarenta
3	tres	41	cuarenta y uno (un, una)
4	cuatro	50	cincuenta
5	cinco	52	cincuenta y dos
6	seis	60	sesenta
7	siete	65	sesenta y cinco
8	ocho	70	setenta
9	nueve	76	setenta y seis
10	diez	80	ochenta
11	once	87	ochenta y siete
12	doce	90	noventa
13	trece	99	noventa y nueve
14	catorce	100	cien (ciento)
15	quince	101	ciento uno (un, una)
16	dieciséis	200	doscientos/doscientas
17	diecisiete	212	doscientos/doscientas doce
18	dieciocho	300	trescientos/trescientas
19	diecinueve	400	cuatrocientos/cuatrocientas
20	veinte	500	quinientos/quinientas
21	veintiuno (veintiún, veintiuna)	600	seiscientos/seiscientas
22	veintidós	700	setecientos/setecientas
23	veintitrés	800	ochocientos/ochocientas
24	veinticuatro	900	novecientos/novecientas
25	veinticinco	1000	mil
26	veintiséis	1001	mil (y) uno (un, una)
27	veintisiete	2000	dos mil
28	veintiocho	2500	dos mil quinientos/quinientas
29	veintinueve	1.000.000	un millón
30	treinta		(*in English*: 1,000,000)

EJEMPLOS	EXAMPLES
Vive en el número diez.	He lives at number ten.
en la página diecinueve	on page nineteen
un diez por ciento	10%
un cien por cien(to)	100%

For further explanation of grammatical terms, please see pages viii-xii.

1 | uno, un or una?

➤ Use uno when counting, unless referring to something or someone feminine.

➤ Use un before a masculine noun and una before a feminine noun even when the nouns are plural.

un hombre	one man
una mujer	one woman
treinta y **un** días	thirty-one days
treinta y **una** noches	thirty-one nights
veintiún años	twenty-one years
veintiuna chicas	twenty-one girls

2 | cien or ciento?

➤ Use cien before both masculine and feminine nouns as well as before mil (meaning *thousand*) and millones (meaning *million* in the plural):

cien libros	one hundred books
cien mil hombres	one hundred thousand men
cien millones	one hundred million

➤ Use ciento before other numbers.

ciento un perros	one hundred and one dogs
ciento una ovejas	one hundred and one sheep
ciento cincuenta	one hundred and fifty

i Note that you don't translate the *and* in 101, 220 and so on.

➤ Make doscientos/doscientas, trescientos/trescientas, quinientos/quinientas and so on agree with the noun in question.

doscientas veinte libras	two hundred and twenty pounds
quinientos alumnos	five hundred students

i Note that setecientos and setecientas have no i after the first s. Similarly, novecientos and novecientas have an o rather than the ue you might expect.

3 | Full stop or comma?

➤ Use a full stop, not a comma, to separate thousands and millions in figures.

700.000 (setecientos mil)	700,000 (seven hundred thousand)
5.000.000 (cinco millones)	5,000,000 (five million)

➤ Use a comma instead of a decimal point to show decimals in Spanish.

0,5 (cero coma cinco)	0.5 (nought point five)
3,4 (tres coma cuatro)	3.4 (three point four)

1st	**primero (1º)**, **primer (1er)**, **primera (1ª)**
2nd	**segundo (2º)**, **segunda (2ª)**
3rd	**tercero (3º)**, **tercer (3er)**, **tercera (3ª)**
4th	**cuarto (4º)**, **cuarta (4ª)**
5th	**quinto (5º)**, **quinta (5ª)**
6th	**sexto (6º)**, **sexta (6ª)**
7th	**séptimo (7º)**, **séptima (7ª)**
8th	**octavo (8º)**, **octava (8ª)**
9th	**noveno (9º)**, **novena (9ª)**
10th	**décimo (10º)**, **décima (10ª)**
100th	**centésimo (100º)**, **centésima (100ª)**
101st	**centésimo primero (101º)**, **centésima primera (101ª)**
1000th	**milésimo (1000º)**, **milésima (1000ª)**

EJEMPLOS	EXAMPLES
Vive en el quinto (piso).	He lives on the fifth floor.
Llegó tercero.	He came in third.

Tip

Shorten **primero** (meaning *first*) to **primer**, and **tercero** (meaning *third*) to **tercer** before a <u>masculine singular noun</u>.

su <u>primer</u> cumpleaños	his first birthday
el <u>tercer</u> premio	the third prize

---

[i] Note that when you are writing these numbers in figures, don't write *1st*, *2nd*, *3rd* as in English. Use **1º**, **1ª**, **1er**, **2º**, **2ª** and **3º**, **3ª**, **3er** as required by the noun.

la **2ª** lección	the 2nd lesson
el **3er** premio	the 3rd prize

---

[4] **primero, segundo, tercero or uno, dos, tres?**

➤ Apart from **primero** (meaning *first*) up to **décimo** (meaning *tenth*), as well as **centésimo** (meaning *one hundredth*) and **milésimo** (meaning *one thousandth*), the ordinal numbers tend not to be used very much in Spanish. Cardinal numbers (ordinary numbers) are used instead.

Carlos <u>tercero</u>	Carlos the third
Alfonso <u>trece</u>	Alfonso the thirteenth

⇨ *For numbers used in dates, see page 211.*

LA HORA	THE TIME
¿Qué hora es?	**What time is it?**
Es la una menos veinte.	It's twenty to one.
Es la una menos cuarto.	It's (a) quarter to one.
Es la una.	It's one o'clock.
Es la una y diez.	It's ten past one.
Es la una y cuarto.	It's (a) quarter past one.
Es la una y media.	It's half past one.
Son las dos menos veinticinco.	It's twenty-five to two.
Son las dos menos cuarto.	It's (a) quarter to two.
Son las dos.	It's two o'clock.
Son las dos y diez.	It's ten past two.
Son las dos y cuarto.	It's (a) quarter past two.
Son las dos y media.	It's half past two.
Son las tres.	It's three o'clock.

Típ

Use **son las** for all times not involving **una** (meaning *one*).

¿A qué hora?	**At what time?**
a medianoche	at midnight
a mediodía	at midday
a la una (del mediodía)	at one o'clock (in the afternoon)
a las ocho (de la tarde)	at eight o'clock (in the evening)
a las 9:25 *or* **a las nueve (y) veinticinco**	at nine twenty-five
a las 16:50 *or* **a las dieciséis (y) cincuenta**	at 16:50 *or* sixteen fifty

Note that in Spanish, as in English, you can also tell the time using the figures you see on a digital clock or watch or on a 24-hour timetable.

LA FECHA	THE DATE
Los días de la semana	**The days of the week**
lunes	Monday
martes	Tuesday
miércoles	Wednesday
jueves	Thursday
viernes	Friday
sábado	Saturday
domingo	Sunday

¿Cuándo?	When?
el lunes	on Monday
los lunes	on Mondays
todos los lunes	every Monday
el martes pasado	last Tuesday
el viernes que viene	next Friday
el sábado que viene no, el otro	a week on Saturday
dentro de tres sábados	two weeks on Saturday

i Note that days of the week <u>DON'T</u> have a capital letter in Spanish.

Los meses	Months of the year
enero	January
febrero	February
marzo	March
abril	April
mayo	May
junio	June
julio	July
agosto	August
septiembre	September
octubre	October
noviembre	November
diciembre	December

¿Cuándo?	When?
en febrero	in February
el 1 *or* **uno de diciembre**	on December 1st *or* first December
en 1998 (mil novecientos noventa y ocho)	in 1998 (nineteen ninety-eight)
el 15 de diciembre de 2003	on 15th December, 2003
el año dos mil	(the year) two thousand
dos mil cinco	two thousand and five

¿Qué día es hoy?	What day is it today?
Es...	It's...
lunes 26 de febrero	Monday, 26th February
domingo 1 de octubre	Sunday, 1st October
lunes veintiséis de febrero	Monday, the twenty-sixth of February
domingo uno de octubre	Sunday, the first of October

i Note that months of the year are <u>DON'T</u> have a capital letter in Spanish.

For further explanation of grammatical terms, please see pages viii-xii.

Tip

Although in English we use *first, second, third* and so on in dates, in Spanish you use the equivalent of *one, two, three* and so on.

el dos de mayo   the second of May

FRASES ÚTILES	**USEFUL PHRASES**
¿Cuándo?	**When?**
hoy	today
esta mañana	this morning
esta tarde	this afternoon
esta noche	this evening
¿Con qué frecuencia?	**How often?**
todos los días	every day
cada dos días	every other day
una vez por semana	once a week
dos veces por semana	twice a week
una vez al mes	once a month
¿Cuándo pasó?	**When did it happen?**
por la mañana	in the morning
por la noche	in the evening
ayer	yesterday
ayer por la mañana	yesterday morning
ayer por la tarde	yesterday afternoon/evening
ayer por la noche	yesterday evening/last night
anoche	last night
anteayer	the day before yesterday
hace una semana	a week ago
hace quince días	two weeks ago
la semana pasada	last week
el año pasado	last year
¿Cuándo va a pasar?	**When is it going to happen?**
mañana	tomorrow
mañana por la mañana	tomorrow morning
mañana por la tarde	tomorrow afternoon/evening
mañana por la noche	tomorrow evening/night
pasado mañana	the day after tomorrow
dentro de dos días	in two days' time
dentro de una semana	in a week's time
dentro de quince días	in two weeks' time
el mes que viene	next month
el año que viene	next year

MAIN INDEX

Introduction

The **Verb Tables** in the following section contain 83 tables of Spanish verbs (some regular and some irregular) in alphabetical order. Each table shows you the following forms: **Present, Preterite, Future, Present Subjunctive, Imperfect, Conditional, Imperative** and the **Past Participle** and **Gerund**. For more information on these tenses, how they are formed, when they are used and so on, you should look at the section on **Verbs** in the main text on pages 69–156.

In order to help you use the verbs shown in Verb Tables correctly, there are also a number of example phrases at the bottom of each page to show the verb as it is used in context.

In Spanish there are both **regular** verbs (their forms follow the normal rules) and **irregular** verbs (their forms do not follow the normal rules). The regular verbs in these tables are:

hablar (regular -**ar** verb, Verb Table 39)
comer (regular -**er** verb, Verb Table 16)
vivir (regular -**ir** verb, Verb Table 81)

The irregular verbs are shown in full.

The **Verb Index** at the end of this section contains over 1200 verbs, each of which is cross-referred to one of the verbs given in the Verb Tables. The table shows the patterns that the verb listed in the index follows.

abolir (to abolish)

PRESENT

(nosotros/as)	abolimos
(vosotros/as)	abolís

* Present tense only used in persons shown

PRESENT SUBJUNCTIVE

not used

PRETERITE

(yo)	abolí
(tú)	aboliste
(él/ella/usted)	abolió
(nosotros/as)	abolimos
(vosotros/as)	abolisteis
(ellos/ellas/ustedes)	abolieron

IMPERFECT

(yo)	abolía
(tú)	abolías
(él/ella/usted)	abolía
(nosotros/as)	abolíamos
(vosotros/as)	abolíais
(ellos/ellas/ustedes)	abolían

FUTURE

(yo)	aboliré
(tú)	abolirás
(él/ella/usted)	abolirá
(nosotros/as)	aboliremos
(vosotros/as)	aboliréis
(ellos/ellas/ustedes)	abolirán

CONDITIONAL

(yo)	aboliría
(tú)	abolirías
(él/ella/usted)	aboliría
(nosotros/as)	aboliríamos
(vosotros/as)	aboliríais
(ellos/ellas/ustedes)	abolirían

IMPERATIVE

abolid

PAST PARTICIPLE

abolido

GERUND

aboliendo

EXAMPLE PHRASES

Hay que **abolirlo**. It ought to be abolished.
Han abolido la pena de muerte. They have abolished the death penalty.
Abolieron la esclavitud. They abolished slavery.

▶ **abrir** (to open)

PRESENT

(yo)	abro
(tú)	abres
(él/ella/usted)	abre
(nosotros/as)	abrimos
(vosotros/as)	abrís
(ellos/ellas/ustedes)	abren

PRESENT SUBJUNCTIVE

(yo)	abra
(tú)	abras
(él/ella/usted)	abra
(nosotros/as)	abramos
(vosotros/as)	abráis
(ellos/ellas/ustedes)	abran

PRETERITE

(yo)	abrí
(tú)	abriste
(él/ella/usted)	abrió
(nosotros/as)	abrimos
(vosotros/as)	abristeis
(ellos/ellas/ustedes)	abrieron

IMPERFECT

(yo)	abría
(tú)	abrías
(él/ella/usted)	abría
(nosotros/as)	abríamos
(vosotros/as)	abríais
(ellos/ellas/ustedes)	abrían

FUTURE

(yo)	abriré
(tú)	abrirás
(él/ella/usted)	abrirá
(nosotros/as)	abriremos
(vosotros/as)	abriréis
(ellos/ellas/ustedes)	abrirán

CONDITIONAL

(yo)	abriría
(tú)	abrirías
(él/ella/usted)	abriría
(nosotros/as)	abriríamos
(vosotros/as)	abriríais
(ellos/ellas/ustedes)	abrirían

IMPERATIVE

abre / abrid

PAST PARTICIPLE

abierto

GERUND

abriendo

EXAMPLE PHRASES

No **abras** ese grifo. Don't turn on that tap.
Han abierto un restaurante cerca de aquí. They've opened a new restaurant near here.
Abrirán todas las puertas de la catedral. They'll open all the doors of the cathedral.

Remember that subject pronouns are not used very often in Spanish.

▶ actuar (to act)

PRESENT

(yo)	actúo
(tú)	actúas
(él/ella/usted)	actúa
(nosotros/as)	actuamos
(vosotros/as)	actuáis
(ellos/ellas/ustedes)	actúan

PRESENT SUBJUNCTIVE

(yo)	actúe
(tú)	actúes
(él/ella/usted)	actúe
(nosotros/as)	actuemos
(vosotros/as)	actuéis
(ellos/ellas/ustedes)	actúen

PRETERITE

(yo)	actué
(tú)	actuaste
(él/ella/usted)	actuó
(nosotros/as)	actuamos
(vosotros/as)	actuasteis
(ellos/ellas/ustedes)	actuaron

IMPERFECT

(yo)	actuaba
(tú)	actuabas
(él/ella/usted)	actuaba
(nosotros/as)	actuábamos
(vosotros/as)	actuabais
(ellos/ellas/ustedes)	actuaban

FUTURE

(yo)	actuaré
(tú)	actuarás
(él/ella/usted)	actuará
(nosotros/as)	actuaremos
(vosotros/as)	actuaréis
(ellos/ellas/ustedes)	actuarán

CONDITIONAL

(yo)	actuaría
(tú)	actuarías
(él/ella/usted)	actuaría
(nosotros/as)	actuaríamos
(vosotros/as)	actuaríais
(ellos/ellas/ustedes)	actuarían

IMPERATIVE

actúa / actuad

PAST PARTICIPLE

actuado

GERUND

actuando

EXAMPLE PHRASES

Actúa *de una forma muy rara.* He's acting very strangely.
Actuó *en varias películas.* He was in several films.
¿Quién **actuará** *en su próxima película?* Who will be in his next film?

▶ adquirir (to acquire)

PRESENT		PRESENT SUBJUNCTIVE	
(yo)	adquiero	(yo)	adquiera
(tú)	adquieres	(tú)	adquieras
(él/ella/usted)	adquiere	(él/ella/usted)	adquiera
(nosotros/as)	adquirimos	(nosotros/as)	adquiramos
(vosotros/as)	adquirís	(vosotros/as)	adquiráis
(ellos/ellas/ustedes)	adquieren	(ellos/ellas/ustedes)	adquieran

PRETERITE		IMPERFECT	
(yo)	adquirí	(yo)	adquiría
(tú)	adquiriste	(tú)	adquirías
(él/ella/usted)	adquirió	(él/ella/usted)	adquiría
(nosotros/as)	adquirimos	(nosotros/as)	adquiríamos
(vosotros/as)	adquiristeis	(vosotros/as)	adquiríais
(ellos/ellas/ustedes)	adquirieron	(ellos/ellas/ustedes)	adquirían

FUTURE		CONDITIONAL	
(yo)	adquiriré	(yo)	adquiriría
(tú)	adquirirás	(tú)	adquirirías
(él/ella/usted)	adquirirá	(él/ella/usted)	adquiriría
(nosotros/as)	adquiriremos	(nosotros/as)	adquiriríamos
(vosotros/as)	adquiriréis	(vosotros/as)	adquiriríais
(ellos/ellas/ustedes)	adquirirán	(ellos/ellas/ustedes)	adquirirían

IMPERATIVE

adquiere / adquirid

PAST PARTICIPLE

adquirido

GERUND

adquiriendo

EXAMPLE PHRASES

Hemos adquirido una colección de sellos. We've bought a stamp collection.
Al final **adquirirán** los derechos de publicación. They will get the publishing rights in the end.
¿Lo **adquirirías** por ese precio? Would you buy it for that price?

Remember that subject pronouns are not used very often in Spanish.

► **almorzar** (to have lunch)

PRESENT

(yo)	almuerzo
(tú)	almuerzas
(él/ella/usted)	almuerza
(nosotros/as)	almorzamos
(vosotros/as)	almorzáis
(ellos/ellas/ustedes)	almuerzan

PRESENT SUBJUNCTIVE

(yo)	almuerce
(tú)	almuerces
(él/ella/usted)	almuerce
(nosotros/as)	almorcemos
(vosotros/as)	almorcéis
(ellos/ellas/ustedes)	almuercen

PRETERITE

(yo)	almorcé
(tú)	almorzaste
(él/ella/usted)	almorzó
(nosotros/as)	almorzamos
(vosotros/as)	almorzasteis
(ellos/ellas/ustedes)	almorzaron

IMPERFECT

(yo)	almorzaba
(tú)	almorzabas
(él/ella/usted)	almorzaba
(nosotros/as)	almorzábamos
(vosotros/as)	almorzabais
(ellos/ellas/ustedes)	almorzaban

FUTURE

(yo)	almorzaré
(tú)	almorzarás
(él/ella/usted)	almorzará
(nosotros/as)	almorzaremos
(vosotros/as)	almorzaréis
(ellos/ellas/ustedes)	almorzarán

CONDITIONAL

(yo)	almorzaría
(tú)	almorzarías
(él/ella/usted)	almorzaría
(nosotros/as)	almorzaríamos
(vosotros/as)	almorzaríais
(ellos/ellas/ustedes)	almorzarían

IMPERATIVE

almuerza / almorzad

PAST PARTICIPLE

almorzado

GERUND

almorzando

EXAMPLE PHRASES

*¿A qué hora **almuerzas**?* What time do you have lunch?
***Almorcé** en un bar.* I had lunch in a bar.
*Mañana **almorzaremos** todos juntos.* We'll all have lunch together tomorrow.

Remember that subject pronouns are not used very often in Spanish.

▶ andar (to walk)

PRESENT

(yo)	ando
(tú)	andas
(él/ella/usted)	anda
(nosotros/as)	andamos
(vosotros/as)	andáis
(ellos/ellas/ustedes)	andan

PRESENT SUBJUNCTIVE

(yo)	ande
(tú)	andes
(él/ella/usted)	ande
(nosotros/as)	andemos
(vosotros/as)	andéis
(ellos/ellas/ustedes)	anden

PRETERITE

(yo)	anduve
(tú)	anduviste
(él/ella/usted)	anduvo
(nosotros/as)	anduvimos
(vosotros/as)	anduvisteis
(ellos/ellas/ustedes)	anduvieron

IMPERFECT

(yo)	andaba
(tú)	andabas
(él/ella/usted)	andaba
(nosotros/as)	andábamos
(vosotros/as)	andabais
(ellos/ellas/ustedes)	andaban

FUTURE

(yo)	andaré
(tú)	andarás
(él/ella/usted)	andará
(nosotros/as)	andaremos
(vosotros/as)	andaréis
(ellos/ellas/ustedes)	andarán

CONDITIONAL

(yo)	andaría
(tú)	andarías
(él/ella/usted)	andaría
(nosotros/as)	andaríamos
(vosotros/as)	andaríais
(ellos/ellas/ustedes)	andarían

IMPERATIVE

anda / andad

PAST PARTICIPLE

andado

GERUND

andando

EXAMPLE PHRASES

Voy andando al trabajo todos los días. I walk to work every day.
Anduvimos al menos 10 km. We walked at least 10 km.
No sé por dónde **andará**. I don't know where he will be.

Remember that subject pronouns are not used very often in Spanish.

▶ aunar (to join together)

PRESENT

(yo)	aúno
(tú)	aúnas
(él/ella/usted)	aúna
(nosotros/as)	aunamos
(vosotros/as)	aunáis
(ellos/ellas/ustedes)	aúnan

PRESENT SUBJUNCTIVE

(yo)	aúne
(tú)	aúnes
(él/ella/usted)	aúne
(nosotros/as)	aunemos
(vosotros/as)	aunéis
(ellos/ellas/ustedes)	aúnen

PRETERITE

(yo)	auné
(tú)	aunaste
(él/ella/usted)	aunó
(nosotros/as)	aunamos
(vosotros/as)	aunasteis
(ellos/ellas/ustedes)	aunaron

IMPERFECT

(yo)	aunaba
(tú)	aunabas
(él/ella/usted)	aunaba
(nosotros/as)	aunábamos
(vosotros/as)	aunabais
(ellos/ellas/ustedes)	aunaban

FUTURE

(yo)	aunaré
(tú)	aunarás
(él/ella/usted)	aunará
(nosotros/as)	aunaremos
(vosotros/as)	aunaréis
(ellos/ellas/ustedes)	aunarán

CONDITIONAL

(yo)	aunaría
(tú)	aunarías
(él/ella/usted)	aunaría
(nosotros/as)	aunaríamos
(vosotros/as)	aunaríais
(ellos/ellas/ustedes)	aunarían

IMPERATIVE

aúna / aunad

PAST PARTICIPLE

aunado

GERUND

aunando

EXAMPLE PHRASES

*El candidato **aúna** experiencia y entusiasmo.* The candidate has both experience and enthusiasm.
*Han **aúnado** fuerzas para combatir la violencia.* They've joined forces to combat violence.
*Este organismo **aunará** a todos los países europeos.* This organization will bring together all the countries of Europe.

Remember that subject pronouns are not used very often in Spanish.

▶ avergonzar (to shame)

PRESENT

(yo)	avergüenzo
(tú)	avergüenzas
(él/ella/usted)	avergüenza
(nosotros/as)	avergonzamos
(vosotros/as)	avergonzáis
(ellos/ellas/ustedes)	avergüenzan

PRESENT SUBJUNCTIVE

(yo)	avergüence
(tú)	avergüences
(él/ella/usted)	avergüence
(nosotros/as)	avergoncemos
(vosotros/as)	avergoncéis
(ellos/ellas/ustedes)	avergüencen

PRETERITE

(yo)	avergoncé
(tú)	avergonzaste
(él/ella/usted)	avergonzó
(nosotros/as)	avergonzamos
(vosotros/as)	avergonzasteis
(ellos/ellas/ustedes)	avergonzaron

IMPERFECT

(yo)	avergonzaba
(tú)	avergonzabas
(él/ella/usted)	avergonzaba
(nosotros/as)	avergonzábamos
(vosotros/as)	avergonzabais
(ellos/ellas/ustedes)	avergonzaban

FUTURE

(yo)	avergonzaré
(tú)	avergonzarás
(él/ella/usted)	avergonzará
(nosotros/as)	avergonzaremos
(vosotros/as)	avergonzaréis
(ellos/ellas/ustedes)	avergonzarán

CONDITIONAL

(yo)	avergonzaría
(tú)	avergonzarías
(él/ella/usted)	avergonzaría
(nosotros/as)	avergonzaríamos
(vosotros/as)	avergonzaríais
(ellos/ellas/ustedes)	avergonzarían

IMPERATIVE

avergüenza / avergonzad

PAST PARTICIPLE

avergonzado

GERUND

avergonzando

EXAMPLE PHRASES

No **me avergüenzo** de nada. I'm not ashamed of anything.
Cuando me lo dijo **me avergoncé.** I was embarrassed when he told me.
Te **avergonzarás** de eso. You'll be ashamed of that.
Su actitud **avergonzó** a sus padres. His attitude embarrassed his parents.

Remember that subject pronouns are not used very often in Spanish.

▶ averiguar (to find out)

PRESENT

(yo)	averiguo
(tú)	averiguas
(él/ella/usted)	averigua
(nosotros/as)	averiguamos
(vosotros/as)	averiguáis
(ellos/ellas/ustedes)	averiguan

PRESENT SUBJUNCTIVE

(yo)	averigüe
(tú)	averigües
(él/ella/usted)	averigüe
(nosotros/as)	averigüemos
(vosotros/as)	averigüéis
(ellos/ellas/ustedes)	averigüen

PRETERITE

(yo)	averigüé
(tú)	averiguaste
(él/ella/usted)	averiguó
(nosotros/as)	averiguamos
(vosotros/as)	averiguasteis
(ellos/ellas/ustedes)	averiguaron

IMPERFECT

(yo)	averiguaba
(tú)	averiguabas
(él/ella/usted)	averiguaba
(nosotros/as)	averiguábamos
(vosotros/as)	averiguabais
(ellos/ellas/ustedes)	averiguaban

FUTURE

(yo)	averiguaré
(tú)	averiguarás
(él/ella/usted)	averiguará
(nosotros/as)	averiguaremos
(vosotros/as)	averiguaréis
(ellos/ellas/ustedes)	averiguarán

CONDITIONAL

(yo)	averiguaría
(tú)	averiguarías
(él/ella/usted)	averiguaría
(nosotros/as)	averiguaríamos
(vosotros/as)	averiguaríais
(ellos/ellas/ustedes)	averiguarían

IMPERATIVE

averigua / averiguad

PAST PARTICIPLE

averiguado

GERUND

averiguando

EXAMPLE PHRASES

¿Cuándo lo averiguaron? When did they find out?
Lo averiguaré pronto. I'll find out soon.
En cuanto lo averigüe te lo digo. I'll tell you as soon as I find out.

▶ bendecir (to bless)

PRESENT

(yo)	bendigo
(tú)	bendices
(él/ella/usted)	bendice
(nosotros/as)	bendecimos
(vosotros/as)	bendecís
(ellos/ellas/ustedes)	bendicen

PRESENT SUBJUNCTIVE

(yo)	bendiga
(tú)	bendigas
(él/ella/usted)	bendiga
(nosotros/as)	bendigamos
(vosotros/as)	bendigáis
(ellos/ellas/ustedes)	bendigan

PRETERITE

(yo)	bendije
(tú)	bendijiste
(él/ella/usted)	bendijo
(nosotros/as)	bendijimos
(vosotros/as)	bendijisteis
(ellos/ellas/ustedes)	bendijeron

IMPERFECT

(yo)	bendecía
(tú)	bendecías
(él/ella/usted)	bendecía
(nosotros/as)	bendecíamos
(vosotros/as)	bendecíais
(ellos/ellas/ustedes)	bendecían

FUTURE

(yo)	bendeciré
(tú)	bendecirás
(él/ella/usted)	bendecirá
(nosotros/as)	bendeciremos
(vosotros/as)	bendeciréis
(ellos/ellas/ustedes)	bendecirán

CONDITIONAL

(yo)	bendeciría
(tú)	bendecirías
(él/ella/usted)	bendeciría
(nosotros/as)	bendeciríamos
(vosotros/as)	bendeciríais
(ellos/ellas/ustedes)	bendecirían

IMPERATIVE

bendice / bendecid

PAST PARTICIPLE

bendecido

GERUND

bendiciendo

EXAMPLE PHRASES

*Dios te **bendiga**.* God bless you!
*El sacerdote **ha bendecido** la nueva tienda.* The priest has blessed the new shop.
*Mi padre **bendijo** la comida.* My father said grace.

Remember that subject pronouns are not used very often in Spanish.

▶ caber (to fit)

PRESENT

(yo)	quepo
(tú)	cabes
(él/ella/usted)	cabe
(nosotros/as)	cabemos
(vosotros/as)	cabéis
(ellos/ellas/ustedes)	caben

PRESENT SUBJUNCTIVE

(yo)	quepa
(tú)	quepas
(él/ella/usted)	quepa
(nosotros/as)	quepamos
(vosotros/as)	quepáis
(ellos/ellas/ustedes)	quepan

PRETERITE

(yo)	cupe
(tú)	cupiste
(él/ella/usted)	cupo
(nosotros/as)	cupimos
(vosotros/as)	cupisteis
(ellos/ellas/ustedes)	cupieron

IMPERFECT

(yo)	cabía
(tú)	cabías
(él/ella/usted)	cabía
(nosotros/as)	cabíamos
(vosotros/as)	cabíais
(ellos/ellas/ustedes)	cabían

FUTURE

(yo)	cabré
(tú)	cabrás
(él/ella/usted)	cabrá
(nosotros/as)	cabremos
(vosotros/as)	cabréis
(ellos/ellas/ustedes)	cabrán

CONDITIONAL

(yo)	cabría
(tú)	cabrías
(él/ella/usted)	cabría
(nosotros/as)	cabríamos
(vosotros/as)	cabríais
(ellos/ellas/ustedes)	cabrían

IMPERATIVE

cabe / cabed

PAST PARTICIPLE

cabido

GERUND

cabiendo

EXAMPLE PHRASES

*Aquí no **cabe**.* There's not enough room here for it.
*No **cabíamos** todos.* There wasn't enough room for all of us.
*¿Crees que **cabrá**?* Do you think there will be enough room for it?

▶ caer (to fall)

PRESENT

(yo)	caigo
(tú)	caes
(él/ella/usted)	cae
(nosotros/as)	caemos
(vosotros/as)	caéis
(ellos/ellas/ustedes)	caen

PRESENT SUBJUNCTIVE

(yo)	caiga
(tú)	caigas
(él/ella/usted)	caiga
(nosotros/as)	caigamos
(vosotros/as)	caigáis
(ellos/ellas/ustedes)	caigan

PRETERITE

(yo)	caí
(tú)	caíste
(él/ella/usted)	cayó
(nosotros/as)	caímos
(vosotros/as)	caísteis
(ellos/ellas/ustedes)	cayeron

IMPERFECT

(yo)	caía
(tú)	caías
(él/ella/usted)	caía
(nosotros/as)	caíamos
(vosotros/as)	caíais
(ellos/ellas/ustedes)	caían

FUTURE

(yo)	caeré
(tú)	caerás
(él/ella/usted)	caerá
(nosotros/as)	caeremos
(vosotros/as)	caeréis
(ellos/ellas/ustedes)	caerán

CONDITIONAL

(yo)	caería
(tú)	caerías
(él/ella/usted)	caería
(nosotros/as)	caeríamos
(vosotros/as)	caeríais
(ellos/ellas/ustedes)	caerían

IMPERATIVE

cae / caed

PAST PARTICIPLE

caído

GERUND

cayendo

EXAMPLE PHRASES

Me caí por las escaleras. I fell down the stairs.
Ese edificio se está cayendo. That building is falling down.
Se me ha caído un guante. I've dropped one of my gloves.

Remember that subject pronouns are not used very often in Spanish.

▶ **cocer** (to boil)

PRESENT

(yo)	cuezo
(tú)	cueces
(él/ella/usted)	cuece
(nosotros/as)	cocemos
(vosotros/as)	cocéis
(ellos/ellas/ustedes)	cuecen

PRESENT SUBJUNCTIVE

(yo)	cueza
(tú)	cuezas
(él/ella/usted)	cueza
(nosotros/as)	cozamos
(vosotros/as)	cozáis
(ellos/ellas/ustedes)	cuezan

PRETERITE

(yo)	cocí
(tú)	cociste
(él/ella/usted)	coció
(nosotros/as)	cocimos
(vosotros/as)	cocisteis
(ellos/ellas/ustedes)	cocieron

IMPERFECT

(yo)	cocía
(tú)	cocías
(él/ella/usted)	cocía
(nosotros/as)	cocíamos
(vosotros/as)	cocíais
(ellos/ellas/ustedes)	cocían

FUTURE

(yo)	coceré
(tú)	cocerás
(él/ella/usted)	cocerá
(nosotros/as)	coceremos
(vosotros/as)	coceréis
(ellos/ellas/ustedes)	cocerán

CONDITIONAL

(yo)	cocería
(tú)	cocerías
(él/ella/usted)	cocería
(nosotros/as)	coceríamos
(vosotros/as)	coceríais
(ellos/ellas/ustedes)	cocerían

IMPERATIVE

cuece / coced

PAST PARTICIPLE

cocido

GERUND

cociendo

EXAMPLE PHRASES

Cuécelo *a fuego lento.* Cook it over a gentle heat.
Aquí nos **estamos cociendo.** It's boiling in here.
No lo **cuezas** *demasiado.* Don't overcook it.

Remember that subject pronouns are not used very often in Spanish.

▶ **coger** (to catch)

PRESENT

(yo)	cojo
(tú)	coges
(él/ella/usted)	coge
(nosotros/as)	cogemos
(vosotros/as)	cogéis
(ellos/ellas/ustedes)	cogen

PRESENT SUBJUNCTIVE

(yo)	coja
(tú)	cojas
(él/ella/usted)	coja
(nosotros/as)	cojamos
(vosotros/as)	cojáis
(ellos/ellas/ustedes)	cojan

PRETERITE

(yo)	cogí
(tú)	cogiste
(él/ella/usted)	cogió
(nosotros/as)	cogimos
(vosotros/as)	cogisteis
(ellos/ellas/ustedes)	cogieron

IMPERFECT

(yo)	cogía
(tú)	cogías
(él/ella/usted)	cogía
(nosotros/as)	cogíamos
(vosotros/as)	cogíais
(ellos/ellas/ustedes)	cogían

FUTURE

(yo)	cogeré
(tú)	cogerás
(él/ella/usted)	cogerá
(nosotros/as)	cogeremos
(vosotros/as)	cogeréis
(ellos/ellas/ustedes)	cogerán

CONDITIONAL

(yo)	cogería
(tú)	cogerías
(él/ella/usted)	cogería
(nosotros/as)	cogeríamos
(vosotros/as)	cogeríais
(ellos/ellas/ustedes)	cogerían

IMPERATIVE

coge / coged

PAST PARTICIPLE

cogido

GERUND

cogiendo

EXAMPLE PHRASES

La **cogí** entre mis brazos. I took her in my arms.
Estuvimos cogiendo setas. We were picking mushrooms.
¿Por qué no **coges** el tren de las seis? Why don't you get the six o'clock train?

Remember that subject pronouns are not used very often in Spanish.

▶ **comer** (to eat)

PRESENT

(yo)	como
(tú)	comes
(él/ella/usted)	come
(nosotros/as)	comemos
(vosotros/as)	coméis
(ellos/ellas/ustedes)	comen

PRESENT SUBJUNCTIVE

(yo)	coma
(tú)	comas
(él/ella/usted)	coma
(nosotros/as)	comamos
(vosotros/as)	comáis
(ellos/ellas/ustedes)	coman

PRETERITE

(yo)	comí
(tú)	comiste
(él/ella/usted)	comió
(nosotros/as)	comimos
(vosotros/as)	comisteis
(ellos/ellas/ustedes)	comieron

IMPERFECT

(yo)	comía
(tú)	comías
(él/ella/usted)	comía
(nosotros/as)	comíamos
(vosotros/as)	comíais
(ellos/ellas/ustedes)	comían

FUTURE

(yo)	comeré
(tú)	comerás
(él/ella/usted)	comerá
(nosotros/as)	comeremos
(vosotros/as)	comeréis
(ellos/ellas/ustedes)	comerán

CONDITIONAL

(yo)	comería
(tú)	comerías
(él/ella/usted)	comería
(nosotros/as)	comeríamos
(vosotros/as)	comeríais
(ellos/ellas/ustedes)	comerían

IMPERATIVE

come / comed

PAST PARTICIPLE

comido

GERUND

comiendo

EXAMPLE PHRASES

No **come** carne. He doesn't eat meat.
No **comas** tan deprisa. Don't eat so fast.
Se ha comido todo. He's eaten it all.

Remember that subject pronouns are not used very often in Spanish.

▶ **conducir** (to drive, to lead)

PRESENT

(yo)	conduzco
(tú)	conduces
(él/ella/usted)	conduce
(nosotros/as)	conducimos
(vosotros/as)	conducís
(ellos/ellas/ustedes)	conducen

PRESENT SUBJUNCTIVE

(yo)	conduzca
(tú)	conduzcas
(él/ella/usted)	conduzca
(nosotros/as)	conduzcamos
(vosotros/as)	conduzcáis
(ellos/ellas/ustedes)	conduzcan

PRETERITE

(yo)	conduje
(tú)	condujiste
(él/ella/usted)	condujo
(nosotros/as)	condujimos
(vosotros/as)	condujisteis
(ellos/ellas/ustedes)	condujeron

IMPERFECT

(yo)	conducía
(tú)	conducías
(él/ella/usted)	conducía
(nosotros/as)	conducíamos
(vosotros/as)	conducíais
(ellos/ellas/ustedes)	conducían

FUTURE

(yo)	conduciré
(tú)	conducirás
(él/ella/usted)	conducirá
(nosotros/as)	conduciremos
(vosotros/as)	conduciréis
(ellos/ellas/ustedes)	conducirán

CONDITIONAL

(yo)	conduciría
(tú)	conducirías
(él/ella/usted)	conduciría
(nosotros/as)	conduciríamos
(vosotros/as)	conduciríais
(ellos/ellas/ustedes)	conducirían

IMPERATIVE

conduce / conducid

PAST PARTICIPLE

conducido

GERUND

conduciendo

EXAMPLE PHRASES

Conduces muy bien. You are a really good driver.
¿*Condujiste* tú? Was it you driving?
Él los *conducirá* a la mesa. He'll show you to your table.

Remember that subject pronouns are not used very often in Spanish.

▶ **construir** (to build)

PRESENT

(yo)	construyo
(tú)	construyes
(él/ella/usted)	construye
(nosotros/as)	construimos
(vosotros/as)	construís
(ellos/ellas/ustedes)	construyen

PRESENT SUBJUNCTIVE

(yo)	construya
(tú)	construyas
(él/ella/usted)	construya
(nosotros/as)	construyamos
(vosotros/as)	construyáis
(ellos/ellas/ustedes)	construyan

PRETERITE

(yo)	construí
(tú)	construiste
(él/ella/usted)	construyó
(nosotros/as)	construimos
(vosotros/as)	construisteis
(ellos/ellas/ustedes)	construyeron

IMPERFECT

(yo)	construía
(tú)	construías
(él/ella/usted)	construía
(nosotros/as)	construíamos
(vosotros/as)	construíais
(ellos/ellas/ustedes)	construían

FUTURE

(yo)	construiré
(tú)	construirás
(él/ella/usted)	construirá
(nosotros/as)	construiremos
(vosotros/as)	construiréis
(ellos/ellas/ustedes)	construirán

CONDITIONAL

(yo)	construiría
(tú)	construirías
(él/ella/usted)	construiría
(nosotros/as)	construiríamos
(vosotros/as)	construiríais
(ellos/ellas/ustedes)	construirían

IMPERATIVE

construye / construid

PAST PARTICIPLE

construido

GERUND

construyendo

EXAMPLE PHRASES

Están construyendo una escuela. They are building a new school.
Yo solo construí el puzzle. I did the jigsaw puzzle on my own.
Aquí construirán una autopista. They're going to build a new motorway here.

Remember that subject pronouns are not used very often in Spanish.

▶ contar (to tell, to count)

PRESENT

(yo)	cuento
(tú)	cuentas
(él/ella/usted)	cuenta
(nosotros/as)	contamos
(vosotros/as)	contáis
(ellos/ellas/ustedes)	cuentan

PRESENT SUBJUNCTIVE

(yo)	cuente
(tú)	cuentes
(él/ella/usted)	cuente
(nosotros/as)	contemos
(vosotros/as)	contéis
(ellos/ellas/ustedes)	cuenten

PRETERITE

(yo)	conté
(tú)	contaste
(él/ella/usted)	contó
(nosotros/as)	contamos
(vosotros/as)	contasteis
(ellos/ellas/ustedes)	contaron

IMPERFECT

(yo)	contaba
(tú)	contabas
(él/ella/usted)	contaba
(nosotros/as)	contábamos
(vosotros/as)	contabais
(ellos/ellas/ustedes)	contaban

FUTURE

(yo)	contaré
(tú)	contarás
(él/ella/usted)	contará
(nosotros/as)	contaremos
(vosotros/as)	contaréis
(ellos/ellas/ustedes)	contarán

CONDITIONAL

(yo)	contaría
(tú)	contarías
(él/ella/usted)	contaría
(nosotros/as)	contaríamos
(vosotros/as)	contaríais
(ellos/ellas/ustedes)	contarían

IMPERATIVE

cuenta / contad

PAST PARTICIPLE

contado

GERUND

contando

EXAMPLE PHRASES

*Venga, **cuéntamelo**.* Come on, tell me.
*Nos **contó** un secreto.* He told us a secret.
*Prométeme que no se lo **contarás** a nadie.* Promise you won't tell anyone.

Remember that subject pronouns are not used very often in Spanish.

▶ **crecer** (to grow)

PRESENT

(yo)	crezco
(tú)	creces
(él/ella/usted)	crece
(nosotros/as)	crecemos
(vosotros/as)	crecéis
(ellos/ellas/ustedes)	crecen

PRESENT SUBJUNCTIVE

(yo)	crezca
(tú)	crezcas
(él/ella/usted)	crezca
(nosotros/as)	crezcamos
(vosotros/as)	crezcáis
(ellos/ellas/ustedes)	crezcan

PRETERITE

(yo)	crecí
(tú)	creciste
(él/ella/usted)	creció
(nosotros/as)	crecimos
(vosotros/as)	crecisteis
(ellos/ellas/ustedes)	crecieron

IMPERFECT

(yo)	crecía
(tú)	crecías
(él/ella/usted)	crecía
(nosotros/as)	crecíamos
(vosotros/as)	crecíais
(ellos/ellas/ustedes)	crecían

FUTURE

(yo)	creceré
(tú)	crecerás
(él/ella/usted)	crecerá
(nosotros/as)	creceremos
(vosotros/as)	creceréis
(ellos/ellas/ustedes)	crecerán

CONDITIONAL

(yo)	crecería
(tú)	crecerías
(él/ella/usted)	crecería
(nosotros/as)	creceríamos
(vosotros/as)	creceríais
(ellos/ellas/ustedes)	crecerían

IMPERATIVE

crece / creced

PAST PARTICIPLE

crecido

GERUND

creciendo

EXAMPLE PHRASES

Esas plantas **crecen** *en Chile.* Those plants grow in Chile.
Crecimos *juntos.* We grew up together.
Cuando **crezca,** *ya verás.* You'll see, when he grows up.

▶ **cruzar** (to cross)

PRESENT

(yo)	cruzo
(tú)	cruzas
(él/ella/usted)	cruza
(nosotros/as)	cruzamos
(vosotros/as)	cruzáis
(ellos/ellas/ustedes)	cruzan

PRESENT SUBJUNCTIVE

(yo)	cruce
(tú)	cruces
(él/ella/usted)	cruce
(nosotros/as)	crucemos
(vosotros/as)	crucéis
(ellos/ellas/ustedes)	crucen

PRETERITE

(yo)	crucé
(tú)	cruzaste
(él/ella/usted)	cruzó
(nosotros/as)	cruzamos
(vosotros/as)	cruzasteis
(ellos/ellas/ustedes)	cruzaron

IMPERFECT

(yo)	cruzaba
(tú)	cruzabas
(él/ella/usted)	cruzaba
(nosotros/as)	cruzábamos
(vosotros/as)	cruzabais
(ellos/ellas/ustedes)	cruzaban

FUTURE

(yo)	cruzaré
(tú)	cruzarás
(él/ella/usted)	cruzará
(nosotros/as)	cruzaremos
(vosotros/as)	cruzaréis
(ellos/ellas/ustedes)	cruzarán

CONDITIONAL

(yo)	cruzaría
(tú)	cruzarías
(él/ella/usted)	cruzaría
(nosotros/as)	cruzaríamos
(vosotros/as)	cruzaríais
(ellos/ellas/ustedes)	cruzarían

IMPERATIVE

cruza / cruzad

PAST PARTICIPLE

cruzado

GERUND

cruzando

EXAMPLE PHRASES

No **cruces** la calle con el semáforo en rojo. Don't cross the road when the signal's at red.
Cruzaron la carretera. They crossed the road.
Hace tiempo que no **me cruzo** con él. I haven't seen him for a long time.

Remember that subject pronouns are not used very often in Spanish.

▶ cubrir (to cover)

PRESENT

(yo)	cubro
(tú)	cubres
(él/ella/usted)	cubre
(nosotros/as)	cubrimos
(vosotros/as)	cubrís
(ellos/ellas/ustedes)	cubren

PRESENT SUBJUNCTIVE

(yo)	cubra
(tú)	cubras
(él/ella/usted)	cubra
(nosotros/as)	cubramos
(vosotros/as)	cubráis
(ellos/ellas/ustedes)	cubran

PRETERITE

(yo)	cubrí
(tú)	cubriste
(él/ella/usted)	cubrió
(nosotros/as)	cubrimos
(vosotros/as)	cubristeis
(ellos/ellas/ustedes)	cubrieron

IMPERFECT

(yo)	cubría
(tú)	cubrías
(él/ella/usted)	cubría
(nosotros/as)	cubríamos
(vosotros/as)	cubríais
(ellos/ellas/ustedes)	cubrían

FUTURE

(yo)	cubriré
(tú)	cubrirás
(él/ella/usted)	cubrirá
(nosotros/as)	cubriremos
(vosotros/as)	cubriréis
(ellos/ellas/ustedes)	cubrirán

CONDITIONAL

(yo)	cubriría
(tú)	cubrirías
(él/ella/usted)	cubriría
(nosotros/as)	cubriríamos
(vosotros/as)	cubriríais
(ellos/ellas/ustedes)	cubrirían

IMPERATIVE

cubre / cubrid

PAST PARTICIPLE

cubierto

GERUND

cubriendo

EXAMPLE PHRASES

*Lo **cubrieron** con una manta.* They covered him with a blanket.
***Estaba** todo **cubierto** de nieve.* Everything was covered in snow.
*Se **cubrió** de gloria.* He covered himself in glory.

▶ **dar** (to give)

PRESENT

(yo)	doy
(tú)	das
(él/ella/usted)	da
(nosotros/as)	damos
(vosotros/as)	dais
(ellos/ellas/ustedes)	dan

PRESENT SUBJUNCTIVE

(yo)	dé
(tú)	des
(él/ella/usted)	dé
(nosotros/as)	demos
(vosotros/as)	deis
(ellos/ellas/ustedes)	den

PRETERITE

(yo)	di
(tú)	diste
(él/ella/usted)	dio
(nosotros/as)	dimos
(vosotros/as)	disteis
(ellos/ellas/ustedes)	dieron

IMPERFECT

(yo)	daba
(tú)	dabas
(él/ella/usted)	daba
(nosotros/as)	dábamos
(vosotros/as)	dabais
(ellos/ellas/ustedes)	daban

FUTURE

(yo)	daré
(tú)	darás
(él/ella/usted)	dará
(nosotros/as)	daremos
(vosotros/as)	daréis
(ellos/ellas/ustedes)	darán

CONDITIONAL

(yo)	daría
(tú)	darías
(él/ella/usted)	daría
(nosotros/as)	daríamos
(vosotros/as)	daríais
(ellos/ellas/ustedes)	darían

IMPERATIVE

da / dad

PAST PARTICIPLE

dado

GERUND

dando

EXAMPLE PHRASES

Me **da** miedo la oscuridad. I'm scared of the dark.
Nos **dieron** un par de entradas gratis. They gave us a couple of free tickets.
Te **daré** el número de mi móvil. I'll give you my mobile-phone number.

Remember that subject pronouns are not used very often in Spanish.

▶ **decir** (to say)

PRESENT

(yo)	digo
(tú)	dices
(él/ella/usted)	dice
(nosotros/as)	decimos
(vosotros/as)	decís
(ellos/ellas/ustedes)	dicen

PRESENT SUBJUNCTIVE

(yo)	diga
(tú)	digas
(él/ella/usted)	diga
(nosotros/as)	digamos
(vosotros/as)	digáis
(ellos/ellas/ustedes)	digan

PRETERITE

(yo)	dije
(tú)	dijiste
(él/ella/usted)	dijo
(nosotros/as)	dijimos
(vosotros/as)	dijisteis
(ellos/ellas/ustedes)	dijeron

IMPERFECT

(yo)	decía
(tú)	decías
(él/ella/usted)	decía
(nosotros/as)	decíamos
(vosotros/as)	decíais
(ellos/ellas/ustedes)	decían

FUTURE

(yo)	diré
(tú)	dirás
(él/ella/usted)	dirá
(nosotros/as)	diremos
(vosotros/as)	diréis
(ellos/ellas/ustedes)	dirán

CONDITIONAL

(yo)	diría
(tú)	dirías
(él/ella/usted)	diría
(nosotros/as)	diríamos
(vosotros/as)	diríais
(ellos/ellas/ustedes)	dirían

IMPERATIVE

di / decid

PAST PARTICIPLE

dicho

GERUND

diciendo

EXAMPLE PHRASES

*Pero ¿qué **dices**?* What are you saying?
*Me lo **dijo** ayer.* He told me yesterday.
*¿Te **ha dicho** lo de la boda?* Has he told you about the wedding?

Remember that subject pronouns are not used very often in Spanish.

▶ **dirigir** (to direct)

PRESENT

(yo)	dirijo
(tú)	diriges
(él/ella/usted)	dirige
(nosotros/as)	dirigimos
(vosotros/as)	dirigís
(ellos/ellas/ustedes)	dirigen

PRESENT SUBJUNCTIVE

(yo)	dirija
(tú)	dirijas
(él/ella/usted)	dirija
(nosotros/as)	dirijamos
(vosotros/as)	dirijáis
(ellos/ellas/ustedes)	dirijan

PRETERITE

(yo)	dirigí
(tú)	dirigiste
(él/ella/usted)	dirigió
(nosotros/as)	dirigimos
(vosotros/as)	dirigisteis
(ellos/ellas/ustedes)	dirigieron

IMPERFECT

(yo)	dirigía
(tú)	dirigías
(él/ella/usted)	dirigía
(nosotros/as)	dirigíamos
(vosotros/as)	dirigíais
(ellos/ellas/ustedes)	dirigían

FUTURE

(yo)	dirigiré
(tú)	dirigirás
(él/ella/usted)	dirigirá
(nosotros/as)	dirigiremos
(vosotros/as)	dirigiréis
(ellos/ellas/ustedes)	dirigirán

CONDITIONAL

(yo)	dirigiría
(tú)	dirigirías
(él/ella/usted)	dirigiría
(nosotros/as)	dirigiríamos
(vosotros/as)	dirigiríais
(ellos/ellas/ustedes)	dirigirían

IMPERATIVE

dirige / dirigid

PAST PARTICIPLE

dirigido

GERUND

dirigiendo

EXAMPLE PHRASES

Dirijo esta empresa desde hace dos años. I've been running this company for two years.

Hace días que no me **dirige** la palabra. He hasn't spoken to me for days.

Se **dirigía** a la parada del autobús. He was making his way to the bus stop.

Remember that subject pronouns are not used very often in Spanish.

▶ distinguir (to distinguish)

PRESENT

(yo)	distingo
(tú)	distingues
(él/ella/usted)	distingue
(nosotros/as)	distinguimos
(vosotros/as)	distinguís
(ellos/ellas/ustedes)	distinguen

PRESENT SUBJUNCTIVE

(yo)	distinga
(tú)	distingas
(él/ella/usted)	distinga
(nosotros/as)	distingamos
(vosotros/as)	distingáis
(ellos/ellas/ustedes)	distingan

PRETERITE

(yo)	distinguí
(tú)	distinguiste
(él/ella/usted)	distinguió
(nosotros/as)	distinguimos
(vosotros/as)	distinguisteis
(ellos/ellas/ustedes)	distinguieron

IMPERFECT

(yo)	distinguía
(tú)	distinguías
(él/ella/usted)	distinguía
(nosotros/as)	distinguíamos
(vosotros/as)	distinguíais
(ellos/ellas/ustedes)	distinguían

FUTURE

(yo)	distinguiré
(tú)	distinguirás
(él/ella/usted)	distinguirá
(nosotros/as)	distinguiremos
(vosotros/as)	distinguiréis
(ellos/ellas/ustedes)	distinguirán

CONDITIONAL

(yo)	distinguiría
(tú)	distinguirías
(él/ella/usted)	distinguiría
(nosotros/as)	distinguiríamos
(vosotros/as)	distinguiríais
(ellos/ellas/ustedes)	distinguirían

IMPERATIVE

distingue / distinguid

PAST PARTICIPLE

distinguido

GERUND

distinguiendo

EXAMPLE PHRASES

No lo **distingo** del azul. I can't tell the difference between it and the blue one.
Se **distinguía** desde lejos. You could see it from the distance.
No los **distinguiría**. I wouldn't be able to tell them apart.

Remember that subject pronouns are not used very often in Spanish.

▶ dormir (to sleep)

PRESENT

(yo)	duermo
(tú)	duermes
(él/ella/usted)	duerme
(nosotros/as)	dormimos
(vosotros/as)	dormís
(ellos/ellas/ustedes)	duermen

PRESENT SUBJUNCTIVE

(yo)	duerma
(tú)	duermas
(él/ella/usted)	duerma
(nosotros/as)	durmamos
(vosotros/as)	durmáis
(ellos/ellas/ustedes)	duerman

PRETERITE

(yo)	dormí
(tú)	dormiste
(él/ella/usted)	durmió
(nosotros/as)	dormimos
(vosotros/as)	dormisteis
(ellos/ellas/ustedes)	durmieron

IMPERFECT

(yo)	dormía
(tú)	dormías
(él/ella/usted)	dormía
(nosotros/as)	dormíamos
(vosotros/as)	dormíais
(ellos/ellas/ustedes)	dormían

FUTURE

(yo)	dormiré
(tú)	dormirás
(él/ella/usted)	dormirá
(nosotros/as)	dormiremos
(vosotros/as)	dormiréis
(ellos/ellas/ustedes)	dormirán

CONDITIONAL

(yo)	dormiría
(tú)	dormirías
(él/ella/usted)	dormiría
(nosotros/as)	dormiríamos
(vosotros/as)	dormiríais
(ellos/ellas/ustedes)	dormirían

IMPERATIVE

duerme / dormid

PAST PARTICIPLE

dormido

GERUND

durmiendo

EXAMPLE PHRASES

No **duermo** muy bien. I don't sleep very well.
Nos dormimos en el cine. We fell asleep at the cinema.
Durmió durante doce horas. He slept for twelve hours.

Remember that subject pronouns are not used very often in Spanish.

▶ **elegir** (to choose)

PRESENT

(yo)	elijo
(tú)	eliges
(él/ella/usted)	elige
(nosotros/as)	elegimos
(vosotros/as)	elegís
(ellos/ellas/ustedes)	eligen

PRESENT SUBJUNCTIVE

(yo)	elija
(tú)	elijas
(él/ella/usted)	elija
(nosotros/as)	elijamos
(vosotros/as)	elijáis
(ellos/ellas/ustedes)	elijan

PRETERITE

(yo)	elegí
(tú)	elegiste
(él/ella/usted)	eligió
(nosotros/as)	elegimos
(vosotros/as)	elegisteis
(ellos/ellas/ustedes)	eligieron

IMPERFECT

(yo)	elegía
(tú)	elegías
(él/ella/usted)	elegía
(nosotros/as)	elegíamos
(vosotros/as)	elegíais
(ellos/ellas/ustedes)	elegían

FUTURE

(yo)	elegiré
(tú)	elegirás
(él/ella/usted)	elegirá
(nosotros/as)	elegiremos
(vosotros/as)	elegiréis
(ellos/ellas/ustedes)	elegirán

CONDITIONAL

(yo)	elegiría
(tú)	elegirías
(él/ella/usted)	elegiría
(nosotros/as)	elegiríamos
(vosotros/as)	elegiríais
(ellos/ellas/ustedes)	elegirían

IMPERATIVE

elige / elegid

PAST PARTICIPLE

elegido

GERUND

eligiendo

EXAMPLE PHRASES

*Nosotros no **elegimos** a nuestros padres, ni ellos nos **eligen** a nosotros.* We don't choose our parents and neither do they choose us.
*Creo que **ha elegido** bien.* I think he's made a good choice.
*No lo **eligieron** ellos.* It wasn't they who chose it.

Remember that subject pronouns are not used very often in Spanish.

▶ empezar (to begin)

PRESENT

(yo)	empiezo
(tú)	empiezas
(él/ella/usted)	empieza
(nosotros/as)	empezamos
(vosotros/as)	empezáis
(ellos/ellas/ustedes)	empiezan

PRESENT SUBJUNCTIVE

(yo)	empiece
(tú)	empieces
(él/ella/usted)	empiece
(nosotros/as)	empecemos
(vosotros/as)	empecéis
(ellos/ellas/ustedes)	empiecen

PRETERITE

(yo)	empecé
(tú)	empezaste
(él/ella/usted)	empezó
(nosotros/as)	empezamos
(vosotros/as)	empezasteis
(ellos/ellas/ustedes)	empezaron

IMPERFECT

(yo)	empezaba
(tú)	empezabas
(él/ella/usted)	empezaba
(nosotros/as)	empezábamos
(vosotros/as)	empezabais
(ellos/ellas/ustedes)	empezaban

FUTURE

(yo)	empezaré
(tú)	empezarás
(él/ella/usted)	empezará
(nosotros/as)	empezaremos
(vosotros/as)	empezaréis
(ellos/ellas/ustedes)	empezarán

CONDITIONAL

(yo)	empezaría
(tú)	empezarías
(él/ella/usted)	empezaría
(nosotros/as)	empezaríamos
(vosotros/as)	empezaríais
(ellos/ellas/ustedes)	empezarían

IMPERATIVE

empieza / empezad

PAST PARTICIPLE

empezado

GERUND

empezando

EXAMPLE PHRASES

Empieza por aquí. Start here.
¿Cuándo **empiezas** a trabajar en el sitio nuevo? When do you start work at the new place?
La semana que viene **empezaremos** un curso nuevo. We'll start a new course next week.

Remember that subject pronouns are not used very often in Spanish.

▶ **entender** (to understand)

PRESENT

(yo)	entiendo
(tú)	entiendes
(él/ella/usted)	entiende
(nosotros/as)	entendemos
(vosotros/as)	entendéis
(ellos/ellas/ustedes)	entienden

PRESENT SUBJUNCTIVE

(yo)	entienda
(tú)	entiendas
(él/ella/usted)	entienda
(nosotros/as)	entendamos
(vosotros/as)	entendáis
(ellos/ellas/ustedes)	entiendan

PRETERITE

(yo)	entendí
(tú)	entendiste
(él/ella/usted)	entendió
(nosotros/as)	entendimos
(vosotros/as)	entendisteis
(ellos/ellas/ustedes)	entendieron

IMPERFECT

(yo)	entendía
(tú)	entendías
(él/ella/usted)	entendía
(nosotros/as)	entendíamos
(vosotros/as)	entendíais
(ellos/ellas/ustedes)	entendían

FUTURE

(yo)	entenderé
(tú)	entenderás
(él/ella/usted)	entenderá
(nosotros/as)	entenderemos
(vosotros/as)	entenderéis
(ellos/ellas/ustedes)	entenderán

CONDITIONAL

(yo)	entendería
(tú)	entenderías
(él/ella/usted)	entendería
(nosotros/as)	entenderíamos
(vosotros/as)	entenderíais
(ellos/ellas/ustedes)	entenderían

IMPERATIVE

entiende / entended

PAST PARTICIPLE

entendido

GERUND

entendiendo

EXAMPLE PHRASES

*No lo **entiendo**.* I don't understand.
*¿**Entendiste** lo que dijo?* Did you understand what she said?
*Con el tiempo lo **entenderás**.* You'll understand one day.

Remember that subject pronouns are not used very often in Spanish.

▶ **enviar** (to send)

PRESENT

(yo)	envío
(tú)	envías
(él/ella/usted)	envía
(nosotros/as)	enviamos
(vosotros/as)	enviáis
(ellos/ellas/ustedes)	envían

PRESENT SUBJUNCTIVE

(yo)	envíe
(tú)	envíes
(él/ella/usted)	envíe
(nosotros/as)	enviemos
(vosotros/as)	enviéis
(ellos/ellas/ustedes)	envíen

PRETERITE

(yo)	envié
(tú)	enviaste
(él/ella/usted)	envió
(nosotros/as)	enviamos
(vosotros/as)	enviasteis
(ellos/ellas/ustedes)	enviaron

IMPERFECT

(yo)	enviaba
(tú)	enviabas
(él/ella/usted)	enviaba
(nosotros/as)	enviábamos
(vosotros/as)	enviabais
(ellos/ellas/ustedes)	enviaban

FUTURE

(yo)	enviaré
(tú)	enviarás
(él/ella/usted)	enviará
(nosotros/as)	enviaremos
(vosotros/as)	enviaréis
(ellos/ellas/ustedes)	enviarán

CONDITIONAL

(yo)	enviaría
(tú)	enviarías
(él/ella/usted)	enviaría
(nosotros/as)	enviaríamos
(vosotros/as)	enviaríais
(ellos/ellas/ustedes)	enviarían

IMPERATIVE

envía / enviad

PAST PARTICIPLE

enviado

GERUND

enviando

EXAMPLE PHRASES

Envíe todos sus datos personales. Send all your personal details.
La han **enviado** a Guatemala. They've sent her to Guatemala.
Nos **enviarán** más información. They'll send us further information.

Remember that subject pronouns are not used very often in Spanish.

▶ erguir (to erect)

PRESENT

(yo)	yergo
(tú)	yergues
(él/ella/usted)	yergue
(nosotros/as)	erguimos
(vosotros/as)	erguís
(ellos/ellas/ustedes)	yerguen

PRESENT SUBJUNCTIVE

(yo)	yerga
(tú)	yergas
(él/ella/usted)	yerga
(nosotros/as)	irgamos
(vosotros/as)	irgáis
(ellos/ellas/ustedes)	yergan

PRETERITE

(yo)	erguí
(tú)	erguiste
(él/ella/usted)	irguió
(nosotros/as)	erguimos
(vosotros/as)	erguisteis
(ellos/ellas/ustedes)	irguieron

IMPERFECT

(yo)	erguía
(tú)	erguías
(él/ella/usted)	erguía
(nosotros/as)	erguíamos
(vosotros/as)	erguíais
(ellos/ellas/ustedes)	erguían

FUTURE

(yo)	erguiré
(tú)	erguirás
(él/ella/usted)	erguirá
(nosotros/as)	erguiremos
(vosotros/as)	erguiréis
(ellos/ellas/ustedes)	erguirán

CONDITIONAL

(yo)	erguiría
(tú)	erguirías
(él/ella/usted)	erguiría
(nosotros/as)	erguiríamos
(vosotros/as)	erguiríais
(ellos/ellas/ustedes)	erguirían

IMPERATIVE

yergue / erguid

PAST PARTICIPLE

erguido

GERUND

irguiendo

EXAMPLE PHRASES

Irguió la cabeza con orgullo. She lifted her head up proudly.
El rascacielos se erguía sobre la ciudad. The skyscraper towered over the city.
Erguirán dos nuevas torres en el centro. They're going to put up two new tower
  blocks in the centre.

Remember that subject pronouns are not used very often in Spanish.

▶ **errar** (to err)

PRESENT

(yo)	yerro
(tú)	yerras
(él/ella/usted)	yerra
(nosotros/as)	erramos
(vosotros/as)	erráis
(ellos/ellas/ustedes)	yerran

PRESENT SUBJUNCTIVE

(yo)	yerre
(tú)	yerres
(él/ella/usted)	yerre
(nosotros/as)	erremos
(vosotros/as)	erréis
(ellos/ellas/ustedes)	yerren

PRETERITE

(yo)	erré
(tú)	erraste
(él/ella/usted)	erró
(nosotros/as)	erramos
(vosotros/as)	errasteis
(ellos/ellas/ustedes)	erraron

IMPERFECT

(yo)	erraba
(tú)	errabas
(él/ella/usted)	erraba
(nosotros/as)	errábamos
(vosotros/as)	errabais
(ellos/ellas/ustedes)	erraban

FUTURE

(yo)	erraré
(tú)	errarás
(él/ella/usted)	errará
(nosotros/as)	erraremos
(vosotros/as)	erraréis
(ellos/ellas/ustedes)	errarán

CONDITIONAL

(yo)	erraría
(tú)	errarías
(él/ella/usted)	erraría
(nosotros/as)	erraríamos
(vosotros/as)	erraríais
(ellos/ellas/ustedes)	errarían

IMPERATIVE

yerra / errad

PAST PARTICIPLE

errado

GERUND

errando

EXAMPLE PHRASES

Erró todas las preguntas. He got all the questions wrong.
Erró el tiro. He missed the shot.
*Ha **errado** el camino.* He's lost his way.

Remember that subject pronouns are not used very often in Spanish.

▶ escribir (to write)

PRESENT

(yo)	escribo
(tú)	escribes
(él/ella/usted)	escribe
(nosotros/as)	escribimos
(vosotros/as)	escribís
(ellos/ellas/ustedes)	escriben

PRESENT SUBJUNCTIVE

(yo)	escriba
(tú)	escribas
(él/ella/usted)	escriba
(nosotros/as)	escribamos
(vosotros/as)	escribáis
(ellos/ellas/ustedes)	escriban

PRETERITE

(yo)	escribí
(tú)	escribiste
(él/ella/usted)	escribió
(nosotros/as)	escribimos
(vosotros/as)	escribisteis
(ellos/ellas/ustedes)	escribieron

IMPERFECT

(yo)	escribía
(tú)	escribías
(él/ella/usted)	escribía
(nosotros/as)	escribíamos
(vosotros/as)	escribíais
(ellos/ellas/ustedes)	escribían

FUTURE

(yo)	escribiré
(tú)	escribirás
(él/ella/usted)	escribirá
(nosotros/as)	escribiremos
(vosotros/as)	escribiréis
(ellos/ellas/ustedes)	escribirán

CONDITIONAL

(yo)	escribiría
(tú)	escribirías
(él/ella/usted)	escribiría
(nosotros/as)	escribiríamos
(vosotros/as)	escribiríais
(ellos/ellas/ustedes)	escribirían

IMPERATIVE

escribe / escribid

PAST PARTICIPLE

escrito

GERUND

escribiendo

EXAMPLE PHRASES

*Eso lo **he escrito** yo.* I've written that.
***Escríbelo** en la pizarra.* Write it on the blackboard.
***Nos escribimos** durante un tiempo.* We wrote to each other for a while.

▶ estar (to be)

PRESENT

(yo)	estoy
(tú)	estás
(él/ella/usted)	está
(nosotros/as)	estamos
(vosotros/as)	estáis
(ellos/ellas/ustedes)	están

PRESENT SUBJUNCTIVE

(yo)	esté
(tú)	estés
(él/ella/usted)	esté
(nosotros/as)	estemos
(vosotros/as)	estéis
(ellos/ellas/ustedes)	estén

PRETERITE

(yo)	estuve
(tú)	estuviste
(él/ella/usted)	estuvo
(nosotros/as)	estuvimos
(vosotros/as)	estuvisteis
(ellos/ellas/ustedes)	estuvieron

IMPERFECT

(yo)	estaba
(tú)	estabas
(él/ella/usted)	estaba
(nosotros/as)	estábamos
(vosotros/as)	estabais
(ellos/ellas/ustedes)	estaban

FUTURE

(yo)	estaré
(tú)	estarás
(él/ella/usted)	estará
(nosotros/as)	estaremos
(vosotros/as)	estaréis
(ellos/ellas/ustedes)	estarán

CONDITIONAL

(yo)	estaría
(tú)	estarías
(él/ella/usted)	estaría
(nosotros/as)	estaríamos
(vosotros/as)	estaríais
(ellos/ellas/ustedes)	estarían

IMPERATIVE

está / estad

PAST PARTICIPLE

estado

GERUND

estando

EXAMPLE PHRASES

Estoy cansado. I'm tired.
Estuvimos en casa de mis padres. We went to my parents.
¿A qué hora *estarás* en casa? What time will you be home?

▶ freír (to fry)

PRESENT

(yo)	frío
(tú)	fríes
(él/ella/usted)	fríe
(nosotros/as)	freímos
(vosotros/as)	freís
(ellos/ellas/ustedes)	fríen

PRESENT SUBJUNCTIVE

(yo)	fría
(tú)	frías
(él/ella/usted)	fría
(nosotros/as)	friamos
(vosotros/as)	friáis
(ellos/ellas/ustedes)	frían

PRETERITE

(yo)	freí
(tú)	freíste
(él/ella/usted)	frió
(nosotros/as)	freímos
(vosotros/as)	freísteis
(ellos/ellas/ustedes)	frieron

IMPERFECT

(yo)	freía
(tú)	freías
(él/ella/usted)	freía
(nosotros/as)	freíamos
(vosotros/as)	freíais
(ellos/ellas/ustedes)	freían

FUTURE

(yo)	freiré
(tú)	freirás
(él/ella/usted)	freirá
(nosotros/as)	freiremos
(vosotros/as)	freiréis
(ellos/ellas/ustedes)	freirán

CONDITIONAL

(yo)	freiría
(tú)	freirías
(él/ella/usted)	freiría
(nosotros/as)	freiríamos
(vosotros/as)	freiríais
(ellos/ellas/ustedes)	freirían

IMPERATIVE

fríe / freíd

PAST PARTICIPLE

frito

GERUND

friendo

EXAMPLE PHRASES

Fríelo en esta sartén. Fry it in this pan.
He frito el pescado. I've fried the fish.
Nos freíamos de calor. We were roasting in the heat.

▶ **gruñir** (to grunt)

PRESENT

(yo)	gruño
(tú)	gruñes
(él/ella/usted)	gruñe
(nosotros/as)	gruñimos
(vosotros/as)	gruñís
(ellos/ellas/ustedes)	gruñen

PRESENT SUBJUNCTIVE

(yo)	gruña
(tú)	gruñas
(él/ella/usted)	gruña
(nosotros/as)	gruñamos
(vosotros/as)	gruñáis
(ellos/ellas/ustedes)	gruñan

PRETERITE

(yo)	gruñí
(tú)	gruñiste
(él/ella/usted)	gruñó
(nosotros/as)	gruñimos
(vosotros/as)	gruñisteis
(ellos/ellas/ustedes)	gruñeron

IMPERFECT

(yo)	gruñía
(tú)	gruñías
(él/ella/usted)	gruñía
(nosotros/as)	gruñíamos
(vosotros/as)	gruñíais
(ellos/ellas/ustedes)	gruñían

FUTURE

(yo)	gruñiré
(tú)	gruñirás
(él/ella/usted)	gruñirá
(nosotros/as)	gruñiremos
(vosotros/as)	gruñiréis
(ellos/ellas/ustedes)	gruñirán

CONDITIONAL

(yo)	gruñiría
(tú)	gruñirías
(él/ella/usted)	gruñiría
(nosotros/as)	gruñiríamos
(vosotros/as)	gruñiríais
(ellos/ellas/ustedes)	gruñirían

IMPERATIVE

gruñe / gruñid

PAST PARTICIPLE

gruñido

GERUND

gruñendo

EXAMPLE PHRASES

*Siempre **está gruñendo**.* He's always grumbling.
*¡No **gruñas**!.* Don't grumble!
*No creo que el oso nos **gruña**.* I don't think the bear will growl at us.

Remember that subject pronouns are not used very often in Spanish.

▶ **haber** (to have (auxiliary))

PRESENT

(yo)	he
(tú)	has
(él/ella/usted)	ha
(nosotros/as)	hemos
(vosotros/as)	habéis
(ellos/ellas/ustedes)	han

PRESENT SUBJUNCTIVE

(yo)	haya
(tú)	hayas
(él/ella/usted)	haya
(nosotros/as)	hayamos
(vosotros/as)	hayáis
(ellos/ellas/ustedes)	hayan

PRETERITE

(yo)	hube
(tú)	hubiste
(él/ella/usted)	hubo
(nosotros/as)	hubimos
(vosotros/as)	hubisteis
(ellos/ellas/ustedes)	hubieron

IMPERFECT

(yo)	había
(tú)	habías
(él/ella/usted)	había
(nosotros/as)	habíamos
(vosotros/as)	habíais
(ellos/ellas/ustedes)	habían

FUTURE

(yo)	habré
(tú)	habrás
(él/ella/usted)	habrá
(nosotros/as)	habremos
(vosotros/as)	habréis
(ellos/ellas/ustedes)	habrán

CONDITIONAL

(yo)	habría
(tú)	habrías
(él/ella/usted)	habría
(nosotros/as)	habríamos
(vosotros/as)	habríais
(ellos/ellas/ustedes)	habrían

IMPERATIVE

not used

PAST PARTICIPLE

habido

GERUND

habiendo

EXAMPLE PHRASES

¿Has visto eso? Did you see that?
Ya hemos ido a ver esa película. We've already been to see that film.
Eso nunca había pasado antes. That had never happened before.

Remember that subject pronouns are not used very often in Spanish.

▶ **hablar** (to speak, to talk)

PRESENT

(yo)	hablo
(tú)	hablas
(él/ella/usted)	habla
(nosotros/as)	hablamos
(vosotros/as)	habláis
(ellos/ellas/ustedes)	hablan

PRESENT SUBJUNCTIVE

(yo)	hable
(tú)	hables
(él/ella/usted)	hable
(nosotros/as)	hablemos
(vosotros/as)	habléis
(ellos/ellas/ustedes)	hablen

PRETERITE

(yo)	hablé
(tú)	hablaste
(él/ella/usted)	habló
(nosotros/as)	hablamos
(vosotros/as)	hablasteis
(ellos/ellas/ustedes)	hablaron

IMPERFECT

(yo)	hablaba
(tú)	hablabas
(él/ella/usted)	hablaba
(nosotros/as)	hablábamos
(vosotros/as)	hablabais
(ellos/ellas/ustedes)	hablaban

FUTURE

(yo)	hablaré
(tú)	hablarás
(él/ella/usted)	hablará
(nosotros/as)	hablaremos
(vosotros/as)	hablaréis
(ellos/ellas/ustedes)	hablarán

CONDITIONAL

(yo)	hablaría
(tú)	hablarías
(él/ella/usted)	hablaría
(nosotros/as)	hablaríamos
(vosotros/as)	hablaríais
(ellos/ellas/ustedes)	hablarían

IMPERATIVE

habla / hablad

PAST PARTICIPLE

hablado

GERUND

hablando

EXAMPLE PHRASES

Hoy **he hablado** con mi hermana. I've spoken to my sister today.
No **hables** tan alto. Don't talk so loud.
No **se hablan.** They don't talk to each other.

Remember that subject pronouns are not used very often in Spanish.

▶ **hacer** (to do, to make)

PRESENT

(yo)	hago
(tú)	haces
(él/ella/usted)	hace
(nosotros/as)	hacemos
(vosotros/as)	hacéis
(ellos/ellas/ustedes)	hacen

PRESENT SUBJUNCTIVE

(yo)	haga
(tú)	hagas
(él/ella/usted)	haga
(nosotros/as)	hagamos
(vosotros/as)	hagáis
(ellos/ellas/ustedes)	hagan

PRETERITE

(yo)	hice
(tú)	hiciste
(él/ella/usted)	hizo
(nosotros/as)	hicimos
(vosotros/as)	hicisteis
(ellos/ellas/ustedes)	hicieron

IMPERFECT

(yo)	hacía
(tú)	hacías
(él/ella/usted)	hacía
(nosotros/as)	hacíamos
(vosotros/as)	hacíais
(ellos/ellas/ustedes)	hacían

FUTURE

(yo)	haré
(tú)	harás
(él/ella/usted)	hará
(nosotros/as)	haremos
(vosotros/as)	haréis
(ellos/ellas/ustedes)	harán

CONDITIONAL

(yo)	haría
(tú)	harías
(él/ella/usted)	haría
(nosotros/as)	haríamos
(vosotros/as)	haríais
(ellos/ellas/ustedes)	harían

IMPERATIVE

haz / haced

PAST PARTICIPLE

hecho

GERUND

haciendo

EXAMPLE PHRASES

*Lo **haré** yo mismo.* I'll do it myself.
*¿Quién **hizo** eso?* Who did that?
*Quieres que **haga** las camas?* Do you want me to make the beds?

▶ hay (there is, there are)

PRESENT

hay

PRESENT SUBJUNCTIVE

haya

PRETERITE

hubo

IMPERFECT

había

FUTURE

habrá

CONDITIONAL

habría

IMPERATIVE

not used

PAST PARTICIPLE

habido

GERUND

habiendo

EXAMPLE PHRASES

¿Hay más galletas? Are there any biscuits left?
No había nadie. There wasn't anybody there.
El domingo habrá una manifestación. There will be a demonstration on Sunday.

Remember that subject pronouns are not used very often in Spanish.

▶ ir (to go)

PRESENT

(yo)	voy
(tú)	vas
(él/ella/usted)	va
(nosotros/as)	vamos
(vosotros/as)	vais
(ellos/ellas/ustedes)	van

PRESENT SUBJUNCTIVE

(yo)	vaya
(tú)	vayas
(él/ella/usted)	vaya
(nosotros/as)	vayamos
(vosotros/as)	vayáis
(ellos/ellas/ustedes)	vayan

PRETERITE

(yo)	fui
(tú)	fuiste
(él/ella/usted)	fue
(nosotros/as)	fuimos
(vosotros/as)	fuisteis
(ellos/ellas/ustedes)	fueron

IMPERFECT

(yo)	iba
(tú)	ibas
(él/ella/usted)	iba
(nosotros/as)	íbamos
(vosotros/as)	ibais
(ellos/ellas/ustedes)	iban

FUTURE

(yo)	iré
(tú)	irás
(él/ella/usted)	irá
(nosotros/as)	iremos
(vosotros/as)	iréis
(ellos/ellas/ustedes)	irán

CONDITIONAL

(yo)	iría
(tú)	irías
(él/ella/usted)	iría
(nosotros/as)	iríamos
(vosotros/as)	iríais
(ellos/ellas/ustedes)	irían

IMPERATIVE

ve / id

PAST PARTICIPLE

ido

GERUND

yendo

EXAMPLE PHRASES

¿**Vamos** a comer al campo? Shall we have a picnic in the country?
El domingo **iré** a Edimburgo. I'll go to Edinburgh on Sunday.
Yo no **voy** con ellos. I'm not going with them.

Remember that subject pronouns are not used very often in Spanish.

▶ jugar (to play)

PRESENT

(yo)	juego
(tú)	juegas
(él/ella/usted)	juega
(nosotros/as)	jugamos
(vosotros/as)	jugáis
(ellos/ellas/ustedes)	juegan

PRESENT SUBJUNCTIVE

(yo)	juegue
(tú)	juegues
(él/ella/usted)	juegue
(nosotros/as)	juguemos
(vosotros/as)	juguéis
(ellos/ellas/ustedes)	jueguen

PRETERITE

(yo)	jugué
(tú)	jugaste
(él/ella/usted)	jugó
(nosotros/as)	jugamos
(vosotros/as)	jugasteis
(ellos/ellas/ustedes)	jugaron

IMPERFECT

(yo)	jugaba
(tú)	jugabas
(él/ella/usted)	jugaba
(nosotros/as)	jugábamos
(vosotros/as)	jugabais
(ellos/ellas/ustedes)	jugaban

FUTURE

(yo)	jugaré
(tú)	jugarás
(él/ella/usted)	jugará
(nosotros/as)	jugaremos
(vosotros/as)	jugaréis
(ellos/ellas/ustedes)	jugarán

CONDITIONAL

(yo)	jugaría
(tú)	jugarías
(él/ella/usted)	jugaría
(nosotros/as)	jugaríamos
(vosotros/as)	jugaríais
(ellos/ellas/ustedes)	jugarían

IMPERATIVE

juega / jugad

PAST PARTICIPLE

jugado

GERUND

jugando

EXAMPLE PHRASES

Juego al fútbol todos los domingos. I play football every Sunday.
Están jugando en el jardín. They're playing in the garden.
Jugarán contra el Real Madrid. They'll play Real Madrid.

Remember that subject pronouns are not used very often in Spanish.

▶ leer (to read)

PRESENT

(yo)	leo
(tú)	lees
(él/ella/usted)	lee
(nosotros/as)	leemos
(vosotros/as)	leéis
(ellos/ellas/ustedes)	leen

PRESENT SUBJUNCTIVE

(yo)	lea
(tú)	leas
(él/ella/usted)	lea
(nosotros/as)	leamos
(vosotros/as)	leáis
(ellos/ellas/ustedes)	lean

PRETERITE

(yo)	leí
(tú)	leíste
(él/ella/usted)	leyó
(nosotros/as)	leímos
(vosotros/as)	leísteis
(ellos/ellas/ustedes)	leyeron

IMPERFECT

(yo)	leía
(tú)	leías
(él/ella/usted)	leía
(nosotros/as)	leíamos
(vosotros/as)	leíais
(ellos/ellas/ustedes)	leían

FUTURE

(yo)	leeré
(tú)	leerás
(él/ella/usted)	leerá
(nosotros/as)	leeremos
(vosotros/as)	leeréis
(ellos/ellas/ustedes)	leerán

CONDITIONAL

(yo)	leería
(tú)	leerías
(él/ella/usted)	leería
(nosotros/as)	leeríamos
(vosotros/as)	leeríais
(ellos/ellas/ustedes)	leerían

IMPERATIVE

lee / leed

PAST PARTICIPLE

leído

GERUND

leyendo

EXAMPLE PHRASES

*Hace mucho tiempo que no **leo**.* I haven't read anything for ages.
*¿**Has leído** esta novela?* Have you read this novel?
*Lo **leí** hace tiempo.* I read it a while ago.

Remember that subject pronouns are not used very often in Spanish.

▶ lucir (to shine)

PRESENT

(yo)	luzco
(tú)	luces
(él/ella/usted)	luce
(nosotros/as)	lucimos
(vosotros/as)	lucís
(ellos/ellas/ustedes)	lucen

PRESENT SUBJUNCTIVE

(yo)	luzca
(tú)	luzcas
(él/ella/usted)	luzca
(nosotros/as)	luzcamos
(vosotros/as)	luzcáis
(ellos/ellas/ustedes)	luzcan

PRETERITE

(yo)	lucí
(tú)	luciste
(él/ella/usted)	lució
(nosotros/as)	lucimos
(vosotros/as)	lucisteis
(ellos/ellas/ustedes)	lucieron

IMPERFECT

(yo)	lucía
(tú)	lucías
(él/ella/usted)	lucía
(nosotros/as)	lucíamos
(vosotros/as)	lucíais
(ellos/ellas/ustedes)	lucían

FUTURE

(yo)	luciré
(tú)	lucirás
(él/ella/usted)	lucirá
(nosotros/as)	luciremos
(vosotros/as)	luciréis
(ellos/ellas/ustedes)	lucirán

CONDITIONAL

(yo)	luciría
(tú)	lucirías
(él/ella/usted)	luciría
(nosotros/as)	luciríamos
(vosotros/as)	luciríais
(ellos/ellas/ustedes)	lucirían

IMPERATIVE

luce / lucid

PAST PARTICIPLE

lucido

GERUND

luciendo

EXAMPLE PHRASES

Lucirá un traje muy elegante. She will be wearing a very smart dress.
Se lució en el examen. He excelled in the exam.
Lucían las estrellas. The stars were shining.

Remember that subject pronouns are not used very often in Spanish.

▶ **llover** (to rain)

PRESENT

llueve

PRESENT SUBJUNCTIVE

llueva

PRETERITE

llovió

IMPERFECT

llovía

FUTURE

lloverá

CONDITIONAL

llovería

IMPERATIVE

not used

PAST PARTICIPLE

llovido

GERUND

lloviendo

EXAMPLE PHRASES

Está lloviendo. It's raining.
Llovió sin parar. It rained non-stop.
*Hace semanas que no **llueve**.* It hasn't rained for weeks.

Remember that subject pronouns are not used very often in Spanish.

▶ morir (to die)

PRESENT

(yo)	muero
(tú)	mueres
(él/ella/usted)	muere
(nosotros/as)	morimos
(vosotros/as)	morís
(ellos/ellas/ustedes)	mueren

PRESENT SUBJUNCTIVE

(yo)	muera
(tú)	mueras
(él/ella/usted)	muera
(nosotros/as)	muramos
(vosotros/as)	muráis
(ellos/ellas/ustedes)	mueran

PRETERITE

(yo)	morí
(tú)	moriste
(él/ella/usted)	murió
(nosotros/as)	morimos
(vosotros/as)	moristeis
(ellos/ellas/ustedes)	murieron

IMPERFECT

(yo)	moría
(tú)	morías
(él/ella/usted)	moría
(nosotros/as)	moríamos
(vosotros/as)	moríais
(ellos/ellas/ustedes)	morían

FUTURE

(yo)	moriré
(tú)	morirás
(él/ella/usted)	morirá
(nosotros/as)	moriremos
(vosotros/as)	moriréis
(ellos/ellas/ustedes)	morirán

CONDITIONAL

(yo)	moriría
(tú)	morirías
(él/ella/usted)	moriría
(nosotros/as)	moriríamos
(vosotros/as)	moriríais
(ellos/ellas/ustedes)	morirían

IMPERATIVE

muere / morid

PAST PARTICIPLE

muerto

GERUND

muriendo

EXAMPLE PHRASES

Murió a las cinco de la madrugada. He died at five in the morning.
Cuando **me muera**... When I die...
Se le **ha muerto** el gato. His cat has died.

▶ **mover** (to move)

PRESENT

(yo)	muevo
(tú)	mueves
(él/ella/usted)	mueve
(nosotros/as)	movemos
(vosotros/as)	movéis
(ellos/ellas/ustedes)	mueven

PRESENT SUBJUNCTIVE

(yo)	mueva
(tú)	muevas
(él/ella/usted)	mueva
(nosotros/as)	movamos
(vosotros/as)	mováis
(ellos/ellas/ustedes)	muevan

PRETERITE

(yo)	moví
(tú)	moviste
(él/ella/usted)	movió
(nosotros/as)	movimos
(vosotros/as)	movisteis
(ellos/ellas/ustedes)	movieron

IMPERFECT

(yo)	movía
(tú)	movías
(él/ella/usted)	movía
(nosotros/as)	movíamos
(vosotros/as)	movíais
(ellos/ellas/ustedes)	movían

FUTURE

(yo)	moveré
(tú)	moverás
(él/ella/usted)	moverá
(nosotros/as)	moveremos
(vosotros/as)	moveréis
(ellos/ellas/ustedes)	moverán

CONDITIONAL

(yo)	movería
(tú)	moverías
(él/ella/usted)	movería
(nosotros/as)	moveríamos
(vosotros/as)	moveríais
(ellos/ellas/ustedes)	moverían

IMPERATIVE

mueve / moved

PAST PARTICIPLE

movido

GERUND

moviendo

EXAMPLE PHRASES

Mueve la mesa hacia la derecha. Move the table over to the right.
Se está **moviendo**. It's moving.
No **se movieron** de casa. They didn't leave the house.

Remember that subject pronouns are not used very often in Spanish.

▶ **nacer** (to be born)

PRESENT

(yo)	nazco
(tú)	naces
(él/ella/usted)	nace
(nosotros/as)	nacemos
(vosotros/as)	nacéis
(ellos/ellas/ustedes)	nacen

PRESENT SUBJUNCTIVE

(yo)	nazca
(tú)	nazcas
(él/ella/usted)	nazca
(nosotros/as)	nazcamos
(vosotros/as)	nazcáis
(ellos/ellas/ustedes)	nazcan

PRETERITE

(yo)	nací
(tú)	naciste
(él/ella/usted)	nació
(nosotros/as)	nacimos
(vosotros/as)	nacisteis
(ellos/ellas/ustedes)	nacieron

IMPERFECT

(yo)	nacía
(tú)	nacías
(él/ella/usted)	nacía
(nosotros/as)	nacíamos
(vosotros/as)	nacíais
(ellos/ellas/ustedes)	nacían

FUTURE

(yo)	naceré
(tú)	nacerás
(él/ella/usted)	nacerá
(nosotros/as)	naceremos
(vosotros/as)	naceréis
(ellos/ellas/ustedes)	nacerán

CONDITIONAL

(yo)	nacería
(tú)	nacerías
(él/ella/usted)	nacería
(nosotros/as)	naceríamos
(vosotros/as)	naceríais
(ellos/ellas/ustedes)	nacerían

IMPERATIVE

nace / naced

PAST PARTICIPLE

nacido

GERUND

naciendo

EXAMPLE PHRASES

Nació en 1967. He was born in 1967.
Nacerá el año que viene. It will be born next year.
¿Cuándo *naciste*? When were you born?

Remember that subject pronouns are not used very often in Spanish.

▶ negar (to deny)

PRESENT

(yo)	niego
(tú)	niegas
(él/ella/usted)	niega
(nosotros/as)	negamos
(vosotros/as)	negáis
(ellos/ellas/ustedes)	niegan

PRESENT SUBJUNCTIVE

(yo)	niegue
(tú)	niegues
(él/ella/usted)	niegue
(nosotros/as)	neguemos
(vosotros/as)	neguéis
(ellos/ellas/ustedes)	nieguen

PRETERITE

(yo)	negué
(tú)	negaste
(él/ella/usted)	negó
(nosotros/as)	negamos
(vosotros/as)	negasteis
(ellos/ellas/ustedes)	negaron

IMPERFECT

(yo)	negaba
(tú)	negabas
(él/ella/usted)	negaba
(nosotros/as)	negábamos
(vosotros/as)	negabais
(ellos/ellas/ustedes)	negaban

FUTURE

(yo)	negaré
(tú)	negarás
(él/ella/usted)	negará
(nosotros/as)	negaremos
(vosotros/as)	negaréis
(ellos/ellas/ustedes)	negarán

CONDITIONAL

(yo)	negaría
(tú)	negarías
(él/ella/usted)	negaría
(nosotros/as)	negaríamos
(vosotros/as)	negaríais
(ellos/ellas/ustedes)	negarían

IMPERATIVE

niega / negad

PAST PARTICIPLE

negado

GERUND

negando

EXAMPLE PHRASES

*No lo **niegues**.* Don't deny it.
*Se **negó** a venir con nosotros.* She refused to come with us.
*No me **negarás** que es barato.* You can't say it's not cheap.

Remember that subject pronouns are not used very often in Spanish.

▶ **oír** (to hear)

PRESENT

(yo)	oigo
(tú)	oyes
(él/ella/usted)	oye
(nosotros/as)	oímos
(vosotros/as)	oís
(ellos/ellas/ustedes)	oyen

PRESENT SUBJUNCTIVE

(yo)	oiga
(tú)	oigas
(él/ella/usted)	oiga
(nosotros/as)	oigamos
(vosotros/as)	oigáis
(ellos/ellas/ustedes)	oigan

PRETERITE

(yo)	oí
(tú)	oíste
(él/ella/usted)	oyó
(nosotros/as)	oímos
(vosotros/as)	oísteis
(ellos/ellas/ustedes)	oyeron

IMPERFECT

(yo)	oía
(tú)	oías
(él/ella/usted)	oía
(nosotros/as)	oíamos
(vosotros/as)	oíais
(ellos/ellas/ustedes)	oían

FUTURE

(yo)	oiré
(tú)	oirás
(él/ella/usted)	oirá
(nosotros/as)	oiremos
(vosotros/as)	oiréis
(ellos/ellas/ustedes)	oirán

CONDITIONAL

(yo)	oiría
(tú)	oirías
(él/ella/usted)	oiría
(nosotros/as)	oiríamos
(vosotros/as)	oiríais
(ellos/ellas/ustedes)	oirían

IMPERATIVE

oye / oíd

PAST PARTICIPLE

oído

GERUND

oyendo

EXAMPLE PHRASES

No **oigo** nada. I can't hear anything.
Si no **oyes** bien, ve al médico. If you can't hear properly, go and see the doctor.
¿Has **oído** eso? Did you hear that?

Remember that subject pronouns are not used very often in Spanish.

▶ **oler** (to smell)

PRESENT

(yo)	huelo
(tú)	hueles
(él/ella/usted)	huele
(nosotros/as)	olemos
(vosotros/as)	oléis
(ellos/ellas/ustedes)	huelen

PRESENT SUBJUNCTIVE

(yo)	huela
(tú)	huelas
(él/ella/usted)	huela
(nosotros/as)	olamos
(vosotros/as)	oláis
(ellos/ellas/ustedes)	huelan

PRETERITE

(yo)	olí
(tú)	oliste
(él/ella/usted)	olió
(nosotros/as)	olimos
(vosotros/as)	olisteis
(ellos/ellas/ustedes)	olieron

IMPERFECT

(yo)	olía
(tú)	olías
(él/ella/usted)	olía
(nosotros/as)	olíamos
(vosotros/as)	olíais
(ellos/ellas/ustedes)	olían

FUTURE

(yo)	oleré
(tú)	olerás
(él/ella/usted)	olerá
(nosotros/as)	oleremos
(vosotros/as)	oleréis
(ellos/ellas/ustedes)	olerán

CONDITIONAL

(yo)	olería
(tú)	olerías
(él/ella/usted)	olería
(nosotros/as)	oleríamos
(vosotros/as)	oleríais
(ellos/ellas/ustedes)	olerían

IMPERATIVE

huele / oled

PAST PARTICIPLE

olido

GERUND

oliendo

EXAMPLE PHRASES

Huele a pescado. It smells of fish.
Olía muy bien. It smelled really nice.
Con esto ya no **olerá**. This will take the smell away.

▶ **pagar** (to pay)

PRESENT

(yo)	pago
(tú)	pagas
(él/ella/usted)	paga
(nosotros/as)	pagamos
(vosotros/as)	pagáis
(ellos/ellas/ustedes)	pagan

PRESENT SUBJUNCTIVE

(yo)	pague
(tú)	pagues
(él/ella/usted)	pague
(nosotros/as)	paguemos
(vosotros/as)	paguéis
(ellos/ellas/ustedes)	paguen

PRETERITE

(yo)	pagué
(tú)	pagaste
(él/ella/usted)	pagó
(nosotros/as)	pagamos
(vosotros/as)	pagasteis
(ellos/ellas/ustedes)	pagaron

IMPERFECT

(yo)	pagaba
(tú)	pagabas
(él/ella/usted)	pagaba
(nosotros/as)	pagábamos
(vosotros/as)	pagabais
(ellos/ellas/ustedes)	pagaban

FUTURE

(yo)	pagaré
(tú)	pagarás
(él/ella/usted)	pagará
(nosotros/as)	pagaremos
(vosotros/as)	pagaréis
(ellos/ellas/ustedes)	pagarán

CONDITIONAL

(yo)	pagaría
(tú)	pagarías
(él/ella/usted)	pagaría
(nosotros/as)	pagaríamos
(vosotros/as)	pagaríais
(ellos/ellas/ustedes)	pagarían

IMPERATIVE

paga / pagad

PAST PARTICIPLE

pagado

GERUND

pagando

EXAMPLE PHRASES

¿*Cuánto te* **pagan** *al mes?* How much do they pay you a month?
Lo **pagué** *en efectivo.* I paid for it in cash.
Yo te **pagaré** *la entrada.* I'll pay for your ticket.

Remember that subject pronouns are not used very often in Spanish.

▶ **pedir** (to ask for)

PRESENT

(yo)	pido
(tú)	pides
(él/ella/usted)	pide
(nosotros/as)	pedimos
(vosotros/as)	pedís
(ellos/ellas/ustedes)	piden

PRESENT SUBJUNCTIVE

(yo)	pida
(tú)	pidas
(él/ella/usted)	pida
(nosotros/as)	pidamos
(vosotros/as)	pidáis
(ellos/ellas/ustedes)	pidan

PRETERITE

(yo)	pedí
(tú)	pediste
(él/ella/usted)	pidió
(nosotros/as)	pedimos
(vosotros/as)	pedisteis
(ellos/ellas/ustedes)	pidieron

IMPERFECT

(yo)	pedía
(tú)	pedías
(él/ella/usted)	pedía
(nosotros/as)	pedíamos
(vosotros/as)	pedíais
(ellos/ellas/ustedes)	pedían

FUTURE

(yo)	pediré
(tú)	pedirás
(él/ella/usted)	pedirá
(nosotros/as)	pediremos
(vosotros/as)	pediréis
(ellos/ellas/ustedes)	pedirán

CONDITIONAL

(yo)	pediría
(tú)	pedirías
(él/ella/usted)	pediría
(nosotros/as)	pediríamos
(vosotros/as)	pediríais
(ellos/ellas/ustedes)	pedirían

IMPERATIVE

pide / pedid

PAST PARTICIPLE

pedido

GERUND

pidiendo

EXAMPLE PHRASES

*No nos **pidieron** el pasaporte.* They didn't ask us for our passports.
***Hemos pedido** dos cervezas.* We've ordered two beers.
***Pídele** el teléfono.* Ask her for her telephone number.

Remember that subject pronouns are not used very often in Spanish.

▶ **pensar** (to think)

PRESENT

(yo)	pienso
(tú)	piensas
(él/ella/usted)	piensa
(nosotros/as)	pensamos
(vosotros/as)	pensáis
(ellos/ellas/ustedes)	piensan

PRESENT SUBJUNCTIVE

(yo)	piense
(tú)	pienses
(él/ella/usted)	piense
(nosotros/as)	pensemos
(vosotros/as)	penséis
(ellos/ellas/ustedes)	piensen

PRETERITE

(yo)	pensé
(tú)	pensaste
(él/ella/usted)	pensó
(nosotros/as)	pensamos
(vosotros/as)	pensasteis
(ellos/ellas/ustedes)	pensaron

IMPERFECT

(yo)	pensaba
(tú)	pensabas
(él/ella/usted)	pensaba
(nosotros/as)	pensábamos
(vosotros/as)	pensabais
(ellos/ellas/ustedes)	pensaban

FUTURE

(yo)	pensaré
(tú)	pensarás
(él/ella/usted)	pensará
(nosotros/as)	pensaremos
(vosotros/as)	pensaréis
(ellos/ellas/ustedes)	pensarán

CONDITIONAL

(yo)	pensaría
(tú)	pensarías
(él/ella/usted)	pensaría
(nosotros/as)	pensaríamos
(vosotros/as)	pensaríais
(ellos/ellas/ustedes)	pensarían

IMPERATIVE

piensa / pensad

PAST PARTICIPLE

pensado

GERUND

pensando

EXAMPLE PHRASES

*No lo **pienses** más.* Don't think any more about it.
***Está pensando** en comprarse un piso.* He's thinking of buying a flat.
***Pensaba** que vendrías.* I thought you'd come.

Remember that subject pronouns are not used very often in Spanish.

▶ **poder** (to be able)

PRESENT

(yo)	puedo
(tú)	puedes
(él/ella/usted)	puede
(nosotros/as)	podemos
(vosotros/as)	podéis
(ellos/ellas/ustedes)	pueden

PRESENT SUBJUNCTIVE

(yo)	pueda
(tú)	puedas
(él/ella/usted)	pueda
(nosotros/as)	podamos
(vosotros/as)	podáis
(ellos/ellas/ustedes)	puedan

PRETERITE

(yo)	pude
(tú)	pudiste
(él/ella/usted)	pudo
(nosotros/as)	pudimos
(vosotros/as)	pudisteis
(ellos/ellas/ustedes)	pudieron

IMPERFECT

(yo)	podía
(tú)	podías
(él/ella/usted)	podía
(nosotros/as)	podíamos
(vosotros/as)	podíais
(ellos/ellas/ustedes)	podían

FUTURE

(yo)	podré
(tú)	podrás
(él/ella/usted)	podrá
(nosotros/as)	podremos
(vosotros/as)	podréis
(ellos/ellas/ustedes)	podrán

CONDITIONAL

(yo)	podría
(tú)	podrías
(él/ella/usted)	podría
(nosotros/as)	podríamos
(vosotros/as)	podríais
(ellos/ellas/ustedes)	podrían

IMPERATIVE

puede / poded

PAST PARTICIPLE

podido

GERUND

pudiendo

EXAMPLE PHRASES

¿Puedo entrar? Can I come in?
Puedes venir cuando quieras. You can come when you like.
¿Podrías ayudarme? Could you help me?

Remember that subject pronouns are not used very often in Spanish.

▶ **poner** (to put)

PRESENT

(yo)	pongo
(tú)	pones
(él/ella/usted)	pone
(nosotros/as)	ponemos
(vosotros/as)	ponéis
(ellos/ellas/ustedes)	ponen

PRESENT SUBJUNCTIVE

(yo)	ponga
(tú)	pongas
(él/ella/usted)	ponga
(nosotros/as)	pongamos
(vosotros/as)	pongáis
(ellos/ellas/ustedes)	pongan

PRETERITE

(yo)	puse
(tú)	pusiste
(él/ella/usted)	puso
(nosotros/as)	pusimos
(vosotros/as)	pusisteis
(ellos/ellas/ustedes)	pusieron

IMPERFECT

(yo)	ponía
(tú)	ponías
(él/ella/usted)	ponía
(nosotros/as)	poníamos
(vosotros/as)	poníais
(ellos/ellas/ustedes)	ponían

FUTURE

(yo)	pondré
(tú)	pondrás
(él/ella/usted)	pondrá
(nosotros/as)	pondremos
(vosotros/as)	pondréis
(ellos/ellas/ustedes)	pondrán

CONDITIONAL

(yo)	pondría
(tú)	pondrías
(él/ella/usted)	pondría
(nosotros/as)	pondríamos
(vosotros/as)	pondríais
(ellos/ellas/ustedes)	pondrían

IMPERATIVE

pon / poned

PAST PARTICIPLE

puesto

GERUND

poniendo

EXAMPLE PHRASES

Ponlo *ahí encima.* Put it on there.
Lo **pondré** *aquí.* I'll put it here.
Todos **nos pusimos** *de acuerdo.* We all agreed.

Remember that subject pronouns are not used very often in Spanish.

▶ prohibir (to forbid)

PRESENT

(yo)	prohíbo
(tú)	prohíbes
(él/ella/usted)	prohíbe
(nosotros/as)	prohibimos
(vosotros/as)	prohibís
(ellos/ellas/ustedes)	prohíben

PRESENT SUBJUNCTIVE

(yo)	prohíba
(tú)	prohíbas
(él/ella/usted)	prohíba
(nosotros/as)	prohibamos
(vosotros/as)	prohibáis
(ellos/ellas/ustedes)	prohíban

PRETERITE

(yo)	prohibí
(tú)	prohibiste
(él/ella/usted)	prohibió
(nosotros/as)	prohibimos
(vosotros/as)	prohibisteis
(ellos/ellas/ustedes)	prohibieron

IMPERFECT

(yo)	prohibía
(tú)	prohibías
(él/ella/usted)	prohibía
(nosotros/as)	prohibíamos
(vosotros/as)	prohibíais
(ellos/ellas/ustedes)	prohibían

FUTURE

(yo)	prohibiré
(tú)	prohibirás
(él/ella/usted)	prohibirá
(nosotros/as)	prohibiremos
(vosotros/as)	prohibiréis
(ellos/ellas/ustedes)	prohibirán

CONDITIONAL

(yo)	prohibiría
(tú)	prohibirías
(él/ella/usted)	prohibiría
(nosotros/as)	prohibiríamos
(vosotros/as)	prohibiríais
(ellos/ellas/ustedes)	prohibirían

IMPERATIVE

prohíbe / prohibid

PAST PARTICIPLE

prohibido

GERUND

prohibiendo

EXAMPLE PHRASES

*Le **prohibieron** la entrada en el bingo.* She was not allowed into the bingo hall.
*Han **prohibido** el acceso a la prensa.* The press have been banned.
*Te **prohíbo** que me hables así.* I won't have you talking to me like that!

▶ querer (to want)

PRESENT

(yo)	quiero
(tú)	quieres
(él/ella/usted)	quiere
(nosotros/as)	queremos
(vosotros/as)	queréis
(ellos/ellas/ustedes)	quieren

PRESENT SUBJUNCTIVE

(yo)	quiera
(tú)	quieras
(él/ella/usted)	quiera
(nosotros/as)	queramos
(vosotros/as)	queráis
(ellos/ellas/ustedes)	quieran

PRETERITE

(yo)	quise
(tú)	quisiste
(él/ella/usted)	quiso
(nosotros/as)	quisimos
(vosotros/as)	quisisteis
(ellos/ellas/ustedes)	quisieron

IMPERFECT

(yo)	quería
(tú)	querías
(él/ella/usted)	quería
(nosotros/as)	queríamos
(vosotros/as)	queríais
(ellos/ellas/ustedes)	querían

FUTURE

(yo)	querré
(tú)	querrás
(él/ella/usted)	querrá
(nosotros/as)	querremos
(vosotros/as)	querréis
(ellos/ellas/ustedes)	querrán

CONDITIONAL

(yo)	querría
(tú)	querrías
(él/ella/usted)	querría
(nosotros/as)	querríamos
(vosotros/as)	querríais
(ellos/ellas/ustedes)	querrían

IMPERATIVE

quiere / quered

PAST PARTICIPLE

querido

GERUND

queriendo

EXAMPLE PHRASES

*Te **quiero**.* I love you.
***Quisiera** preguntar una cosa.* I'd like to ask something.
*No **quería** decírmelo.* She didn't want to tell me.

Remember that subject pronouns are not used very often in Spanish.

▶ **rehusar** (to refuse)

PRESENT

(yo)	rehúso
(tú)	rehúsas
(él/ella/usted)	rehúsa
(nosotros/as)	rehusamos
(vosotros/as)	rehusáis
(ellos/ellas/ustedes)	rehúsan

PRESENT SUBJUNCTIVE

(yo)	rehúse
(tú)	rehúses
(él/ella/usted)	rehúse
(nosotros/as)	rehusemos
(vosotros/as)	rehuséis
(ellos/ellas/ustedes)	rehúsen

PRETERITE

(yo)	rehusé
(tú)	rehusaste
(él/ella/usted)	rehusó
(nosotros/as)	rehusamos
(vosotros/as)	rehusasteis
(ellos/ellas/ustedes)	rehusaron

IMPERFECT

(yo)	rehusaba
(tú)	rehusabas
(él/ella/usted)	rehusaba
(nosotros/as)	rehusábamos
(vosotros/as)	rehusabais
(ellos/ellas/ustedes)	rehusaban

FUTURE

(yo)	rehusaré
(tú)	rehusarás
(él/ella/usted)	rehusará
(nosotros/as)	rehusaremos
(vosotros/as)	rehusaréis
(ellos/ellas/ustedes)	rehusarán

CONDITIONAL

(yo)	rehusaría
(tú)	rehusarías
(él/ella/usted)	rehusaría
(nosotros/as)	rehusaríamos
(vosotros/as)	rehusaríais
(ellos/ellas/ustedes)	rehusarían

IMPERATIVE

rehúsa / rehusad

PAST PARTICIPLE

rehusado

GERUND

rehusando

EXAMPLE PHRASES

***Rehusó** hacer declaraciones.* He declined to make a statement.
***Ha rehusado** el premio.* He's turned down the award.
*Le **rehusaron** la posibilidad de reclamar.* They denied her the possibility of appealing.

▶ reír (to laugh)

PRESENT

(yo)	río
(tú)	ríes
(él/ella/usted)	ríe
(nosotros/as)	reímos
(vosotros/as)	reís
(ellos/ellas/ustedes)	ríen

PRESENT SUBJUNCTIVE

(yo)	ría
(tú)	rías
(él/ella/usted)	ría
(nosotros/as)	riamos
(vosotros/as)	riáis
(ellos/ellas/ustedes)	rían

PRETERITE

(yo)	reí
(tú)	reíste
(él/ella/usted)	rió
(nosotros/as)	reímos
(vosotros/as)	reísteis
(ellos/ellas/ustedes)	rieron

IMPERFECT

(yo)	reía
(tú)	reías
(él/ella/usted)	reía
(nosotros/as)	reíamos
(vosotros/as)	reíais
(ellos/ellas/ustedes)	reían

FUTURE

(yo)	reiré
(tú)	reirás
(él/ella/usted)	reirá
(nosotros/as)	reiremos
(vosotros/as)	reiréis
(ellos/ellas/ustedes)	reirán

CONDITIONAL

(yo)	reiría
(tú)	reirías
(él/ella/usted)	reiría
(nosotros/as)	reiríamos
(vosotros/as)	reiríais
(ellos/ellas/ustedes)	reirían

IMPERATIVE

ríe / reíd

PAST PARTICIPLE

reído

GERUND

riendo

EXAMPLE PHRASES

No *te rías* de mí. Don't laugh at me.
Si *ríes* mucho te saldrán arrugas. If you laugh too much you'll get lines.
Se ríe de cualquier cosa. She laughs at anything.

Remember that subject pronouns are not used very often in Spanish.

▶ reñir (to scold)

PRESENT

(yo)	riño
(tú)	riñes
(él/ella/usted)	riñe
(nosotros/as)	reñimos
(vosotros/as)	reñís
(ellos/ellas/ustedes)	riñen

PRESENT SUBJUNCTIVE

(yo)	riña
(tú)	riñas
(él/ella/usted)	riña
(nosotros/as)	riñamos
(vosotros/as)	riñáis
(ellos/ellas/ustedes)	riñan

PRETERITE

(yo)	reñí
(tú)	reñiste
(él/ella/usted)	riñó
(nosotros/as)	reñimos
(vosotros/as)	reñisteis
(ellos/ellas/ustedes)	riñeron

IMPERFECT

(yo)	reñía
(tú)	reñías
(él/ella/usted)	reñía
(nosotros/as)	reñíamos
(vosotros/as)	reñíais
(ellos/ellas/ustedes)	reñían

FUTURE

(yo)	reñiré
(tú)	reñirás
(él/ella/usted)	reñirá
(nosotros/as)	reñiremos
(vosotros/as)	reñiréis
(ellos/ellas/ustedes)	reñirán

CONDITIONAL

(yo)	reñiría
(tú)	reñirías
(él/ella/usted)	reñiría
(nosotros/as)	reñiríamos
(vosotros/as)	reñiríais
(ellos/ellas/ustedes)	reñirían

IMPERATIVE

riñe / reñid

PAST PARTICIPLE

reñido

GERUND

riñendo

EXAMPLE PHRASES

*Les **riñó** por llegar tarde a casa.* She told them off for getting home late.
*Nos **reñía** sin motivo.* She used to tell us off for no reason.

Remember that subject pronouns are not used very often in Spanish.

▶ resolver (to solve)

PRESENT

(yo)	resuelvo
(tú)	resuelves
(él/ella/usted)	resuelve
(nosotros/as)	resolvemos
(vosotros/as)	resolvéis
(ellos/ellas/ustedes)	resuelven

PRESENT SUBJUNCTIVE

(yo)	resuelva
(tú)	resuelvas
(él/ella/usted)	resuelva
(nosotros/as)	resolvamos
(vosotros/as)	resolváis
(ellos/ellas/ustedes)	resuelvan

PRETERITE

(yo)	resolví
(tú)	resolviste
(él/ella/usted)	resolvió
(nosotros/as)	resolvimos
(vosotros/as)	resolvisteis
(ellos/ellas/ustedes)	resolvieron

IMPERFECT

(yo)	resolvía
(tú)	resolvías
(él/ella/usted)	resolvía
(nosotros/as)	resolvíamos
(vosotros/as)	resolvíais
(ellos/ellas/ustedes)	resolvían

FUTURE

(yo)	resolveré
(tú)	resolverás
(él/ella/usted)	resolverá
(nosotros/as)	resolveremos
(vosotros/as)	resolveréis
(ellos/ellas/ustedes)	resolverán

CONDITIONAL

(yo)	resolvería
(tú)	resolverías
(él/ella/usted)	resolvería
(nosotros/as)	resolveríamos
(vosotros/as)	resolveríais
(ellos/ellas/ustedes)	resolverían

IMPERATIVE

resuelve / resolved

PAST PARTICIPLE

resuelto

GERUND

resolviendo

EXAMPLE PHRASES

Resolvimos el problema entre todos. We solved the problem together.
No hemos **resuelto** los problemas. We haven't solved the problems.
Hasta que no lo **resuelva** no descansaré. I won't rest until I've sorted it out.

▶ reunir (to put together, to gather)

PRESENT

(yo)	reúno
(tú)	reúnes
(él/ella/usted)	reúne
(nosotros/as)	reunimos
(vosotros/as)	reunís
(ellos/ellas/ustedes)	reúnen

PRESENT SUBJUNCTIVE

(yo)	reúna
(tú)	reúnas
(él/ella/usted)	reúna
(nosotros/as)	reunamos
(vosotros/as)	reunáis
(ellos/ellas/ustedes)	reúnan

PRETERITE

(yo)	reuní
(tú)	reuniste
(él/ella/usted)	reunió
(nosotros/as)	reunimos
(vosotros/as)	reunisteis
(ellos/ellas/ustedes)	reunieron

IMPERFECT

(yo)	reunía
(tú)	reunías
(él/ella/usted)	reunía
(nosotros/as)	reuníamos
(vosotros/as)	reuníais
(ellos/ellas/ustedes)	reunían

FUTURE

(yo)	reuniré
(tú)	reunirás
(él/ella/usted)	reunirá
(nosotros/as)	reuniremos
(vosotros/as)	reuniréis
(ellos/ellas/ustedes)	reunirán

CONDITIONAL

(yo)	reuniría
(tú)	reunirías
(él/ella/usted)	reuniría
(nosotros/as)	reuniríamos
(vosotros/as)	reuniríais
(ellos/ellas/ustedes)	reunirían

IMPERATIVE

reúne / reunid

PAST PARTICIPLE

reunido

GERUND

reuniendo

EXAMPLE PHRASES

Han reunido suficientes pruebas. They have gathered enough evidence.
No **reúne** las condiciones necesarias. He doesn't meet the necessary requirements.
Se reunían una vez por semana. They used to meet once a week.

▶ rogar (to beg)

PRESENT

(yo)	ruego
(tú)	ruegas
(él/ella/usted)	ruega
(nosotros/as)	rogamos
(vosotros/as)	rogáis
(ellos/ellas/ustedes)	ruegan

PRESENT SUBJUNCTIVE

(yo)	ruegue
(tú)	ruegues
(él/ella/usted)	ruegue
(nosotros/as)	roguemos
(vosotros/as)	roguéis
(ellos/ellas/ustedes)	rueguen

PRETERITE

(yo)	rogué
(tú)	rogaste
(él/ella/usted)	rogó
(nosotros/as)	rogamos
(vosotros/as)	rogasteis
(ellos/ellas/ustedes)	rogaron

IMPERFECT

(yo)	rogaba
(tú)	rogabas
(él/ella/usted)	rogaba
(nosotros/as)	rogábamos
(vosotros/as)	rogabais
(ellos/ellas/ustedes)	rogaban

FUTURE

(yo)	rogaré
(tú)	rogarás
(él/ella/usted)	rogará
(nosotros/as)	rogaremos
(vosotros/as)	rogaréis
(ellos/ellas/ustedes)	rogarán

CONDITIONAL

(yo)	rogaría
(tú)	rogarías
(él/ella/usted)	rogaría
(nosotros/as)	rogaríamos
(vosotros/as)	rogaríais
(ellos/ellas/ustedes)	rogarían

IMPERATIVE

ruega / rogad

PAST PARTICIPLE

rogado

GERUND

rogando

EXAMPLE PHRASES

Te **ruego** que me lo devuelvas. Please give it back to me.
"Se **ruega** no fumar" "Please do not smoke"
Les **rogamos** acepten nuestras disculpas. Please accept our apologies.

Remember that subject pronouns are not used very often in Spanish.

▶ romper (to break)

PRESENT

(yo)	rompo
(tú)	rompes
(él/ella/usted)	rompe
(nosotros/as)	rompemos
(vosotros/as)	rompéis
(ellos/ellas/ustedes)	rompen

PRESENT SUBJUNCTIVE

(yo)	rompa
(tú)	rompas
(él/ella/usted)	rompa
(nosotros/as)	rompamos
(vosotros/as)	rompáis
(ellos/ellas/ustedes)	rompan

PRETERITE

(yo)	rompí
(tú)	rompiste
(él/ella/usted)	rompió
(nosotros/as)	rompimos
(vosotros/as)	rompisteis
(ellos/ellas/ustedes)	rompieron

IMPERFECT

(yo)	rompía
(tú)	rompías
(él/ella/usted)	rompía
(nosotros/as)	rompíamos
(vosotros/as)	rompíais
(ellos/ellas/ustedes)	rompían

FUTURE

(yo)	romperé
(tú)	romperás
(él/ella/usted)	romperá
(nosotros/as)	romperemos
(vosotros/as)	romperéis
(ellos/ellas/ustedes)	romperán

CONDITIONAL

(yo)	rompería
(tú)	romperías
(él/ella/usted)	rompería
(nosotros/as)	romperíamos
(vosotros/as)	romperíais
(ellos/ellas/ustedes)	romperían

IMPERATIVE

rompe / romped

PAST PARTICIPLE

roto

GERUND

rompiendo

EXAMPLE PHRASES

Siempre **están rompiendo** cosas. They're always breaking things.
Cuidado, no lo **rompas**. Careful you don't break it.
Se rompió el jarrón. The vase broke.

▶ **saber** (to know)

PRESENT

(yo)	sé
(tú)	sabes
(él/ella/usted)	sabe
(nosotros/as)	sabemos
(vosotros/as)	sabéis
(ellos/ellas/ustedes)	saben

PRESENT SUBJUNCTIVE

(yo)	sepa
(tú)	sepas
(él/ella/usted)	sepa
(nosotros/as)	sepamos
(vosotros/as)	sepáis
(ellos/ellas/ustedes)	sepan

PRETERITE

(yo)	supe
(tú)	supiste
(él/ella/usted)	supo
(nosotros/as)	supimos
(vosotros/as)	supisteis
(ellos/ellas/ustedes)	supieron

IMPERFECT

(yo)	sabía
(tú)	sabías
(él/ella/usted)	sabía
(nosotros/as)	sabíamos
(vosotros/as)	sabíais
(ellos/ellas/ustedes)	sabían

FUTURE

(yo)	sabré
(tú)	sabrás
(él/ella/usted)	sabrá
(nosotros/as)	sabremos
(vosotros/as)	sabréis
(ellos/ellas/ustedes)	sabrán

CONDITIONAL

(yo)	sabría
(tú)	sabrías
(él/ella/usted)	sabría
(nosotros/as)	sabríamos
(vosotros/as)	sabríais
(ellos/ellas/ustedes)	sabrían

IMPERATIVE

sabe / sabed

PAST PARTICIPLE

sabido

GERUND

sabiendo

EXAMPLE PHRASES

*No lo **sé**.* I don't know.
*¿**Sabes** una cosa?* Do you know what?
*Pensaba que lo **sabías**.* I thought you knew.

Remember that subject pronouns are not used very often in Spanish.

▶ **sacar** (to take out)

PRESENT

(yo)	saco
(tú)	sacas
(él/ella/usted)	saca
(nosotros/as)	sacamos
(vosotros/as)	sacáis
(ellos/ellas/ustedes)	sacan

PRESENT SUBJUNCTIVE

(yo)	saque
(tú)	saques
(él/ella/usted)	saque
(nosotros/as)	saquemos
(vosotros/as)	saqueís
(ellos/ellas/ustedes)	saquen

PRETERITE

(yo)	saqué
(tú)	sacaste
(él/ella/usted)	sacó
(nosotros/as)	sacamos
(vosotros/as)	sacasteis
(ellos/ellas/ustedes)	sacaron

IMPERFECT

(yo)	sacaba
(tú)	sacabas
(él/ella/usted)	sacaba
(nosotros/as)	sacábamos
(vosotros/as)	sacabais
(ellos/ellas/ustedes)	sacaban

FUTURE

(yo)	sacaré
(tú)	sacarás
(él/ella/usted)	sacará
(nosotros/as)	sacaremos
(vosotros/as)	sacaréis
(ellos/ellas/ustedes)	sacarán

CONDITIONAL

(yo)	sacaría
(tú)	sacarías
(él/ella/usted)	sacaría
(nosotros/as)	sacaríamos
(vosotros/as)	sacaríais
(ellos/ellas/ustedes)	sacarían

IMPERATIVE

saca / sacad

PAST PARTICIPLE

sacado

GERUND

sacando

EXAMPLE PHRASES

Ya **he sacado** las entradas. I've already bought the tickets.
Saqué un 7 en el examen. I got 7 points in the exam.
No **saques** la cabeza por la ventanilla. Don't lean out of the window.

▶ salir (to go out)

PRESENT

(yo)	salgo
(tú)	sales
(él/ella/usted)	sale
(nosotros/as)	salimos
(vosotros/as)	salís
(ellos/ellas/ustedes)	salen

PRESENT SUBJUNCTIVE

(yo)	salga
(tú)	salgas
(él/ella/usted)	salga
(nosotros/as)	salgamos
(vosotros/as)	salgáis
(ellos/ellas/ustedes)	salgan

PRETERITE

(yo)	salí
(tú)	saliste
(él/ella/usted)	salió
(nosotros/as)	salimos
(vosotros/as)	salisteis
(ellos/ellas/ustedes)	salieron

IMPERFECT

(yo)	salía
(tú)	salías
(él/ella/usted)	salía
(nosotros/as)	salíamos
(vosotros/as)	salíais
(ellos/ellas/ustedes)	salían

FUTURE

(yo)	saldré
(tú)	saldrás
(él/ella/usted)	saldrá
(nosotros/as)	saldremos
(vosotros/as)	saldréis
(ellos/ellas/ustedes)	saldrán

CONDITIONAL

(yo)	saldría
(tú)	saldrías
(él/ella/usted)	saldría
(nosotros/as)	saldríamos
(vosotros/as)	saldríais
(ellos/ellas/ustedes)	saldrían

IMPERATIVE

sal / salid

PAST PARTICIPLE

salido

GERUND

saliendo

EXAMPLE PHRASES

*Hace tiempo que no **salimos**.* We haven't been out for a while.
*Por favor, **salgan** por la puerta de atrás.* Please leave via the back door.
Salió un par de veces con nosotros. He went out with us a couple of times.

Remember that subject pronouns are not used very often in Spanish.

▶ **satisfacer** (to satisfy)

PRESENT

(yo)	satisfago
(tú)	satisfaces
(él/ella/usted)	satisface
(nosotros/as)	satisfacemos
(vosotros/as)	satisfacéis
(ellos/ellas/ustedes)	satisfacen

PRESENT SUBJUNCTIVE

(yo)	satisfaga
(tú)	satisfagas
(él/ella/usted)	satisfaga
(nosotros/as)	satisfagamos
(vosotros/as)	satisfagáis
(ellos/ellas/ustedes)	satisfagan

PRETERITE

(yo)	satisfice
(tú)	satisficiste
(él/ella/usted)	satisfizo
(nosotros/as)	satisficimos
(vosotros/as)	satisficisteis
(ellos/ellas/ustedes)	satisficieron

IMPERFECT

(yo)	satisfacía
(tú)	satisfacías
(él/ella/usted)	satisfacía
(nosotros/as)	satisfacíamos
(vosotros/as)	satisfacíais
(ellos/ellas/ustedes)	satisfacían

FUTURE

(yo)	satisfaré
(tú)	satisfarás
(él/ella/usted)	satisfará
(nosotros/as)	satisfaremos
(vosotros/as)	satisfaréis
(ellos/ellas/ustedes)	satisfarán

CONDITIONAL

(yo)	satisfaría
(tú)	satisfarías
(él/ella/usted)	satisfaría
(nosotros/as)	satisfaríamos
(vosotros/as)	satisfaríais
(ellos/ellas/ustedes)	satisfarían

IMPERATIVE

satisfaz / satisface /satisfaced

PAST PARTICIPLE

satisfecho

GERUND

satisfaciendo

EXAMPLE PHRASES

*No me **satisface** nada el resultado.* I'm not at all satisfied with the result.
*Eso **satisfizo** mi curiosidad.* That satisfied my curiosity.
***Ha satisfecho** mis expectativas.* It came up to my expectations.

▶ **seguir** (to follow)

PRESENT

(yo)	sigo
(tú)	sigues
(él/ella/usted)	sigue
(nosotros/as)	seguimos
(vosotros/as)	seguís
(ellos/ellas/ustedes)	siguen

PRESENT SUBJUNCTIVE

(yo)	siga
(tú)	sigas
(él/ella/usted)	siga
(nosotros/as)	sigamos
(vosotros/as)	sigáis
(ellos/ellas/ustedes)	sigan

PRETERITE

(yo)	seguí
(tú)	seguiste
(él/ella/usted)	siguió
(nosotros/as)	seguimos
(vosotros/as)	seguisteis
(ellos/ellas/ustedes)	siguieron

IMPERFECT

(yo)	seguía
(tú)	seguías
(él/ella/usted)	seguía
(nosotros/as)	seguíamos
(vosotros/as)	seguíais
(ellos/ellas/ustedes)	seguían

FUTURE

(yo)	seguiré
(tú)	seguirás
(él/ella/usted)	seguirá
(nosotros/as)	seguiremos
(vosotros/as)	seguiréis
(ellos/ellas/ustedes)	seguirán

CONDITIONAL

(yo)	seguiría
(tú)	seguirías
(él/ella/usted)	seguiría
(nosotros/as)	seguiríamos
(vosotros/as)	seguiríais
(ellos/ellas/ustedes)	seguirían

IMPERATIVE

sigue / seguid

PAST PARTICIPLE

seguido

GERUND

siguiendo

EXAMPLE PHRASES

Siga por esta calle hasta el final. Go on till you get to the end of the street.
Nos seguiremos viendo. We will go on seeing each other.
Nos siguió todo el camino. He followed us all the way.

Remember that subject pronouns are not used very often in Spanish.

▶ **sentir** (to feel)

PRESENT

(yo)	siento
(tú)	sientes
(él/ella/usted)	siente
(nosotros/as)	sentimos
(vosotros/as)	sentís
(ellos/ellas/ustedes)	sienten

PRESENT SUBJUNCTIVE

(yo)	sienta
(tú)	sientas
(él/ella/usted)	sienta
(nosotros/as)	sintamos
(vosotros/as)	sintáis
(ellos/ellas/ustedes)	sientan

PRETERITE

(yo)	sentí
(tú)	sentiste
(él/ella/usted)	sintió
(nosotros/as)	sentimos
(vosotros/as)	sentisteis
(ellos/ellas/ustedes)	sintieron

IMPERFECT

(yo)	sentía
(tú)	sentías
(él/ella/usted)	sentía
(nosotros/as)	sentíamos
(vosotros/as)	sentíais
(ellos/ellas/ustedes)	sentían

FUTURE

(yo)	sentiré
(tú)	sentirás
(él/ella/usted)	sentirá
(nosotros/as)	sentiremos
(vosotros/as)	sentiréis
(ellos/ellas/ustedes)	sentirán

CONDITIONAL

(yo)	sentiría
(tú)	sentirías
(él/ella/usted)	sentiría
(nosotros/as)	sentiríamos
(vosotros/as)	sentiríais
(ellos/ellas/ustedes)	sentirían

IMPERATIVE

siente / sentid

PAST PARTICIPLE

sentido

GERUND

sintiendo

EXAMPLE PHRASES

Siento mucho lo que pasó. I'm really sorry about what happened.
Sentí un pinchazo en la pierna. I felt a sharp pain in my leg.
No creo que lo **sienta**. I don't think she's sorry.

Remember that subject pronouns are not used very often in Spanish.

▶ **ser** (to be)

PRESENT

(yo)	soy
(tú)	eres
(él/ella/usted)	es
(nosotros/as)	somos
(vosotros/as)	sois
(ellos/ellas/ustedes)	son

PRESENT SUBJUNCTIVE

(yo)	sea
(tú)	seas
(él/ella/usted)	sea
(nosotros/as)	seamos
(vosotros/as)	seáis
(ellos/ellas/ustedes)	sean

PRETERITE

(yo)	fui
(tú)	fuiste
(él/ella/usted)	fue
(nosotros/as)	fuimos
(vosotros/as)	fuisteis
(ellos/ellas/ustedes)	fueron

IMPERFECT

(yo)	era
(tú)	eras
(él/ella/usted)	era
(nosotros/as)	éramos
(vosotros/as)	erais
(ellos/ellas/ustedes)	eran

FUTURE

(yo)	seré
(tú)	serás
(él/ella/usted)	será
(nosotros/as)	seremos
(vosotros/as)	seréis
(ellos/ellas/ustedes)	serán

CONDITIONAL

(yo)	sería
(tú)	serías
(él/ella/usted)	sería
(nosotros/as)	seríamos
(vosotros/as)	seríais
(ellos/ellas/ustedes)	serían

IMPERATIVE

sé / sed

PAST PARTICIPLE

sido

GERUND

siendo

EXAMPLE PHRASES

Soy español. I'm Spanish.
¿*Fuiste* tú el que llamó? Was it you who phoned?
Era de noche. It was dark.

Remember that subject pronouns are not used very often in Spanish.

▶ **tener** (to have)

PRESENT

(yo)	tengo
(tú)	tienes
(él/ella/usted)	tiene
(nosotros/as)	tenemos
(vosotros/as)	tenéis
(ellos/ellas/ustedes)	tienen

PRESENT SUBJUNCTIVE

(yo)	tenga
(tú)	tengas
(él/ella/usted)	tenga
(nosotros/as)	tengamos
(vosotros/as)	tengáis
(ellos/ellas/ustedes)	tengan

PRETERITE

(yo)	tuve
(tú)	tuviste
(él/ella/usted)	tuvo
(nosotros/as)	tuvimos
(vosotros/as)	tuvisteis
(ellos/ellas/ustedes)	tuvieron

IMPERFECT

(yo)	tenía
(tú)	tenías
(él/ella/usted)	tenía
(nosotros/as)	teníamos
(vosotros/as)	teníais
(ellos/ellas/ustedes)	tenían

FUTURE

(yo)	tendré
(tú)	tendrás
(él/ella/usted)	tendrá
(nosotros/as)	tendremos
(vosotros/as)	tendréis
(ellos/ellas/ustedes)	tendrán

CONDITIONAL

(yo)	tendría
(tú)	tendrías
(él/ella/usted)	tendría
(nosotros/as)	tendríamos
(vosotros/as)	tendríais
(ellos/ellas/ustedes)	tendrían

IMPERATIVE

ten / tened

PAST PARTICIPLE

tenido

GERUND

teniendo

EXAMPLE PHRASES

Tengo sed. I'm thirsty.
No **tenía** suficiente dinero. She didn't have enough money.
Tuvimos que irnos. We had to leave.

Remember that subject pronouns are not used very often in Spanish.

▶ **torcer** (to twist)

PRESENT

(yo)	tuerzo
(tú)	tuerces
(él/ella/usted)	tuerce
(nosotros/as)	torcemos
(vosotros/as)	torcéis
(ellos/ellas/ustedes)	tuercen

PRESENT SUBJUNCTIVE

(yo)	tuerza
(tú)	tuerzas
(él/ella/usted)	tuerza
(nosotros/as)	torzamos
(vosotros/as)	torzáis
(ellos/ellas/ustedes)	tuerzan

PRETERITE

(yo)	torcí
(tú)	torciste
(él/ella/usted)	torció
(nosotros/as)	torcimos
(vosotros/as)	torcisteis
(ellos/ellas/ustedes)	torcieron

IMPERFECT

(yo)	torcía
(tú)	torcías
(él/ella/usted)	torcía
(nosotros/as)	torcíamos
(vosotros/as)	torcíais
(ellos/ellas/ustedes)	torcían

FUTURE

(yo)	torceré
(tú)	torcerás
(él/ella/usted)	torcerá
(nosotros/as)	torceremos
(vosotros/as)	torceréis
(ellos/ellas/ustedes)	torcerán

CONDITIONAL

(yo)	torcería
(tú)	torcerías
(él/ella/usted)	torcería
(nosotros/as)	torceríamos
(vosotros/as)	torceríais
(ellos/ellas/ustedes)	torcerían

IMPERATIVE

tuerce / torced

PAST PARTICIPLE

torcido

GERUND

torciendo

EXAMPLE PHRASES

*Se me **torció** el tobillo.* I twisted my ankle.
***Tuerza** a la izquierda.* Turn left.
***Tuércelo** un poco más.* Twist it a little more.

▶ traer (to bring)

PRESENT

(yo)	traigo
(tú)	traes
(él/ella/usted)	trae
(nosotros/as)	traemos
(vosotros/as)	traéis
(ellos/ellas/ustedes)	traen

PRESENT SUBJUNCTIVE

(yo)	traiga
(tú)	traigas
(él/ella/usted)	traiga
(nosotros/as)	traigamos
(vosotros/as)	traigáis
(ellos/ellas/ustedes)	traigan

PRETERITE

(yo)	traje
(tú)	trajiste
(él/ella/usted)	trajo
(nosotros/as)	trajimos
(vosotros/as)	trajisteis
(ellos/ellas/ustedes)	trajeron

IMPERFECT

(yo)	traía
(tú)	traías
(él/ella/usted)	traía
(nosotros/as)	traíamos
(vosotros/as)	traíais
(ellos/ellas/ustedes)	traían

FUTURE

(yo)	traeré
(tú)	traerás
(él/ella/usted)	traerá
(nosotros/as)	traeremos
(vosotros/as)	traeréis
(ellos/ellas/ustedes)	traerán

CONDITIONAL

(yo)	traería
(tú)	traerías
(él/ella/usted)	traería
(nosotros/as)	traeríamos
(vosotros/as)	traeríais
(ellos/ellas/ustedes)	traerían

IMPERATIVE

trae / traed

PAST PARTICIPLE

traído

GERUND

trayendo

EXAMPLE PHRASES

¿**Has traído** lo que te pedí? Have you brought what I asked?
No **trajo** el dinero. He didn't bring the money.
Trae eso. Give that here.

Remember that subject pronouns are not used very often in Spanish.

▶ valer (to be worth)

PRESENT

(yo)	valgo
(tú)	vales
(él/ella/usted)	vale
(nosotros/as)	valemos
(vosotros/as)	valéis
(ellos/ellas/ustedes)	valen

PRESENT SUBJUNCTIVE

(yo)	valga
(tú)	valgas
(él/ella/usted)	valga
(nosotros/as)	valgamos
(vosotros/as)	valgáis
(ellos/ellas/ustedes)	valgan

PRETERITE

(yo)	valí
(tú)	valiste
(él/ella/usted)	valió
(nosotros/as)	valimos
(vosotros/as)	valisteis
(ellos/ellas/ustedes)	valieron

IMPERFECT

(yo)	valía
(tú)	valías
(él/ella/usted)	valía
(nosotros/as)	valíamos
(vosotros/as)	valíais
(ellos/ellas/ustedes)	valían

FUTURE

(yo)	valdré
(tú)	valdrás
(él/ella/usted)	valdrá
(nosotros/as)	valdremos
(vosotros/as)	valdréis
(ellos/ellas/ustedes)	valdrán

CONDITIONAL

(yo)	valdría
(tú)	valdrías
(él/ella/usted)	valdría
(nosotros/as)	valdríamos
(vosotros/as)	valdríais
(ellos/ellas/ustedes)	valdrían

IMPERATIVE

vale / valed

PAST PARTICIPLE

valido

GERUND

valiendo

EXAMPLE PHRASES

*¿Cuánto **vale** eso?* How much is that?
*No **valía** la pena.* It wasn't worth it.
***Valga** lo que **valga**, lo compro.* I'll buy it, no matter how much it costs.

Remember that subject pronouns are not used very often in Spanish.

▶ **vencer** (to win)

PRESENT

(yo)	venzo
(tú)	vences
(él/ella/usted)	vence
(nosotros/as)	vencemos
(vosotros/as)	vencéis
(ellos/ellas/ustedes)	vencen

PRESENT SUBJUNCTIVE

(yo)	venza
(tú)	venzas
(él/ella/usted)	venza
(nosotros/as)	venzamos
(vosotros/as)	venzáis
(ellos/ellas/ustedes)	venzan

PRETERITE

(yo)	vencí
(tú)	venciste
(él/ella/usted)	venció
(nosotros/as)	vencimos
(vosotros/as)	vencisteis
(ellos/ellas/ustedes)	vencieron

IMPERFECT

(yo)	vencía
(tú)	vencías
(él/ella/usted)	vencía
(nosotros/as)	vencíamos
(vosotros/as)	vencíais
(ellos/ellas/ustedes)	vencían

FUTURE

(yo)	venceré
(tú)	vencerás
(él/ella/usted)	vencerá
(nosotros/as)	venceremos
(vosotros/as)	venceréis
(ellos/ellas/ustedes)	vencerán

CONDITIONAL

(yo)	vencería
(tú)	vencerías
(él/ella/usted)	vencería
(nosotros/as)	venceríamos
(vosotros/as)	venceríais
(ellos/ellas/ustedes)	vencerían

IMPERATIVE

vence / venced

PAST PARTICIPLE

vencido

GERUND

venciendo

EXAMPLE PHRASES

*¿Quién crees que **vencerá** en las elecciones?* Who do you think will win the elections?
*Han **vencido** tres veces fuera de casa.* They've had three away wins.
***Vencimos** por dos a uno.* We won two-one.

Remember that subject pronouns are not used very often in Spanish.

▶ **venir** (to come)

PRESENT

(yo)	vengo
(tú)	vienes
(él/ella/usted)	viene
(nosotros/as)	venimos
(vosotros/as)	venís
(ellos/ellas/ustedes)	vienen

PRESENT SUBJUNCTIVE

(yo)	venga
(tú)	vengas
(él/ella/usted)	venga
(nosotros/as)	vengamos
(vosotros/as)	vengáis
(ellos/ellas/ustedes)	vengan

PRETERITE

(yo)	vine
(tú)	viniste
(él/ella/usted)	vino
(nosotros/as)	vinimos
(vosotros/as)	vinisteis
(ellos/ellas/ustedes)	vinieron

IMPERFECT

(yo)	venía
(tú)	venías
(él/ella/usted)	venía
(nosotros/as)	veníamos
(vosotros/as)	veníais
(ellos/ellas/ustedes)	venían

FUTURE

(yo)	vendré
(tú)	vendrás
(él/ella/usted)	vendrá
(nosotros/as)	vendremos
(vosotros/as)	vendréis
(ellos/ellas/ustedes)	vendrán

CONDITIONAL

(yo)	vendría
(tú)	vendrías
(él/ella/usted)	vendría
(nosotros/as)	vendríamos
(vosotros/as)	vendríais
(ellos/ellas/ustedes)	vendrían

IMPERATIVE

ven / venid

PAST PARTICIPLE

venido

GERUND

viniendo

EXAMPLE PHRASES

Vengo andando desde la playa. I've walked all the way from the beach.
¿Vendrás conmigo al cine? Will you come to see a film with me?
Prefiero que no venga. I'd rather he didn't come.

Remember that subject pronouns are not used very often in Spanish.

▶ ver (to see)

PRESENT

(yo)	veo
(tú)	ves
(él/ella/usted)	ve
(nosotros/as)	vemos
(vosotros/as)	veis
(ellos/ellas/ustedes)	ven

PRESENT SUBJUNCTIVE

(yo)	vea
(tú)	veas
(él/ella/usted)	vea
(nosotros/as)	veamos
(vosotros/as)	veáis
(ellos/ellas/ustedes)	vean

PRETERITE

(yo)	vi
(tú)	viste
(él/ella/usted)	vio
(nosotros/as)	vimos
(vosotros/as)	visteis
(ellos/ellas/ustedes)	vieron

IMPERFECT

(yo)	veía
(tú)	veías
(él/ella/usted)	veía
(nosotros/as)	veíamos
(vosotros/as)	veíais
(ellos/ellas/ustedes)	veían

FUTURE

(yo)	veré
(tú)	verás
(él/ella/usted)	verá
(nosotros/as)	veremos
(vosotros/as)	veréis
(ellos/ellas/ustedes)	verán

CONDITIONAL

(yo)	vería
(tú)	verías
(él/ella/usted)	vería
(nosotros/as)	veríamos
(vosotros/as)	veríais
(ellos/ellas/ustedes)	verían

IMPERATIVE

ve / ved

PAST PARTICIPLE

visto

GERUND

viendo

EXAMPLE PHRASES

No **veo** muy bien. I can't see very well.
Los **veía** a todos desde la ventana. I could see them all from the window.
¿**Viste** lo que pasó? Did you see what happened?

Remember that subject pronouns are not used very often in Spanish.

▶ **vivir** (to live)

PRESENT

(yo)	vivo
(tú)	vives
(él/ella/usted)	vive
(nosotros/as)	vivimos
(vosotros/as)	vivís
(ellos/ellas/ustedes)	viven

PRESENT SUBJUNCTIVE

(yo)	viva
(tú)	vivas
(él/ella/usted)	viva
(nosotros/as)	vivamos
(vosotros/as)	viváis
(ellos/ellas/ustedes)	vivan

PRETERITE

(yo)	viví
(tú)	viviste
(él/ella/usted)	vivió
(nosotros/as)	vivimos
(vosotros/as)	vivisteis
(ellos/ellas/ustedes)	vivieron

IMPERFECT

(yo)	vivía
(tú)	vivías
(él/ella/usted)	vivía
(nosotros/as)	vivíamos
(vosotros/as)	vivíais
(ellos/ellas/ustedes)	vivían

FUTURE

(yo)	viviré
(tú)	vivirás
(él/ella/usted)	vivirá
(nosotros/as)	viviremos
(vosotros/as)	viviréis
(ellos/ellas/ustedes)	vivirán

CONDITIONAL

(yo)	viviría
(tú)	vivirías
(él/ella/usted)	viviría
(nosotros/as)	viviríamos
(vosotros/as)	viviríais
(ellos/ellas/ustedes)	vivirían

IMPERATIVE

vive / vivid

PAST PARTICIPLE

vivido

GERUND

viviendo

EXAMPLE PHRASES

Vivo en Valencia. I live in Valencia.
Vivieron juntos dos años. They lived together for two years.
Hemos vivido momentos difíciles. We've had some difficult times.

Remember that subject pronouns are not used very often in Spanish.

▶ volcar (to overturn)

PRESENT

(yo)	vuelco
(tú)	vuelcas
(él/ella/usted)	vuelca
(nosotros/as)	volcamos
(vosotros/as)	volcáis
(ellos/ellas/ustedes)	vuelcan

PRESENT SUBJUNCTIVE

(yo)	vuelque
(tú)	vuelques
(él/ella/usted)	vuelque
(nosotros/as)	volquemos
(vosotros/as)	volquéis
(ellos/ellas/ustedes)	vuelquen

PRETERITE

(yo)	volqué
(tú)	volcaste
(él/ella/usted)	volcó
(nosotros/as)	volcamos
(vosotros/as)	volcasteis
(ellos/ellas/ustedes)	volcaron

IMPERFECT

(yo)	volcaba
(tú)	volcabas
(él/ella/usted)	volcaba
(nosotros/as)	volcábamos
(vosotros/as)	volcabais
(ellos/ellas/ustedes)	volcaban

FUTURE

(yo)	volcaré
(tú)	volcarás
(él/ella/usted)	volcará
(nosotros/as)	volcaremos
(vosotros/as)	volcaréis
(ellos/ellas/ustedes)	volcarán

CONDITIONAL

(yo)	volcaría
(tú)	volcarías
(él/ella/usted)	volcaría
(nosotros/as)	volcaríamos
(vosotros/as)	volcaríais
(ellos/ellas/ustedes)	volcarían

IMPERATIVE

vuelca / volcad

PAST PARTICIPLE

volcado

GERUND

volcando

EXAMPLE PHRASES

El camión volcó. The lorry overturned.
Volcó la basura en el suelo. He emptied the rubbish out on the floor.
Ten cuidado no lo vuelques. Careful not to knock it over.

Remember that subject pronouns are not used very often in Spanish.

▶ **volver** (to return)

PRESENT

(yo)	vuelvo
(tú)	vuelves
(él/ella/usted)	vuelve
(nosotros/as)	volvemos
(vosotros/as)	volvéis
(ellos/ellas/ustedes)	vuelven

PRESENT SUBJUNCTIVE

(yo)	vuelva
(tú)	vuelvas
(él/ella/usted)	vuelva
(nosotros/as)	volvamos
(vosotros/as)	volváis
(ellos/ellas/ustedes)	vuelvan

PRETERITE

(yo)	volví
(tú)	volviste
(él/ella/usted)	volvió
(nosotros/as)	volvimos
(vosotros/as)	volvisteis
(ellos/ellas/ustedes)	volvieron

IMPERFECT

(yo)	volvía
(tú)	volvías
(él/ella/usted)	volvía
(nosotros/as)	volvíamos
(vosotros/as)	volvíais
(ellos/ellas/ustedes)	volvían

FUTURE

(yo)	volveré
(tú)	volverás
(él/ella/usted)	volverá
(nosotros/as)	volveremos
(vosotros/as)	volveréis
(ellos/ellas/ustedes)	volverán

CONDITIONAL

(yo)	volvería
(tú)	volverías
(él/ella/usted)	volvería
(nosotros/as)	volveríamos
(vosotros/as)	volveríais
(ellos/ellas/ustedes)	volverían

IMPERATIVE

vuelve / volved

PAST PARTICIPLE

vuelto

GERUND

volviendo

EXAMPLE PHRASES

*Mi padre **vuelve** mañana.* My father's coming back tomorrow.
*No **vuelvas** por aquí.* Don't come back here.
***Ha vuelto** a casa.* He's gone back home.

Remember that subject pronouns are not used very often in Spanish.

► **zurcir** (to darn)

PRESENT

(yo)	zurzo
(tú)	zurces
(él/ella/usted)	zurce
(nosotros/as)	zurcimos
(vosotros/as)	zurcís
(ellos/ellas/ustedes)	zurcen

PRESENT SUBJUNCTIVE

(yo)	zurza
(tú)	zurzas
(él/ella/usted)	zurza
(nosotros/as)	zurzamos
(vosotros/as)	zurzáis
(ellos/ellas/ustedes)	zurzan

PRETERITE

(yo)	zurcí
(tú)	zurciste
(él/ella/usted)	zurció
(nosotros/as)	zurcimos
(vosotros/as)	zurcisteis
(ellos/ellas/ustedes)	zurcieron

IMPERFECT

(yo)	zurcía
(tú)	zurcías
(él/ella/usted)	zurcía
(nosotros/as)	zurcíamos
(vosotros/as)	zurcíais
(ellos/ellas/ustedes)	zurcían

FUTURE

(yo)	zurciré
(tú)	zurcirás
(él/ella/usted)	zurcirá
(nosotros/as)	zurciremos
(vosotros/as)	zurciréis
(ellos/ellas/ustedes)	zurcirán

CONDITIONAL

(yo)	zurciría
(tú)	zurcirías
(él/ella/usted)	zurciría
(nosotros/as)	zurciríamos
(vosotros/as)	zurciríais
(ellos/ellas/ustedes)	zurcirían

IMPERATIVE

zurce / zurcid

PAST PARTICIPLE

zurcido

GERUND

zurciendo

EXAMPLE PHRASES

*¿Quién le **zurce** las camisas?* Who darns his shirts?
*¡Que te **zurzan**!* Get lost!
*Se pasa el día **zurciéndole** la ropa.* She spends the whole day darning his clothes.

Remember that subject pronouns are not used very often in Spanish.

How to use the Verb Index

The verbs in bold are the model verbs which you will find in the verb tables. All the other verbs follow one of these patterns, so the number next to each verb indicates which pattern fits this particular verb. For example, **acampar** (*to camp*) follows the same pattern as **hablar** (number 39 in the verb tables).

All the verbs are in alphabetical order.

Superior numbers (¹ etc) refer you to notes on page 91. These notes explain any differences between verbs and their model.

abandonar	39	acudir	81	ahorrar	39	anotar	39
abastecer	20	acurrucarse	39	ajustar	39	anticipar	39
abolir	**2**	acusar	39	alabar	39	antojarse	39
abollar	39	adaptar	39	alardear	39	anular	39
abombar	39	adecuar	39	alargar	53	anunciar	39
abonar	39	adelantar	39	alcanzar	21	añadir	81
abortar	39	adelgazar	21	alegrar	39	apagar	53
abrasar	39	adivinar	39	alejar	39	apañar	39
abrazar	21	admirar	39	aliarse	31	aparcar	68
abrigar	53	admitir	81	aligerar	39	aparecer	20
abrir	**3**	adoptar	39	alimentar	39	aparentar	39
abrochar	39	adorar	39	aliviar	39	apartar	39
absorber	16	adornar	39	almacenar	39	apasionarse	39
abstenerse	74	**adquirir**	**5**	**almorzar**	**6**	apearse	39
abultar	39	advertir	72	alojar	39	apellidar	39
aburrir	81	afectar	39	alquilar	39	apestar	39
abusar	39	afeitar	39	alterar	39	apetecer	20
acabar	39	aficionar	39	alternar	39	aplastar	39
acampar	39	afilar	39	alucinar	39	aplaudir	81
acariciar	39	afiliarse	39	aludir	81	aplazar	21
acatarrarse	39	afinar	39	alzar	21	aplicar	68
acceder	16	afirmar	39	amamantar	39	apoderarse	39
acelerar	39	aflojar	39	amanecer¹	20	aportar	39
acentuar	4	afrontar	39	amar	39	apostar	19
aceptar	39	agachar	39	amargar	53	apoyar	39
acercar	68	agarrar	39	amarrar	39	apreciar	39
acertar	55	agitar	39	amenazar	21	aprender	16
aclarar	39	aglomerarse	39	amontonar	39	apresurarse	39
acobardarse	39	agobiar	39	amortiguar	10	apretar	55
acoger	15	agotar	39	ampliar	31	aprobar	19
acompañar	39	agradar	39	amputar	39	aprovechar	39
aconsejar	39	agradecer	20	amueblar	39	aproximar	39
acordar	19	agrupar	39	analizar	21	apuntar	39
acostar	19	aguantar	39	**andar**	**7**	apuñalar	39
acostumbrar	39	ahogar	53	animar	39	apurar	39
actuar	**4**	ahorcar	68	anochecer¹	20	arañar	39

arar	39	averiarse	31	castigar	53	concentrar	39
archivar	39	**averiguar**	**10**	causar	39	concertar	55
arder	16	avisar	39	cavar	39	condenar	39
armar	39	ayudar	39	cazar	21	**conducir**	**17**
arrancar	68	azotar	39	ceder	16	conectar	39
arrasar	39	bailar	39	celebrar	39	confesar	55
arrastrar	39	bajar	39	cenar	39	confiar	31
arrebatar	39	bañar	39	cepillar	39	confirmar	39
arreglar	39	barnizar	21	cerrar	55	conformar	39
arrepentirse	72	barrer	16	chapotear	39	confundir	81
arrestar	39	basar	39	charlar	39	congelar	39
arriesgar	53	bastar	39	chillar	39	conmemorar	39
arrimar	39	batir	81	chirriar	31	conmover	48
arrodillarse	39	beber	16	chocar	68	conocer	20
arrojar	39	**bendecir**	**11**	chupar	39	conquistar	39
arropar	39	beneficiar	39	circular	39	conseguir	71
arrugar	53	besar	39	citar	39	consentir	72
arruinar	39	bloquear	39	clasificar	68	conservar	39
asaltar	39	bombardear	39	clavar	39	considerar	39
asar	39	bordar	39	cobrar	39	consistir	81
ascender	30	borrar	39	**cocer**	**14**	consolar	19
asegurar	39	bostezar	21	cocinar	39	constar	39
asesinar	39	botar	39	**coger**	**15**	**construir**	**18**
asfixiar	39	brillar	39	coincidir	81	consultar	39
asimilar	39	brincar	68	cojear	39	consumar	39
asistir	81	brindar	39	colaborar	39	consumir	81
asociar	39	bromear	39	colar	19	contagiar	39
asolear	39	brotar	39	coleccionar	39	contaminar	39
asomar	39	bucear	39	colgar	65	**contar**	**19**
asombrar	39	burlar	39	colocar	68	contener	74
asumir	81	buscar	68	colonizar	21	contentar	39
asustar	39	**caber**	**12**	combinar	39	contestar	39
atacar	68	caducar	68	comentar	39	continuar	4
atar	39	**caer**	**13**	comenzar	29	contradecir	24
atardecer[1]	20	calar	39	**comer**	**16**	contraer	76
atender	30	calcar	68	compadecer	20	contrastar	39
aterrizar	21	calcular	39	comparar	39	contratar	39
atiborrar	39	calentar	55	compartir	81	contribuir	18
atracar	68	calificar	68	compensar	39	controlar	39
atraer	76	callar	39	competir	54	convencer	20
atrapar	39	calmar	39	complacer	49	convenir	79
atravesar	55	cambiar	39	completar	39	conversar	39
atreverse	16	caminar	39	complicar	68	convertir	72
atropellar	39	cancelar	39	componer	57	convocar	68
aumentar	39	cansar	39	comportarse	39	cooperar	39
aunar	**8**	cantar	39	comprar	39	copiar	39
autorizar	21	capacitar	39	comprender	16	corregir	28
avanzar	21	capturar	39	comprobar	19	correr	16
aventajar	39	cargar	53	comprometer	16	corresponder	16
aventar	55	casar	39	comunicar	68	cortar	39
avergonzar	**9**	cascar	6	concebir	54	cosechar	39

coser	16	desanimar	39	desprender	16	echar	39
costar	19	desaparecer	20	despreocuprase	39	editar	39
crear	39	desaprovechar	39	destacar	68	educar	68
crecer	**20**	desarrollar	39	destapar	39	efectuar	4
creer	44	desatar	39	desteñir	62	ejectuar	39
criar	31	desayunar	39	destinar	39	ejercer	78
criticar	68	decalzar	21	destornillar	39	elaborar	39
crujir	81	descansar	39	destrozar	21	**elegir**	**28**
cruzar	**21**	descargar	53	destruir	18	elevar	39
cuadrar	39	descender	30	desvelar	39	eliminar	39
cuajar	39	descolgar	65	desviar	31	elogiar	39
cubrir	**22**	desconcertar	55	detener	74	embalar	39
cuchichear	39	desconectar	39	deteriorar	39	embarcar	68
cuidar	39	desconfiar	31	determinar	39	emborrachar	39
cultivar	39	descontar	19	detestar	39	embrollar	39
cumplir	81	descoser	16	devolver	83	emigrar	39
curar	39	describir	34	devorar	39	emitir	81
dañar	39	descubrir	22	dibujar	39	emocionar	39
dar	**23**	descuidar	39	diferenciar	39	empalmar	39
debatir	81	desdoblar	39	dificultar	39	empañar	39
deber	16	desear	39	digerir	72	empapar	39
debilitar	39	desembarcar	68	diluir	18	empapelar	39
decepcionar	39	desembocar	68	dimitir	81	empaquetar	39
decidir	81	desempeñar	39	**dirigir**	**25**	empastar	39
decir	**24**	desengañar	39	disculpar	39	empatar	39
declarar	39	desenredar	39	discutir	81	empeñar	39
decorar	39	desenvolver	83	diseñar	39	empeorar	39
dedicar	68	deseperar	39	disfrazar	21	**empezar**	**29**
deducir	17	desfilar	39	disfrutar	39	emplear	39
defender	30	desgastar	39	disgustar	39	empujar	39
definir	81	deshacer	40	disimular	39	enamorar	39
deformar	39	deshinchar	39	disminuir	18	encabezar	21
defraudar	39	desilusionar	39	disolver	63	encajar	39
dejar	39	desinfectar	39	disparar	39	encantar	39
delatar	39	desinflar	39	disponer	57	encarcelar	39
deletrear	39	deslizar	21	disputar	39	encargar	53
demostrar	19	deslumbrar	39	**distinguir**	**26**	encender	30
denunciar	39	desmayar	39	distraer	76	encerrar	55
depender	16	desmontar	39	distribuir	18	encoger	15
deprimir	81	desnudar	39	disuadir	81	encontrar	19
derramar	39	desobedecer	20	divertir	72	enchufar	39
derretir	54	desorientar	39	dividir	81	enderezar	21
derribar	39	despachar	39	divorciarse	39	endulzar	21
derrotar	39	despedir	54	divulgar	53	endurecer	20
derrumbar	39	despegar	53	doblar	39	enemistar	39
desabrochar	39	despejar	39	doler	48	enfadar	39
desacertar	55	desperezarse	21	dominar	39	enfermar	39
desafiar	31	despertar	55	**dormir**	**27**	enfocar	68
desafinar	39	despistar	39	drogar	53	enfrentar	39
desahogar	53	desplegar	50	ducharse	39	enfriar	31
desalojar	39	despreciar	39	durar	39	enganchar	39

Notes

[1]) The verbs **amanecer, anochecer, atardecer, granizar, helar, llover, nevar, nublarse** and **tronar** are used almost exclusively in the infinitive and third person singular forms.

[2]) The **past participle** of the verb **pudrir** is **podrido**.

[3]) The verb **soler** is used only in the **present** and **imperfect indicative**.

THE ALPHABET

➤ The Spanish alphabet is pronounced differently from the way it is pronounced in English. Use the list below to help you sound out the letters.

A, a	[a]	(ah)	like 'a' in 'la'
B, b	[be]	(bay)	
C, c	[θe]	(thay)	
Ch, ch	[tʃe]	(chay)	
D, d	[de]	(day)	
E, e	[e]	(ay)	
F, f	['efe]	(efay)	
G, g	[xe]	(chay)	like 'ch' in Scottish 'loch'
H, h	['atʃe]	(atshay)	
I, i	[i]	(ee)	
J, j	['xota]	(chota)	like 'ch' in Scottish 'loch'
K, k	[ka]	(ka)	
L, l	['ele]	(elay)	
Ll, ll	['eʎe]	(elyay)	
M, m	['eme]	(emay)	
N, n	['ene]	(enay)	
Ñ, ñ	['eɲe]	(enyay)	
O, o	[o]	(oh)	
P, p	[pe]	(pay)	
Q, q	[ku]	(koo)	
R, r	['ere]	(eray)	
Rr, rr	['erre]	(erray)	
S, s	['ese]	(esay)	
T, t	[te]	(tay)	
U, u	[u]	(oo)	
V, v	['uβe]	(oobay)	
W, w	['uβe'doble]	(oobaydoblay)	
X, x	['ekis]	(ekees)	
Y, y	[i'ɣrjeɣa]	(ee-griayga)	
Z, z	['θeta]	(thayta)	